Ideologues and Ideologies in Latin America

**Recent Titles in
Contributions in Latin American Studies**

Modernization and Stagnation: Latin American Agriculture into the 1990's
Michael J. Twomey and Ann Helwege, editors

State Formation in Central America: The Struggle for Autonomy, Development, and
Democracy
Howard H. Lentner

Cuba and the Future
Donald E. Schulz, editor

Ambivalent Anti-Colonialism: The United States and the Genesis of West Indian
Independence, 1940–1964
Cary Fraser

Mexico Faces the 21st Century
Donald E. Schulz and Edward J. Williams, editors

Authoritarianism in Latin America since Independence
Will Fowler, editor

Colombia's Military and Brazil's Monarchy: Undermining the Republican
Foundations of South American Independence
Thomas Millington

Brutality and Benevolence: Human Ethology, Culture, and the Birth of Mexico
Abel A. Alves

Ideologues and Ideologies in Latin America

Edited by **Will Fowler**

Contributions in Latin American Studies, Number 9

Greenwood Press
Westport, Connecticut • London

Library of Congress Cataloging-in-Publication Data

Ideologues and ideologies in Latin America / edited by Will Fowler.
     p. cm. — (Contributions in Latin American studies, ISSN
  1054–6790 ; no. 9)
   Includes bibliographical references and index.
   ISBN 0–313–30063–1 (alk. paper)
   1. Latin America—Politics and government—20th century.
  2. Ideology—Latin America. 3. Social movements—Latin America.
  I. Fowler, Will. II. Series.
  JL966.I34 1997
  320.5′098′0904—dc20   96–41469

British Library Cataloguing in Publication Data is available.

Library of Congress Catalog Card Number: 96–41469
ISBN: 0–313–30063–1
ISSN: 1054–6790

First published in 1997

Greenwood Press, 88 Post Road West, Westport, CT 06881
An imprint of Greenwood Publishing Group, Inc.

Printed in the United States of America

The paper used in this book complies with the
Permanent Paper Standard issued by the National
Information Standards Organization (Z39.48–1984).

10 9 8 7 6 5 4 3 2 1

To Thomas and Eddie
(*¡los ideólogos del mañana!*)

Contents

Preface   ix

1. Introduction: Stressing the Importance of Ideological Discourse   1
   Will Fowler

2. The Rise and Fall of Anarcho-Syndicalism in South America,
   1880–1930   11
   Paul Henderson

3. Cuban Nationalism and Responses to Private Education in Cuba,
   1902–1958   27
   Laurie Johnston

4. Intellectuals and the State in Spanish America: A Comparative
   Perspective   45
   Nicola Miller

5. Ideology and Populism in Latin America: A Gendered Overview   65
   Marta Zabaleta
   Translated by Caroline Fowler and Mike Gatehouse

6. Ideology and the Cuban Revolution: Myth, Icon, and Identity   83
   Antoni Kapcia

7. U.S. Ideology and Central American Revolutions in the Cold War   105
   David Ryan

8. Ideology and Opportunism in the Regime of Alfredo Stroessner,
    1954–1989   125
        Peter Lambert

 9. Feminism, Ideology, and Low-Income Women's Groups in Latin
    America   139
        Anny Brooksbank Jones

10. Jaime Guzmán and the *Gremialistas*: From Catholic Corporatist
    Movement to Free Market Party   151
        Marcelo Pollack

11. *El Mercurio*'s Editorial Page ("La Semana Económica") and
    Neoliberal Policy Making in Today's Chile   171
        David E. Hojman

Selected Bibliography   187

Index   197

Editor and Contributors   209

Preface

Since 1994 my research has focused on political thought in Independent Mexico, 1821–1853. Given that in 1996 I had started to work on a study on *Mexico in the Age of Proposals, 1821–1853*, I was interested, in comparative terms, to see how ideologues and ideologies had, in fact, influenced or not, the political process in other Latin American countries since independence. For what were clearly selfish reasons I was particularly interested in seeing other scholars at work, concentrating on the same issues that were obsessing me, albeit regarding different countries and different historical contexts. The hope of stealing some of their ideas in order to apply them to my own ongoing work, into the ideologies of Mexico during the early national period, formed part of my motivation in inviting other specialists to reassess the importance of ideological discourse in their own fields of interest. Therefore, I organized a symposium on "Ideologues and Ideologies," which was held at the University of Leeds during the annual conference of the Society for Latin American Studies (SLAS), March 29–31, 1996.

At a time of "ideological crisis" it seems apt to reconsider the importance of ideological discourse. This became all the more obvious to me when twenty scholars came forward proposing to give papers in my session, and when, of all the symposia that took place during the conference, this one was the one that attracted most delegates. It is evident that the apparent absence of ideological dialectics in the world at large, at the turn of the century, is a concern shared by the majority of academics. This volume is the result of the symposium. Evidently, in order to present a more coherent and consistent book, only eleven of those twenty papers are included. The process of selection meant that the nineteenth century was left out, and therefore, this volume concentrates specifically on the twentieth century.

For similar reasons, those papers that focused more specifically on disciplines such as literature and geography were also excluded. In brief, the chapters contained in this book are the works of historians and political scientists.

However, the quality of all the papers was exceptional in my mind. The discussion that they generated was also compelling. I would like to thank in particular all of those speakers who regrettably are not included in the volume: Rebecca Earle, Francis Lambert, Stephanie Dennison, Brígida Pastor, Humberto Morales Moreno, Gareth Jones, Simon Naylor, Joel Outtes, Jasmine Gideon, George Lambie, Conrad James, Deborah Shaw, and María Negroni. Furthermore a number of persons and institutions contributed to the success of the meeting and to the publication of this volume. I am grateful to my colleagues at the University of St. Andrews, Gustavo San Román, Bernard Bentley, Louise Haywood, Nigel Dennis, Alan Paterson, and Francisco Soguero, for their support and encouragement. I am grateful to the officers of the SLAS Committee who allowed the symposium to take place: Peter Beardsell, Sylvia Chant, Colin Clarke, David Fox, Gareth Jones, James Dunkerley, Roberto Espíndola, John Fisher, Brian Hamnett, David Stansfield, Paul Garner, Peter Wade, Rory Miller, Elizabeth Allen and Adam Bickersteth. I am also grateful to David Corkill and David Preston for the excellent organization of the conference itself. As in the past, my wife, Caroline, proved invaluable in assisting with the translation of the Spanish quotes into English and in preparing the chapters for publication, as well as being prepared to look after Thomas and Eddie whilst I disappeared yet again to attend another conference.

This volume is dedicated to my sons Thomas and Eddie in the hope that their generation will find the ideological solutions to the problems with which our generation is wrestling.

chapter 1

Introduction: Stressing the Importance of Ideological Discourse

Will Fowler

In Gabriel García Márquez's *One Hundred Years of Solitude*, the character of Colonel Aureliano Buendía leaves the imaginary village of Macondo to start a civil war for what are clearly ideological reasons. While the differences between the conservatives and the liberals in terms of the behavior of their respective political elites in nineteenth-century Colombia appear blurred and confused, at a village level it becomes clear that the two movements represent in the eyes of the people two distinct and opposed ideological discourses. In the words of the character of Don Apolinar Moscote, the conservative mayor of Macondo:

The Liberals, he said, were Freemasons, bad people, wanting to hang priests, to institute civil marriage and divorce, to recognize the rights of illegitimate children as equal to those of legitimate ones, and to cut the country up into a federal system that would take power away from the supreme authority. The Conservatives, on the other hand, who had received their power directly from God, proposed the establishment of public order and family morality. They were the defenders of the faith of Christ, of the principle of authority, and were not prepared to permit the country to be broken down into autonomous entities.[1]

Although the colonel leads thirty-two wars in the novel, initially upholding the liberal principles of the period, it becomes clear to the character, by the end, that his own troops and his allied politicians are no longer concerned with bringing the conflict to an end out of a sincere belief that a war and a subsequent conciliatory treaty are the only means to achieving social and political justice, but that, instead, their main priority is simply that of obtaining power.

"That means," Colonel Aureliano Buendía said, smiling when the reading was over, "that all we're fighting for is power."

"They're tactical changes," one of the delegates replied. "Right now the main thing is to broaden the popular base of the war. Then we'll have another look."

One of Colonel Aureliano Buendía's political advisers hastened to intervene.

"It's a contradiction," he said. "If these changes are good, it means that the Conservative regime is good. If we succeed in broadening the popular base of the war with them, as you people say, it means that the regime has a popular base. It means, in short, that for almost twenty years we've been fighting against the sentiments of the nation."

He was going to go on, but Colonel Aureliano Buendía stopped him with a signal. "Don't waste your time, doctor," he said. "The important thing is that from now on we'll be fighting only for power."[2]

This political loss of innocence Colonel Aureliano Buendía undergoes is evidently one that has tormented people over the last two centuries; ever since, parties and factions have resorted to claiming that they represented ideals and beliefs. García Márquez's novel succeeds in highlighting two of the critical aspects that concern this volume: (1) the importance of ideological discourse, especially at a village level, and (2) the fact that sooner or later, for pragmatic reasons, the parties that claim to represent one ideology or another arrive at a point of what could be defined as ideological betrayal.

At the end of the twentieth century this dialectic or contradiction between political reality and ideological fantasy is evidently reaching its most critical stage. It is significant, in this sense, to quote Roger Eatwell and Anthony Wright that, "in everyday usage, 'ideology' tends to be a pejorative term, synonymous with the dogmatic or fanatical."[3] In Latin America and in the Western world, since the demise of the Soviet Union, government and opposition parties have almost ruthlessly resorted to abandoning their traditional ideological discourses, replacing them with pragmatic policies, which could, to some, appear as a naked quest for power, whether it be retaining it or achieving it at all costs, renouncing in the process any notion of upholding morally uplifting political dreams or a purer form of utopian idealism. The end of the twentieth century could be described as the beginning of a technocratic era, where our so-called democratic systems have ceased to offer the electorate a clear ideological choice of possible future governments. In this sense, managing the country or aspiring to manage the country, responding almost exclusively to world economic pressures, and leaving aside any strong commitments to political philosophies, whether it be socialism, liberalism, conservatism or communism, has become the main priority for governing and opposition parties.

Evidence of this is that from the outside it is difficult to perceive any notable ideological difference between the administrations of Bill Clinton and his predecessor George Bush. Likewise, in Britain, the opposition Labor Party has undergone such a radical change of image under the leadership of Tony Blair, that its current moderate propaganda is such that the electorate could be seen to be voting in the next elections under the impression that a possible Labor government, while bringing to the fore a new team of ministers, would only continue to perpetuate the policies defended by a Conservative government, which in turn, since the fall of Margaret Thatcher, has also abandoned its traditional values for what are defined as pragmatic reasons. In Spain, as well, the electorate were offered in the March elections of 1996 what in essence was a choice between two parties whose historical ideological credentials had long been abandoned. The issue was no longer whether the electorate preferred a right-wing or a left-wing government, given that both parties claimed to be center Christian or social-democratic options, but whether the governing *Partido Socialista Obrero Español* (PSOE) had been in power for too long, and whether it was time for a change of personnel rather than one of policies.

The Spanish case serves as a perfect example of this new technocratic era. The PSOE, from its rise to power in October 1982, almost systematically betrayed its socialist traditions and electoral promises, promoting conservative economic policies that alienated its own union, the *Unión General de Trabajadores*, defending, moreover, Spain staying in NATO after having pledged in 1982 to defend Spanish military neutrality. The originally conservative *Alianza Popular* of Manuel Fraga Iribarne purged its more traditional Francoist members, after asking its supporters to vote in favor of leaving NATO (in order to embarrass the PSOE government) during the 1986 referendum, changed its name becoming the *Partido Popular* (PP), and reached a situation, in 1993, where its executive committee openly stated that its party was not a right wing force (*de derechas*) but a center one (*de centro*), making unlikely alliances while in the opposition with the communist-led *Izquierda Unida* of Julio Anguita.

Although the behavior of the parties has been one of absolute pragmatism, the electorate in most countries has continued to embrace what might be deemed to be anachronistic ideological notions of what the different parties actually represent. To a U.S. citizen to be a Democrat or a Republican at a street level clearly continues to conjure up a whole series of philosophical and historical associations that may no longer be strictly relevant. In Britain a Labor voter will continue to view a Conservative voter, and vice versa, according to ideological principles and prejudices that have been perpetuated over several decades, even when these beliefs may no longer reflect the policies of his or her party or that of his or her antagonist's party. It is significant in this sense that the PSOE, both in the 1993 and 1996 elections insisted in associating the PP with its Francoist past. In fact, during the 1996 campaign the PSOE went to the extreme of producing posters that used La Pasionaria's famous cry of "*No pasarán*" (the fascists will not pass/succeed), publicized during the siege of Madrid that lasted throughout the civil war, as one of their slogans vis-à-vis the predicted landslide victory of the PP. The use of this ideological card illustrates clearly that the PSOE was aware that the electorate was still prepared in 1993 to reject the PP for ideological reasons, and that it hoped that the same would apply in 1996. The association of the PP with Franco and fascism was meant to act as a deterrent, warning possible PP voters that if they voted for the PP, Spain would be run once more by the authoritarian methods of the Franco dictatorship. It was clearly an electoral strategy that could not be sustained convincingly given the dramatic changes the PP had undergone since José María Aznar became its leader in 1990. To quote Gabriel Albendea, "To sully the name of a young conservatism, which has nothing to do with the civil war nor with the Franco dictatorship, associating it with the possibility of future evils akin to those of the past, could only be the desperate strategy of a party which was going to lose the elections."[4] However, the PSOE's repeated accusation that the PP was a right-wing party, and the repeated claim of the PP that is was not *de derechas*, illustrates the extent to which the electorate were perceived to be still affected by ideological beliefs that ran deeper than any awareness that both parties, by 1993, were pursuing almost identical policies.

Evidently to talk about the present as one devoid of ideology is wrong; not only because it is clear that the majority of people continue to perceive politics along traditional right-wing or left-wing ethics, but because the predominant hegemonic and all encompassing technocratic and pragmatic views of the world's main governing or opposition parties, must be evaluated within a capitalist system with a relative stress on the rising and controversial ideology of neoliberalism. While governing and opposition parties from traditional conservative or socialist back-grounds have sought to differ over the extent to which their nations' economies are liberalized, what remains clear is that in both camps there has ceased to be an open attack on neoliberal economics. The unquestioning and unimaginative prevalent defense of pragmatism that maintains a certain apolitical and unideological facade, remains a deeply ideological acceptance of capitalism; and one which, moreover, promotes the notion that there is no other workable or working alternative. Never-theless, as Eatwell and Wright have pointed out, "in the last decade or so, the ideologies which were in the ascendant in the early twentieth century seem to have entered terminal decline."[5]

It is precisely because there has been an absence of emphasis on ideological discourse that nationalism and religion have become so important recently. The war between Croats, Bosnians, Serbs, Muslims, and Christians in the former Yugoslavia is evidence of the extent to which this vacuum of ideologies has found a violent expression, which, rather than being based on political principles and values, has arisen from the different sides' xenophobic and cultural as well as religious intolerance. The increasing nationalism in Europe of its so-called "unrecognized" nations (i.e., Scotland, Wales, Northern Ireland, Catalonia, the Basque Country, Sardinia, etc.) also points to the fact that the younger generations, unable to channel their political energy using ideological premises, have started to burn this energy, defending nationalist or religious aspirations that do not sustain a clear political ideology other than that of achieving independence or religious uniformity. The conflict in Chechnia is but another example of this trend.[6]

In brief, we are faced in the Western world with modern capitalist democracies in which the traditional ideological debates between conservatives and socialists have been replaced by a tendency, on the part of the government and opposition parties, to seek pragmatic policies that merely aim to prolong their survival in power or to bring them to power respectively—accepting and, in fact, promoting, in the process, the main values of neoliberalism. While the glorification of pragmatism that has come with this has promoted the notion that all ideologies are dead, it is also clear that those members of the electorate who continue to think along ideological lines have found that their parties have either betrayed them or ceased to represent them.

Latin America has clearly also been affected by the same crisis of ideologies. Whether it is Fidel Castro's attempts to open up the Cuban pseudo-autarkic economy to free market economics or the general pursuit of neoliberal policies in Argentina, Brazil, Chile, Colombia, Ecuador, Mexico, and Venezuela, it would appear that long gone are the days of the right-left dialectic. The revolt in Chiapas, which started on 1 January 1994, led by the mysterious Subcomandante Marcos, confirms rather than contradicts this assertion. Although Mario Vargas Llosa interpreted the revolt in his article "México en llamas"[7] as an anachronic defense of outdated socialist ideologies, it has become clear that Marcos does not defend socialism per se, but an end to the stagnation of Mexico's questionable democracy (or "70 year old dictatorship").[8] It remains to be asked how long it will be before other armed groups take to emulating Marcos elsewhere.

This question, although somewhat alarmist, is an essential one when given that the governing and opposition parties of the Western world have ceased to represent the electorate in ideological terms, it is evident that sooner or later the resulting vacuum of ideological discourse or integrity will provoke the dissatisfied to follow in Marcos's wake, especially if the impression that there is no true democratic alternative becomes generalized. At a time when there is no notable ideological difference between the governing and opposition parties, the current democratic system ceases to be representative. The electorate has no choice except that of having one face or another as president or prime minister.

Jack Hayward argues, however, that "the 1980s shift from technocratic public management to market forces, [with] the consumer becoming more important than the voter," has created a shift "from a Europe ravaged by war to one in which commerce (is) the concomitant of international peace."[9] There is no doubt a sense in Europe and the more prosperous nations of the world that technocracy and neoliberal market forces are perfectly acceptable and worthy doctrines. Countries that have seen a marked rise in their middle-class populations, and that have had functioning welfare states for at least several decades, clearly have an electorate that, on the whole, approves of this prevalent pragmatism; a pragmatism that is in fact reminiscent of Porfirio Díaz's famous slogan of "plenty of administration and no politics." If this were not the case it would be difficult to understand the move away from ideological discourse that has characterized the behavior of traditionally left-wing and right-wing parties in their bids to gain votes rather than defend historic ideals. However, the case of Mexico, with Chiapas remaining an area of conflict, is indicative of the fact that in less developed countries, where there has not been a long established welfare state to assist the less privileged sectors of society during the recent period of hardship, which came with the implementation of neoliberal economic policies in the 1980s, bloody manifestations are bound to become once more the only option left to those members of society who have ceased to have any state protection or political representation.

Thus it is fundamental that the Latin American situation is analyzed in depth. While the Western world would appear to have adapted to the demands and pressures imposed by the World Bank, the Latin American continent poses a dangerous ideological threat to our current new world order of neoliberal technocracy. The high levels of poverty in the entire Latin American continent will not be cured with drastic neoliberal economic policies. Mexico, with its ongoing conflict in Chiapas, provides evidence of how a Latin American country, which was deemed to be among those that were best prepared to adapt to the demands of the World Bank, has been thrown into a state of turmoil, which has entailed the assassination of one of its presidential candidates, Luis Donaldo Colosio, and the collapse of the peso. If Chile is being hailed as the great success of neoliberalism, it must not be forgotten that even under the Pinochet regime, for clear pragmatic reasons, the role of the state was not entirely dismantled,[10] and that in fact state subsidies are being maintained to avoid the possible provocation of social unrest that has been witnessed in Mexico, and that could be perceived to be an inherent aspect of pure neoliberal policies when applied in the developing world.

A study of the Latin American context is also crucial to our understanding of the importance of ideological discourse, given that with greater emphasis than that which has been apparent in the Anglo-Saxon world, myth and ideology have featured prominently in the political language of the twentieth century. Anarchism, communism, fascism and socialism have all been at one point or another predominant in Latin America, in a way that has not been evident in Britain or the United States. The myth of a Labor "winter of discontent"[11] exploited ideologically by the Conservative party in Britain in the last two general elections, although as effective, does not compare to Latin American myths that have emerged in the wake of civil wars, coups d'état, and revolutions that have clearly involved the kind of bloodshed that has not been suffered by the British or, for that matter, U.S. populations. The glorification or damnification of a previous regime or ideological standpoint, tarnished in one way or another with the deaths and repression of certain sectors of society, has been, and continues to be, for obvious reasons, far more emphatic than that which has been experienced in the Western world, with the exception of the former Soviet Union, Germany, and the Mediterranean countries. In other words, the need for and use of ideologies has been far more acute and extreme in Latin America than it has been in Britain or the United States.

The chapters in this volume provide a varied yet consistent analysis of the ways in which ideologies have been used, misused, or abandoned throughout the twentieth century. The paradox that parties or political leaders invariably abandon ideologies in the name of pragmatism, and yet, at the same time, find the need to exploit or redefine them to justify their political existence is a constant theme in all of the chapters. In this sense, the use or misuse of myths on the behalf of governing or opposition parties has clearly been a central part in the development of political strategies in general. While the politics of the leading parties have been throughout the century one that could be perceived to be, in essence, of a deeply pragmatic, even cynical nature, the need to dress power-oriented objectives with the ideological garments of one altruistic philosophy or another has also always been imperative. What is clear from this is that people in general thrive on dreams, and that for any political group to acquire power at a government level, party, class, gender, religious, or regional interests need to be adorned with promises of dreams and utopias if they want to succeed in power. What also becomes clear is that in a context of acute poverty and social injustice, ideologies become all the more influential as they promote the belief or dream that political change will invariably involve a significant economic and social improvement. In what is a generalized context of misery, injustice, and inequality, in which the majority of the population has nothing to lose by joining a revolution or supporting a coup d'état, dreams of extreme and radical change have been and will continue to be evidently appealing. For the same reasons this population, by being more susceptible to the importance given by politicians to ideological discourse, will also be more susceptible to the betrayal of these ideological hopes and expectations the moment their alleged representatives acquire power and opt for a pragmatic approach to reality.

In Chapter 2, Paul Henderson narrates and analyzes the changes that took place at the turn of the century, transforming what started as a purer form of anarchism with the arrival of Spanish and Italian immigrants to Latin America, into anarcho-syndicalism, and later on, trade-unionism. What becomes apparent in his study is the extent to which this metamorphosis was brought about by the pragmatism of those individuals who assumed the leadership of the anarchist movements in the various countries. What also becomes evident is that these changes were clearly perceived to be, from the very beginning, a major betrayal of the values that the original anarchists had fought for at the end of the nineteenth century. This dialectic between flexible pragmatism and strict ideological aspirations is developed further in Chapter 3, where Laurie Johnston discusses the responses to private education that surfaced in Cuba at the beginning of the twentieth century. The complexity of nationalism as an exponent of ideological discourse is emphasized through the way in which the notion of *cubanidad* hindered rather than assisted Cuban socialists in their attempts to improve public education. As has been noted, the current rise of nationalism does not appear to advocate any clear ideological goals. Johnston's chapter provides, in this sense, an insight into how Cuban nationalism, which was in theory meant to unite left-wing thinkers, blurred rather than clarified their objectives. In Chapter 4, Nicola Miller develops this view that Latin American thinkers or intellectuals, more often than not, throughout the twentieth century, have not been able to propose consistent and viable alternatives to the predominant political systems, by focusing on the role played by the state. If in Chapter 3, concentrating on the Cuban context, the impression is that nationalism ironically subverted the common ideology of the intellectuals, Miller goes on to argue that the different pressures that the state exerted throughout the century were such that intellectuals became concerned with power rather than knowledge. The noted view that ideologies have been exploited to serve the interests of a political elite is pinpointed here in the way that state incentives encouraged intellectuals to sacrifice any notions they may have had of ideological integrity, in order to acquire prestige or even political power. Chapter 5 echoes the sense of betrayal that was felt by socialist women in Peru, Chile, and Argentina, as the leaders and intellectuals of movements that were meant to represent their rights invariably discriminated against them as a result of the kind of pressures that are explored in Miller's chapter. Providing also a parallel to Henderson's and Johnston's analysis of the kind of divisions that prevented whether it be anarchists or educational reformers from upholding a united front, Marta Zabaleta explores the ways in which Peronism undermined a form of feminist populism that was potentially capable of radically changing the situation of women in Latin America in 1945. The use of myths that clearly benefited the *peronistas* and frustrated the attempts at emancipation of those women who initially perceived the possibility of liberation by embracing a populist strategy, finds clear parallels in Chapters 6, 7, and 8. Antoni Kapcia, concentrates on the Castro administration's exploitation of the revolutionary myth in contemporary Cuba to justify current changes in the political system; David Ryan, focuses on the U.S. government's exploitation of an altogether different revolutionary myth in Central America during the Cold War to justify U.S. foreign policy; and Peter Lambert, centers on Stroessner's exploitation of his own personalist myths in Paraguay to perpetuate the longevity of his regime. These three chapters demonstrate the extent to which countries respond to ideological discourse, and the extent to which ideologies are abused for what are clearly calculated cynical and pragmatic purposes. Chapter 9, in contrast, provides an insight into how the perception of Western middle-class ideologies has at times divided movements that could have developed a strong united front. In this case the ideology of feminism serves as a perfect example, given that it was criticized for being a foreign import and mistrusted by working-class female movements that in the end advocated *mujerista* beliefs not too dissimilar from those expressed by European feminists. Paralleling Johnston's interpretation of the problematic of Cuban nationalism, Anny Brooksbank Jones argues that the nationalist and classist distrust felt by Latin American women toward the ideology of feminism probably hindered rather than assisted the development of a united womanist movement. The last two chapters, 10 and 11, focus on the current triumphant ideology of neoliberalism and its impact in present-day Chile. Marcelo Pollack analyzes the roles played by Jaime Guzmán and the *gremialistas* in promoting today's neoliberal drive, illustrating the extent to which, for the sake of power and pragmatism, they were prepared to abandon their traditional corporate ideology in order to forge a profitable alliance with the neoliberal technocratic *Chicago Boys*. Finally, in Chapter 11, David E. Hojman emphasizes the power the newspaper *El Mercurio* has had in promoting and defending the values of neoliberalism in Chile from as early as 1940 to the present. While all of the chapters clearly stress the importance of ideological discourse, Hojman's chapter demonstrates the extent to which the media, in this case the press, has played a crucial role in opinion-making in Latin America throughout the twentieth century.

In brief, this volume stresses the importance of ideological discourse at different levels focusing on the Latin American experience. What emerges from the book as a whole is the view that; (1) ideological discourse has been and remains a key element in the population's development of political thought; (2) ideological discourse is perceived, in general by the population at large, as a definition of values that must be advocated by anyone who wants to represent the interests of a sector of society; (3) ideological discourse is deeply entrenched in historical traditions and myths; (4) ideological discourse and myths have been and continue to be abused for cynical factional/party interests because of their persuasive powers; (5) ideologies in their purest forms are invariably betrayed in the name of pragmatism; (6) ideologies can be misinterpreted and/or hindered by the power of nationalism; and (7) neoliberalism has not brought with it the promised end of ideologies, but an ideology in its own right that is both encountering and causing grave problems in the Latin American continent.

It is to be hoped that at a time of ideological crisis, this volume will offer scholars and students concerned with Latin American politics in the twentieth century a challenging collection of interpretations of and explanations for the ways in which ideologues and ideologies have played a key role in the political development of the continent. While illuminating key reasons for the rise and fall of specific ideologies and their repeated betrayal throughout the century, the following chapters also indicate how much there is still left to learn about the importance of ideological discourse in Latin America.

NOTES

1. Gabriel García Márquez, *One Hundred Years of Solitude* (London: Picador, 1978), pp. 84–85.

2. Ibid., p. 141.

3. Roger Eatwell and Anthony Wright (eds.), *Contemporary Political Ideologies* (London: Pinter Publishers, 1993), p. ix.

4. Gabriel Albendea, *España a la deriva* (Madrid: Huerga y Fierro Editores, 1995), p. 20.

5. Eatwell and Wright, *Contemporary Political Ideologies*, p. ix.

6. Evidently this crisis of ideology has also inspired a more positive quest for what may be deemed to be a new and alternative ideological discourse that is more suited to the needs of the end of the twentieth century. The green movement, as such, could be preceived in its many forms as an attempt on the part of its supporters to find an ideological proposal for a different system. See Rosa M. Laffitte "El grup com a procés d'autoaprentatge," *Papers d'innovació social* 35 (Barcelona: Eco Concern, 1996), pp. 3–11.

7. *El País* (Madrid), 16 January 1994. Vargas Llosa argued that "El distraído querrillero no parecía saber por qué cayó el muro de Berlín ni haberse percatado de que el golfo de México y el mar Caribe hierven de balsas de fortuna en que desesperados cubanos, hartos del escorbuto y las dietas de raíces y flores que les trajo el socialismo, están dispuestos a que se los coman los tiburones con tal de llegar al infierno capitalista, incluso en versión mexicana."

8. See Guiomar Rovira, *¡Zapata vive! La rebelión indígena de Chiapas contada por sus protagonistas* (Barcelona: Virus Editorial, 1995).

9. Jack Hayward, *After the French Revolution, Six Critics of Democracy and Nationalism* (London: Harvester Wheatsheaf, 1991), p. xiv.

10. See Ben Richards, "Proprietors not proletarians: The politics of housing subsidies under military rule in Chile," in Will Fowler (ed.), *Authoritarianism in Latin America since Independence* (Westport, CT: Greenwood Press, 1996).

11. The "winter of discontent" refers to the winter of 1979, when under a Labor government the unions were perceived to be in control. In what in fact was a particularly cold winter the constant strikes and power cuts created a sense that the government could not or did not know how to control the disruption caused by the unsatisfied unions. This year has gone on to form part of a contemporary Conservative British mythology, in which during electoral campaigns, the electorate is reminded time and again that if Labor were to win, Britain would once more find itself run by ruthless union leaders.

chapter 2

The Rise and Fall of Anarcho-Syndicalism in South America, 1880–1930

Paul Henderson

In August 1916, Antero Aspíllaga, the owner of the Cayaltí sugar estate on Peru's northern coast, was becoming increasingly alarmed by the wave of strikes in the area. Fearing that the unrest would spread to Cayaltí itself, he lamented the fact that "today's working class is not as before, as is shown by the strikes and claims, which daily grow more serious and frequent."[1] Four years later in Chile, the *South Pacific Mail,* reviewing the effects of the First World War, noted that

There can be no doubt that the World War has profoundly modified conditions in Chile as in every other country of the world. Attempt to conceal it as we may, class distinctions based on wealth and poverty have become accentuated. . . . Industrial unrest has permeated the country and labor has become, for the first time in Chile, conscious of its organised power.[2]

Labor unrest and anxiety on the part of elite groups were by no means confined to Peru and Chile. All over South America, overt class conflict erupted during the war and immediate postwar years. The foundations of oligarchic rule were rocked as never before and while the region's elites, though forced to modify the forms of their rule, were to emerge relatively unscathed in the 1920s, it was clear that their political power could no longer be exercised without regard to the interests and demands of the working class.[3]

Prominent in the wartime labor unrest, as they had been before the war, were anarcho-syndicalists. Indeed, the strong influence of anarchist-inspired doctrines and organizations had become a major characteristic of the region's labor movements. Where they did not dominate, they represented at least a significant current. The elites chose to portray anarchism and its offshoots as the work of subversive foreign agitators, an unwelcome import from Europe.[4] Laws of residence were passed in Argentina in 1902, in Brazil in 1907, and, after six years delay, in 1918 in Chile to facilitate the deportation of undesirable foreigners. While it is true that immigrants did play a significant role in labor organization and agitation, anarcho-syndicalism should not be seen as merely part of the cultural baggage of European immigrants. As James Morris has noted, "The conditions for worker revolt or adaptation to the industrial order are made at home, and if foreign models are successfully transplanted, it is because they fit these conditions in a greater or less degree and not because they have created them."[5] First anarchism, then anarcho-syndicalism (or revolutionary syndicalism as it is often called) and in some cases a more practical, purely syndicalist variant of the latter appeared to offer to many workers in South America in the late nineteenth and early twentieth centuries a seemingly viable solution to the problems they faced. Class consciousness, as E. P. Thompson has argued, is the way in which workers deal in cultural terms with their experience as proletarians.[6] During this period, when the pace of the region's capitalist transformation accelerated markedly, workers were confronted with a rapidly changing way of life and work. In coming to terms with these changes, some of them found a logical expression for their emerging class consciousness in anarchist-inspired doctrine. Many more, with perhaps little regard for the theory, turned to anarcho-syndicalist practice.[7] In the 1920s, however, the appeal of anarcho-syndicalism declined and new modes of expressing and advancing class interests appeared more viable.

While historians have provided many studies of this important phase in the development of South American labor movements, there have been few attempts to provide a framework for understanding the rise and fall of anarcho-syndicalism in the region as a whole.[8] Of course, the growth and precise nature of working-class movements varied from country to country as a reflection of the different ways in which their economic, social, and political structures were articulated. This itself owed much in the late nineteenth and early twentieth centuries to the differing characteristics of each country's export sectors, through which Latin America was integrated into the world economy. However, as Hobart Spalding has observed, "The impact of external events and domestic-foreign interactions determined that broad trends emerged at roughly the same time throughout Latin America."[9] Anarcho-syndicalism was one of those trends and this chapter therefore aims to offer an overview of its origins, the reasons for its appeal, and the causes of its decline.[10]

Essentially, the evolution of anarcho-syndicalism can be divided into three periods. The first, from roughly 1880 to 1900, witnessed the emergence and spread of anarchist doctrine in its pure or individualist form. Most anarchists would probably have agreed with the Peruvian Manuel Gonzales Prada that "we could accurately define the Anarchists' ideal as unlimited freedom and the highest possible well-being of the individual with the abolition of the State. . . . The Anarchist rejects laws, religions, nationalities and recognizes one power only: that of the individual."[11] Influenced largely by the ideas of Mikhail Bakunin, intellectuals and some groups of workers, notably printers and bakers, espoused anarchism and began to spread the word in a variety of publications. The circulation of these was undoubtedly small and their life-span was often short, but they nevertheless offered an alternative both to the mutual aid societies that sought to work within the existing system and also to the dominant values of the South American elites.[12] This was a period when a working class of sorts was only just beginning to form and come to terms with the new disciplines of the region's brand of capitalist development. In some countries, notably Argentina, this process was more advanced than in others. This should not be taken to mean, however, that anarchism represented merely the prehistory of labor movements. As will be seen, the influence of anarchism continued to be felt long after its heyday had passed.

The second period, from about the turn of the century to 1920, saw the emergence of a more recognizably modern working class and with this the emphasis shifted away from the utopian goals of anarchism and the propagandist activities of small circles of adherents to a more syndicalist outlook, which found a much wider audience. Though the long-term aims of anarchism were still proudly proclaimed in the growing number of anarcho-syndicalist publications, less attention was devoted to the nature of the future society than to the question of how to wage the struggle against the oppressive nature of the present, rapidly changing society. As labor was increasingly organized in larger workplaces and as workers themselves began to demonstrate an awareness of their collective interests, some anarchists began to see trade unions as the vehicle for the revolutionary struggle against capitalism.[13] It should be emphasized that this shift in no way represented some sort of logical, predetermined stage in a teleological process. Workers, as Jeremy Adelman has pointed out, made their own decisions and their own history but, it must be added, using Marx's oft-quoted phrase, not under circumstances of their own choosing.[14] Many of the unions formed were of a local nature and often short-lived, frequently lasting only as long as the duration of a strike. Employers generally had the upper hand as both the labor market and state policy rendered union organization difficult. The nature of unionization varied from country to country. Argentine workers, for example, were much more organized than their counterparts in Peru, where unions were weaker and where it would perhaps be more accurate to speak of a syndicalist impulse within the working class. This can be seen as a consequence of the slower emergence of a proletariat in Peru, itself a reflection of the more limited capitalist transformation underway there.

Nevertheless, evident throughout the region was a commitment on the part of growing numbers of workers to the essential characteristics of anarcho-syndicalism. Van der Linden and Thorpe have defined these as: (1) attitudes of class warfare and professed revolutionary objectives culminating in the overthrow of the state; (2) these objectives to be achieved through the collective, direct action of workers best exemplified by the general strike; and (3) workers organizing at the point of production with trade unions being the vehicle of struggle.[15] Linking these was a rejection of politics that was seen as a diversion from the real struggle of workers. It is rather ironic that the anarcho-syndicalists could throw back at his followers

Marx's own dictum that the emancipation of the workers is the act of the workers themselves.

The third period, the 1920s, saw a rapid decline in the influence of anarcho-syndicalism. An element common to all movements was state repression but the fate of anarcho-syndicalism varied from country to country. The worst repression was experienced in Brazil. Nevertheless, according to Wolfe, textile workers in São Paulo, mostly women, managed to maintain a syndicalist organization at plant level.[16] In Argentina there was a move to a more moderate form of trade unionism that was not unfavorably treated by the Yrigoyen regime. Though the Industrial Workers of the World (Wobblies) retained some influence among Chile's port workers until the late 1920s, workers increasingly turned to politics and the Communist Party and later the Socialist Party (in which many syndicalists were prominent) to give the Chilean working class a potent and durable voice. Workers in Peru also turned to politics, but there Haya de la Torre's APRA and populism found a larger audience among the growing urban masses than Mariátegui's Marxism.

After this brief overview of developments in the late nineteenth and early twentieth centuries, the rest of this chapter offers a more detailed consideration of the factors that drew South American workers to anarcho-syndicalism. It will then look at the reasons for the decline of this distinctive current within the region's labor movements.

ANARCHISM

It was during the last quarter of the nineteenth century that Bakuninist ideas began to exercise some influence in South America. Although some variants of European utopian socialism had followers there from the 1840s, it was precisely when the region was becoming increasingly integrated into the world economy through trade, investment, and finance that anarchism began to have an impact. In the same way that the elites looked to Europe for ideas and culture generally, so too did small, dissident minorities—intellectuals and workers—finding, though, a set of European values that the elites were not so keen to bring to South America.

Immigration played a major part in the transmission of anarchist ideas. As emphasized earlier, although anarchism was not solely another European import, Italians and Spaniards were prominent in spreading the word. For example, the Italian Errico Malatesta who was exiled in Argentina from 1885–1889 engaged in propaganda work and, perhaps representing the more pragmatic wing of anarchism, was involved in drawing up the statutes of a union of bakery workers and several other unions in Buenos Aires.[17] Europeans, followers of Fourier and others, also attempted to set up utopian communities in South America, though it is unlikely that they did much to win support for the anarchist cause. Prominent among these was Giovanni Rossi, who left Italy for Brazil in 1890 and founded the experimental colony "Cecilia," which lasted for four years.[18] Conversely, some South American intellectuals, notably the Peruvian Manuel Gonzales Prada, traveled to Europe where they encountered anarchist ideas and returned to carry out propaganda and agitation.

Massive European immigration into South America, especially Argentina and Brazil, clearly provided people who could spread the word. By 1914 nearly half of the inhabitants of Buenos Aires were immigrants and though in percentage terms immigration was less significant in Brazil, immigrants constituted 51 percent of the industrial labor force and 58 percent of those employed in transport in the state of São Paulo by 1920.[19] Of course, not all immigrants were committed anarchists. Probably the overwhelming majority went with the basic idea of making a better life for themselves and their families. Nevertheless they must have provided a degree of receptivity to anarchist ideas once settled. Evidence for this can be found in the working class press. Of the 144 Brazilian titles listed at the IISH in Amsterdam, thirty-three were in Italian. The Italian language paper *L'Avvenire* was one of the major Argentine anarchist publications. Articles in Russian were also published from time to time. The extensive nature of the anarchist press attests to a degree of adherence to anarchist doctrine on the part of at least a small minority of workers. Without this the movement would have been at best irrelevant, the preserve of a few intellectuals; at worst it would have disappeared.

For a time, therefore, it appears that anarchism did tie in with the consciousness of some groups of workers in South America. Peter Blanchard, drawing on the work of Victor Alba, has argued in the Peruvian case that it appealed to "artisans who valued self-teaching and individual enterprise, and therefore saw in the rise of industry a threat to their way of life and to the proletariat who were the product of this industrialization and found their working and living conditions unbearable."[20] While one should neither exaggerate the extent of industrialization nor assume that artisans were being entirely squeezed out by industry, both groups were to be found in the region in the late nineteenth century. On the whole, though, anarchism attracted support from workers in small-scale establishments. Thus the anarchist press in the period regularly featured reports on the influence of anarchist ideas among bakers, cobblers, tailors, cigarette makers, printers, workers in repair shops, and hotel and restaurant staff.[21]

Much of anarchism's appeal must have been cultural rather than strictly ideological. The espousal of anarchism can be seen as a reaction to the capitalist transformation that was gaining pace throughout the region. It was also a reaction *against* that transformation on the part of workers who were struggling to comprehend their role within it. The society they lived in was harsh and often cruel. Many of them wanted none of it and anarchism offered a beguiling vision of an alternative. As Eric Hobsbawm, discussing the millenarian character of anarchism in southern Spain, has observed, "the conscientious anarchist did not wish to destroy the evil world . . . but rejected it here and now."[22] Anarchism promised a new moral order and its publications regularly urged readers not to wait for the revolution but to develop a new anarchist morality immediately.[23]

As part of this new morality the anarchist press called for a more enlightened attitude toward women on the part of men and also urged women to throw off their shackles and unite with men in the struggle for liberation.[24] The Argentinean paper, *La Voz de la Mujer*, written by women for women, can be described as anarcho-feminist in outlook.[25] Apparently with some opposition from male anarchists, the paper called for free love and the dissolution of the family, which, given the dominant moral and religious values of the time and the fact that the family, though oppressive for some, did provide a certain degree of security for many working class women, meant that the paper was unlikely to attract widespread support.[26] In fact, the problems of working class women are conspicuous by their absence from the pages of *La Voz de la Mujer*. Nevertheless, anarchists and anarcho-syndicalists continued to discuss the position of women, particularly the question of women's work and their attitudes to this were often ambivalent and indeed paternalistic. Many saw women's work as a threat to their health and morals as well as to male employment.[27]

The millenarian vision of anarchism appealed also to immigrants and in particular to their rootlessness and the frustration of their hopes as the conditions they encountered proved to be far from those they expected. The working and living conditions of immigrant workers in the major cities of Argentina and Brazil were dismal and thus, as Gordon, discussing the appeal of anarchism to immigrants in Brazil, has argued, "it was the experience of working in Brazil which brought them to that philosophy."[28] But anarchism was not confined to countries with large immigrant populations, as its influence in Peru and Chile demonstrates. In those countries, workers encountered similar conditions and to many anarchism offered the hope of a better world.

ANARCHO-SYNDICALISM

By the turn of the century, however, anarchism, though it did not disappear entirely as, for example, the involvement of anarchists in Buenos Aires' "*semana trágica*" of January 1919 demonstrated, was evolving into anarcho-syndicalism. There had been debate within anarchist circles over the question of trade unions. On the one hand, the "pure" anarchists regarded trade unions as reformist and limited in that they were not committed to the overthrow of capitalism and its replacement with a new society and so viewed participation in them as a betrayal. On the other hand, a much broader and more pragmatic current had emerged and begun to espouse syndicalism.[29] Ideologues, many union leaders, and no doubt ordinary workers still held to the utopian ideals of anarchism and decidedly revolutionary unions like the IWW in Chile enjoyed considerable support. For most workers, however, utopia was becoming an increasingly distant prospect. They turned to anarcho-syndicalism because it offered more immediate and readily understandable goals.

It is no coincidence that this development came when it did. In much of South America, the years 1900–1914 witnessed spectacular rates of economic growth. This was the golden age of export-led development, characterized by a surge in exports, imports, foreign investment, immigration, urbanization and even some limited industrialization. Argentina presents the classic case but, broadly speaking, the same process was underway elsewhere in the region. The process entailed the emergence of a more fully capitalist economy and society, with class lines becoming more clearly demarcated. To workers throughout South America, the accumulation of capital seemed to outweigh their own gains by far.

Marcel van der Linden and Wayne Thorpe have identified a number of factors that in combination led to the emergence of anarcho-syndicalism as a major current within the labor movement internationally and these have a clear relevance in the South American context.[30]

Growing Radicalization of Workers

The backdrop to the emergence of anarcho-syndicalism was provided by the growing radicalization of workers.[31] Although the formation of unions, the incidence of strikes, and the flourishing of a working class press are just part of the picture, they nevertheless provide a measure of the pace and extent of labor radicalization. In all the countries with which this chapter is concerned, elites viewed the increasingly frequent, violent and large-scale strikes with considerable alarm.[32] These were often coordinated by newly established regional or national federations like Argentina's *Federación Obrera Regional Argentina*, established in 1904. Urban workers were most prominent in the wave of strikes in the first decade of the new century but by World War I organized militancy had reached rural areas in Peru, where sugar estate workers struck in 1912.[33] This period also witnessed the first general strikes in South American cities. These often developed from more limited strikes by particular groups of workers that drew in others by example. Wage increases were the most common demand but workers at times also struck for union recognition, in solidarity with other workers and for a reduction in the working day, a particularly popular demand with syndicalists as it was one around which all workers could unite.[34] Levels of unionization were generally low but many strikes, notes Munck, brought into action nonunionized workers thus giving the unions a degree of influence that extended well beyond their own ranks.[35] Though notable victories were achieved, the success rate of strikes was limited. State repression, the use of strike-breakers, and the ever-present threat of unemployment all made the actual winning of a strike a difficult task. Nevertheless, South America's workers, with anarcho-syndicalists playing a prominent role, ensured that modern class conflict had become a prominent feature of the region's brand of capitalist development.

There are several reasons for the growing radicalization of workers in this period. None of these alone was a sufficient condition of radicalization but taken together they do much to explain it. Firstly, conditions for workers, both in the workplace and at home, were almost universally appalling. Workers in major urban centers across the region lived in unhealthy, overcrowded, and often expensive tenement blocks. Public health problems were abundant and mortality rates were high. For workers in full-time employment, hours were long, pay was low, safety standards were minimal, and the threat of dismissal and unemployment was always present.[36] Short-time working was widespread and brought further insecurities.[37] Company stores, the provision of credit at very high rates of interest, and the iniquities of the *enganche* system were just some of the additional problems faced by miners and rural workers in isolated locations. In such circumstances it is hardly surprising that a growing number of workers throughout the region felt that they had little to lose from militancy.

Secondly, workers found themselves in an unregulated confrontation with capital. The region's elites' commitment to the principles of laissez-faire ensured that labor legislation was minimal before World War I.[38] Employers, however, were in little doubt that the state could be called upon to restore order when required. The "social question" in South America was, as it had been described in Brazil, "one for the police."[39] At times disputes were settled with quite extraordinary levels of repression. The use of violence on the part of the state was common throughout the region but perhaps the most tragic case occurred on the grounds of the *Escuela Santa María* in Iquique, Chile, where in 1907, troops attacked nitrate workers and their families who had gathered to demonstrate for higher wages and better working conditions. The death toll was over a thousand. While such repression dealt severe blows to the labor movement, it also confirmed to many workers that the state, far from being a neutral institution, was, as the anarcho-syndicalists argued, the repressive tool of the employers.

Thirdly, urban workers tended to live in largely homogeneous neighborhoods. Gathered together in miserable *conventillos* and *cortiços*, often with many families occupying just one room, workers were only too aware of their collective plight. These circumstances undoubtedly served to heighten class consciousness and foster a degree of solidarity. In 1907 a rent strike in Buenos Aires, in which anarchists were prominent, involved some 120,000 people and spread to Rosario and Bahía Blanca. The outcome was patchy, but at least some landlords agreed to hold down rents.[40] The attitude of unions, however, was lukewarm. While they professed support for the tenants, they were more concerned with employers than landlords. Moreover, in Buenos Aires at least, improvements in public transport facilitated a move to the suburbs that restricted the likelihood of community and workplace struggles dovetailing.[41]

A final factor partly responsible for the radicalization of workers and one that undoubtedly favored the anarcho-syndicalists was the political exclusion of workers. Throughout South America the franchise was extremely limited and electoral politics remained the preserve of the elite. In Brazil literacy qualifications still disenfranchised the 75.5 percent of the population who were illiterate in 1920.[42] Similar restrictions prevailed in Chile and Peru despite the election of Guillermo Billinghurst in the latter in 1912, which owed more to workers' direct action than to their votes.[43] In Argentina, however, with the passing of the Sáenz Peña Law in 1912, the landed oligarchy extended the franchise to the middle class and to native-born and naturalized male workers. They continued, however, to make the acquisition of Argentine citizenship extremely difficult. Though the anarcho-syndicalists could still make a strong case in denouncing the facade of bourgeois politics, the strength of the working-class vote and the electoral successes of the Socialist Party in Buenos Aires were at least partly responsible for the seemingly more conciliatory policies toward labor of the *Unión Cívica Radical* governments of Hipólito Yrigoyen from 1916.[44] This opening up of the political system, partial, yet more advanced in Argentina than elsewhere at this stage, was to have significant consequences for the future of both anarcho-syndicalism and the wider labor movement. Nevertheless, anarcho-syndicalism's rejection and denunciation of politics appeared logical as most workers in the region continued to be denied access to the political process and had to rely on their own efforts to bring about change.

The Labor Process and the Strike Weapon

The capitalist transformation of South America in the late nineteenth and early twentieth centuries brought with it changes in the composition and structure of the working class. The growth of light industry and the development of transport systems raised the pace of proletarianization and workers were increasingly concentrated in larger enterprises. In economies highly dependent on foreign trade, from which governments derived much of their revenue, workers employed in the export sectors or in occupations servicing them found themselves in a powerful bargaining position. While strikes of textile workers could hit individual employers, those of port workers, railroad workers, and miners went to the very heart of the export economy. There can be little doubt that workers were aware of this and it is hardly coincidental that these groups of workers were responsible for the most important and dramatic strikes of the period.[45] This awareness of their collective strength and the potency of the strike weapon dovetailed closely with the anarcho-syndicalists' emphasis on direct action.

At the center of anarcho-syndicalism lay the general strike. Bringing together workers, not all of whom were unionized, at an industry- or city-wide level, general strikes that often involved considerable violence became an unwanted fact of life for employers and governments between 1900 and the early 1920s. Hostile commentators were quick to draw attention to the influence of anarcho-syndicalists in these highly charged displays of class conflict. For militant workers in key economic sectors the general strike represented a mighty expression of class solidarity. For some it represented a revolutionary challenge to capitalism. Even their less radical colleagues would have seen it as a potent weapon at their disposal if all else failed. In fact their participation in these strikes demonstrated that though they may not have been committed anarcho-syndicalists themselves, they were nonetheless prepared to take action when they felt that the preferred tactic of the anarcho-syndicalists would pay off in terms of improvements in wages and working conditions.

Rejection of Alternative Labor Strategies

The influence of anarcho-syndicalism can also be viewed as a conscious rejection by many workers of alternative strategies for the labor movement. Though anarchism was not entirely exhausted, it was increasingly seen as a blind alley. The strength of workers in industries or services vital to the efficient functioning of export economies lay in their ability to confront capital collectively. The anarchist emphasis on individualism hardly corresponded to the conditions in which they lived and worked. Moreover, the violence associated with anarchism, whether individual or collective, only appeared to result in bloodshed and repression.[46]

Socialist parties had made their appearance in the region around the turn of the century yet, in the circumstances then prevailing, their case was far from persuasive and their success was limited. Socialism in Peru and Brazil made little progress before World War I, but some electoral successes were recorded in Chile and most notably in Argentina.[47] However, with the partial exception of Argentina after 1912, the electoral focus of reformist socialism made little sense to workers, especially immigrants, excluded from the formal political process. If gains were to be made, then they would have to come from the direct action of workers themselves.

As will be seen, anarcho-syndicalism itself came to be largely rejected as a viable labor movement strategy after World War I. In Argentina, however, this process was underway before 1914. The revolutionary aims of the movement there were giving way to a more openly reformist form of syndicalism, represented by the *Confederación Obrera Regional Argentina*, established in 1909. Workers were well aware that improvements in wages and conditions could be won through negotiations with employers. Immigrant workers, realizing that they were unlikely to make their fortunes and return home wealthy, sought instead to make the most of the present. Strikes, therefore, though still militant, were seen as the means to achieve immediate economic gains rather than paving the way for revolution. Union leaders may still have been committed to the overthrow of capitalism but in practice they responded to their members' day-to-day, yet for them more pressing, concerns. This tendency became more pronounced with the election of the radical Yrigoyen in 1916, during whose presidency it was increasingly perceived that the state was not wholly impervious to the demands of labor and indeed could, on occasion, act in its immediate interests.

WORLD WAR I AND ITS AFTERMATH

The emergence of a reformist variant of syndicalism in Argentina notwithstanding, World War I ushered in a period in which the intensity of the battle waged between labor and capital in South America was unprecedented. During the early years of the war, economic dislocation and high levels of unemployment seriously weakened the region's labor movements and the level of strike activity was negligible. By 1917, however, an economic upturn, based on rising prices for primary exports, had significantly reduced unemployment and labor regained its confidence. The experience of Brazil during the war differed somewhat from that of the other countries, but even there workers joined with their colleagues elsewhere in launching an onslaught of militancy.[48] In all countries strikes occurred with increasing frequency and in 1919 general strikes took place in Argentina, Peru, and Brazil.

While inflation, falling real wages, and the high levels of profits being made by employers fueled the fires of labor unrest, the period must also be seen as one in which workers, together with disaffected elements of the urban middle class, mounted the strongest challenge yet seen to the old oligarchies.[49] Furthermore, the battles waged by workers in South America formed part of a worldwide rising of workers symbolized most clearly by the October Revolution. The victory of the Bolsheviks was widely reported in the working class press and it undoubtedly provided encouragement as the confrontation with capital became more bitter and bloody at the end of the war. Anarcho-syndicalists, with their emphasis on direct action and the general strike, were at the peak of their influence at this time and the region's elites were swift to blame them for the unrest.

THE DECLINE OF ANARCHO-SYNDICALISM

Looking back at this period from 1920 to 1921, when the brief postwar boom had subsided, workers would have been justified in asking what immediate benefits their efforts had brought. Notable concessions, such as the eight-hour day in Peru, had been won, but the cost was high and many were soon taken away as even supposedly reformist governments wrested back the initiative. The anarcho-syndicalists, often occupying leading positions in strike movements, had promised much, demanded much, but delivered little. During the 1920s their influence began to decline and by the 1930s they were a spent force as an independent current within the labor movements of South America. Three factors were largely responsible for anarcho-syndicalism's decline.

Firstly, in Argentina and Brazil, employers and the state resorted to the tried and tested methods of repression. The outcome of the *semana trágica* in Buenos Aires was a blood bath.[50] It was also a further manifestation of the isolation of the anarchists who were abandoned by the syndicalists and then left to face the attacks of the newly established, anti-labor, anti-immigrant *Liga Patriótica Argentina*.[51] In Brazil similar organizations, such as the *Liga da Defesa Nacional* and *Ação Social Nacionalista*, combined with the forces of the state in the decimation of the labor movement. Arrests and deportations effectively left it without leadership in the face of continued repression under the state of siege in force from 1922 to 1926.

Secondly, the success of the Bolsheviks in capturing state power in Russia offered a persuasive alternative for militants. While the October Revolution was viewed with considerable alarm by elites, it was reported as a triumph in the labor movement press. Anarcho-syndicalists tended to give "critical support" to the Bolshevik regime, though from 1921, with the suppression of the Kronstadt rising, the persecution of Nestor Makhno and the clamp down on independent workers' organizations, this turned to outright criticism of Bolshevik authoritarianism. Nevertheless, the prestige of the Russian Revolution gave impetus to the region's newly established Communist parties and though small they represented a significant challenge to anarcho-syndicalists who viewed the growing number of *moscovisados* with consternation.[52] Indeed, many anarcho-syndicalists came to accept the need for disciplined political parties along Bolshevik lines. As they had done previously, workers were consciously rejecting a strategy that appeared to have failed them in favor of one that could point to the Russian Revolution as real evidence of its viability and practicality.

Thirdly, and arguably most significantly, the partial opening up of politics to workers after the war, a process which, it has been noted, was already underway in Argentina, reflected a change in the nature of the state in South America. The bitterness and intensity of the battles fought by workers was at least partly responsible for the emergence of reformist sections of the elites who saw the need to integrate the working class into political life in the hope of promoting a more harmonious and conflict-free brand of capitalist development. The victory of Yrigoyen in 1916 was thus followed by the coming to power of Leguía in Peru in 1919, and Alessandri in Chile in 1920.[53] Though under these presidents workers' expectations were hardly satisfied, this process of reform and integration helped strip anarcho-syndicalism of one of the major strengths of its appeal, namely its rejection of politics. Workers increasingly came to believe that they could improve their conditions by putting pressure on and even gaining a voice in government.

Such a strategy necessitated political expression and workers gave their support to a variety of currents that best appeared to articulate their interests in the interwar years. Throughout the region Communist parties and labor unions attracted and organized many but nowhere were they unchallenged. In Peru, Haya de la Torre's APRA gained considerable influence and the urban masses provided a base of support for populist politicians. Confronted by a hostile military regime from 1930, Argentine workers, at the expense of the independence of their union organizations, eventually found a political voice in Peronism. Yet elsewhere, anarcho-syndicalism retained some of its influence for a time. In Brazil's weakened labor movement, particularly in São Paulo, predominantly female textile workers kept the tradition alive at plant level. The Chilean IWW continued to play a leading role in the labor movement in Santiago and Valparaíso until falling victim to the repression of the Ibáñez government in 1927. Even then, the spirit was not entirely crushed as anarcho-syndicalists later came to occupy leading positions in the Socialist party of Chile.[54] The heyday of anarcho-syndicalism in South America, however, had passed. Though once articulating the experiences and aspirations of many of the region's workers, it gave way to movements deemed more appropriate in increasingly complex societies by workers themselves.

NOTES

I would like to thank the University of Wolverhampton and the Nuffield Foundation for financial support for some of the research on which this chapter is based and the staff of the International Institute for Social History, Amsterdam.

1. Antero Aspíllaga, Ramón Aspíllaga, 18 August 1916, *Cartas Reservadas*, Cayaltí Archive, Archivo Agrario, Lima.

2. *The South Pacific Mail*, Valparaíso, 1 July 1920.

3. Arturo Alessandri, elected President of Chile in 1920, expressed the new reformist mood of at least part of the country's elite when he wrote, "I believed that the moment had come to produce harmony between capital and labor on the basis of human solidarity and social justice, to thus defend public order and social salvation. . . . In a word, I felt that it was necessary to have rapid evolution to avoid the revolution and the holocaust which in conformity with a reiterated historical law always takes place when evolution is retarded." R. J. Alexander, *Arturo Alessandri: A Biography*, 2 vols. (Ann Arbor: Rutgers University/University Microfilms International, 1977), p. 18.

4. During World War I, *The Economist* maintained that striking Argentinian railway workers were influenced not only by "Spanish and Italian revolutionary socialism" but also by "German agitators and German money." *The Economist*, London, 13, 20 October 1917.

5. J. O. Morris, *Elites, Intellectuals and Consensus. A Study of the Social Question and the Industrial Relations System in Chile* (Ithaca: Cornell University Press, 1966), p. 113.

6. E. P. Thompson, *The Making of the English Working Class* (Harmondsworth: Penguin, 1968), pp. 9–10.

7. In "The Limitations of Ideology in the Early Argentine Labour Movement: Anarchism in the Trade Unions, 1890–1920," *Journal of Latin American Studies* 16:1 (1984), Ruth Thompson argues forcefully against the assumption that the union rank and file shared the views of the leaders. Most workers, she maintains, were interested in improving their wages and conditions rather than overthrowing the state. This was recognized by union leaders themselves who, despite their rhetoric, negotiated with employers and the state on behalf of their members.

8. A bibliography of Latin American labor history would run to many pages. Essential English language works on the region as a whole are H. Spalding, Jr., *Organized Labor in Latin America. Historical Case Studies of Urban Workers in Dependent Societies* (London: Harper and Row, 1977) and C. Bergquist, *Labor in Latin America. Comparative Essays on Chile, Argentina, Venezuela and Colombia* (Stanford: Stanford University Press, 1986). On Argentina, see J. Adelman (ed.), *Essays in Argentine Labour History 1870–1930* (Basingstoke: Macmillan, 1992); on Peru, P. Blanchard, *The Origins of the Peruvian Labor Movement, 1883–1919* (Pittsburgh: Pittsburgh University Press, 1982); on Chile, P. De Shazo, *Urban Workers and Labor Unions in Chile, 1902–1927*, (Madison: Wisconsin University Press, 1983); on Brazil, J.F.W. Dulles, *Anarchists and Communists in Brazil, 1900–1935*, (Austin: Texas University Press, 1973).

9. Spalding, *Organized Labor*, pp. 50–51.

10. The framework of analysis draws on that developed by Marcel van der Linden and Wayne Thorpe (eds.), *Revolutionary Syndicalism: An International Perspective* (Aldershot: Scolar Press, 1990). This chapter is limited to a discussion of developments in Chile, Peru, Argentina, and Brazil. The influence of anarchist-inspired theory and practice was, of course, felt throughout Latin America; in addition to its extremely substantial collection of periodicals from these four countries, the International Institute for Social History in Amsterdam has significant holdings of publications from Bolivia, Colombia, Cuba, Ecuador, Mexico, Paraguay, Puerto Rico, and Uruguay.

11. M. Gonzales Prada, *Anarchy* (Tucson: IWW, 1972), p. 1.

12. The important Argentinian publication *La Voz de la Mujer*, for example, proclaimed on its masthead that "Aparece cuando puede y por subscripción voluntario." (It appears when it can and by voluntary subscription.) The IISH has nine copies, published in 1896–1897.

13. Many, however, still saw trade unions as inherently reformist.

14. Adelman, *Essays*; J. Adelman, "State and Labour in Argentina: The Portworkers of Buenos Aires, 1910–21," *Journal of Latin American Studies* 25:1 (1993).

15. Van der Linden and Thorpe, *Revolutionary*, pp. 1–2.

16. J. Wolfe, "Anarchist Ideology, Worker Practice: The 1917 General Strike and the Formation of São Paulo's Working Class," *Hispanic American Historical Review* 71:4 (1991); J. Wolfe, *Working Women, Working Men: São Paulo and the Rise of Brazil's Industrial Working Class, 1900–1955* (Durham: Duke University Press, 1993).

17. M. H. Hall and H. A. Spalding, Jr., "The Urban Working Class and Early Latin American Labour Movements, 1880–1930," in L. Bethell (ed.), *The Cambridge History of Latin America*, Vol. 4, (Cambridge: Cambridge University Press, 1986), pp. 345–46.

18. Cecilia seems to have foundered over the colony's female members' reluctance to accept Rossi's ideas on free love. Back home Rossi later considered the possibility of purchasing women from the "semi-savage tribes" with the proceeds of a new colony's distillery. He asked his correspondent to consider the scheme "without giving it any publicity." Giovanni Rossi Archive, IISH, Amsterdam, Rossi, A. G. Sanftleben, 29 November, 1896.

19. B. Albert, *South America and the First World War. The Impact of the War on Brazil, Argentina, Peru and Chile* (Cambridge: Cambridge University Press, 1988), p. 239; S. L. Maram, "Anarchists, Immigrants, and the Brazilian Labor Movement." Unpub. Ph.D. Thesis, University of California at Santa Barbara, 1972, pp. 7–8.

20. Blanchard, *Origins*, p. 49.

21. See also J. Godio, *Historia del Movimiento Obrero Argentino, Migrantes Asalariados y Lucha de Clases, 1880–1910* (Buenos Aires: Editorial Tiempo Contemporáneo, 1973), pp. 78–80, 128–29.

22. E. J. Hobsbawm, *Primitive Rebels* (Manchester: Manchester University Press, 1959), p. 83.

23. As late as 1924, long after the eclipse of anarchism, a Chilean anarchist fortnightly, *El Surco*, was still warning of the dangers of alcohol: "El alcohol es una de las causas de las armas poderosas, para atrofiar el cerebro del obrero, y por lo tanto obstrucciona el camino de su liberación." It urged its readers, when thirsty and in need of company, to drink a glass of water and read a book. *El Surco*, Iquique, 15 November 1924.

24. See, for example, *La Organización Obrera*, Buenos Aires, 24, 1903.

25. M. Molyneux, "No God, No Boss, No Husband. Anarchist Feminism in Nineteenth Century Argentina," *Latin American Perspectives* 13:1 (1986).

26. See the article "El Amor Libre: Por qué lo queremos?" signed by Carmen Lareva in the first issue of the paper, 8 January 1896.

27. A. Lavrin, "Women, Labor and the Left: Argentina and Chile, 1890–1925," *Journal of Women's History* 1:2 (1989), p. 95.

28. E. A. Gordon, "Anarchism in Brazil: Theory and Practice, 1890–1920." Unpub. Ph.D. Thesis, Tulane University, 1978, pp. 18–19. On conditions see Hall and Spalding, "Urban Working Class," pp. 332–37.

29. The Argentinian paper *La Acción Socialista*, which described itself as revolutionary syndicalist (a term often used as an alternative to anarcho-syndicalist), described the ideas of anarchism in no uncertain terms as "una monomanía pseudo-literaria y una masturbación

continua" (pseudo-literary singlemindedness and a continuous masturbation) *La Acción Socialista*, Buenos Aires, 16 February 1908.

30. Van der Linden and Thorpe, *Revolutionary*, Chapter 1.

31. Workers also found other outlets for their radicalism. The *Partido Socialista* had been formed in Argentina in 1896, the Chilean *Partido Obrero Socialista* was formed in 1912, and in that year Peruvian workers were instrumental in the election to the presidency of the populist Guillermo Billinghurst. On Billinghurst see P. Blanchard, "A Populist Precursor: Guillermo Billinghurst," *Journal of Latin American Studies* 9:2 (1977).

32. It is not possible here to discuss the strike wave in detail. For a useful summary see Albert, *South America*, Chapter 6.

33. For details of the strikes, see *El Jornalero,* Trujillo, 1912 (various issues).

34. *La Acción Socialista* also argued that "La jornada de ocho horas no constituye sólo una reforma, ni mucho menos un fin; es ante todo un medio de propaganda. Un medio maravilloso." (The eight-hour working day is not just a reform. It is not just an end either. It is above all a means of propaganda. A wonderful means.) *La Acción Socialista*, Buenos Aires, 21 September 1906.

35. R. Munck, "The Formation and Development of the Working Class in Argentina, 1857–1919," in B. Munslow and H. Finch (eds.), *Proletarianisation in the Third World. Studies in the Creation of a Labour Force under Dependent Capitalism* (London: Croon Helm, 1984), p. 263.

36. Some workers were able to extract concessions over safety matters, most notably in Peru, which in 1911 became the first Latin American country to provide compensation through the Law of Professional Risk for workers who were injured or became ill on the job. Blanchard, *Origins*, pp. 36–40.

37. Shipley has calculated that most Buenos Aires workers with families earned nowhere near enough to meet necessary expenditure. R. E. Shipley, "On the Outside Looking In: A Social History of the Porteño Worker During the 'Golden Age' of Argentine Development 1914–1930." Unpub. Ph.D. Thesis, Rutgers University, 1977, pp. 414–41.

38. An important exception to this was Uruguay under the reformist President José Batlle y Ordóñez, 1903–1907 and 1911–1915.

39. Hall and Spalding, "Urban Working Class," p. 332.

40. Godio, *Historia*, p. 264.

41. Adelman, *Essays*, pp. 15–16. In Chile, however, this tendency was less pronounced and major rent strikes took place in Valparaíso and Santiago (where an IWW member headed the tenant league) in 1925. DeShazo, *Urban Workers,* pp. 223–26.

42. B. Fausto, "Brazil: The Social and Political Structure of the First Republic, 1889–1930," in Bethell (ed.), *Cambridge History*, vol. 6, p. 801.

43. Blanchard, *Origins*, pp. 86–88.

44. The best analysis of these developments is to be found in D. Rock, *Politics in Argentina 1890–1930. The Rise and Fall of Radicalism* (Cambridge: Cambridge University Press, 1975).

45. In contrast to Bergquist, DeShazo maintains that the workers of Santiago and Valparaíso rather than nitrate miners were the driving force of the organized labor movement in early twentieth-century Chile. Nevertheless, a major role was played by the portworkers amongst whom anarcho-syndicalism was highly influential.

46. Such was the case following the assassination of the Buenos Aires police chief Ramón Falcón by the young Russian immigrant Simón Radowitzky in November 1909. *La Protesta*, Buenos Aires, 16 January 1910.

47. Spalding, *Organized Labor*, pp. 20–21.

48. On Brazil see Albert, *South America*, pp. 77–94.

49. Following the establishment of the university reform movement in Córdoba, Argentina in 1918, students elsewhere pressed for change and, like the young Haya de la Torre in Peru, frequently supported workers' organizations. Santiago's *La Nación* recorded "the first strike of teachers in Latin America" on 13 August 1918.

50. *La Protesta* claimed that there were 700 dead and 4, 000 wounded. *La Protesta*, Buenos Aires, 23 January 1919.

51. For contrasting interpretations of the *semana trágica*, see Julio Godio, *La Semana Trágica de Enero de 1919* (Buenos Aires: Granica, 1972) and Rock, *Politics in Argentina*.

52. Marques da Costa, Diego Abad de Santillán, 8 May 1924. Santillán Archive, Korrespondenz, 1924, International Institute for Social History, Amsterdam.

53. In Brazil the reformist Rui Barbosa's presidential campaign of 1919 was unsuccessful. Albert has argued that the lack of national political parties and the country's extreme federalism made the Brazilian state less vulnerable to pressure from below. Albert, *South America*, p. 270.

54. DeShazo, *Urban Workers*, pp. 285–86.

chapter 3

Cuban Nationalism and Responses to Private Education in Cuba, 1902–1958

Laurie Johnston

INTRODUCTION

Cuban nationalism is a central theme in nineteenth- and twentieth-century Cuban history. Nationalist ambitions and frustrations provide important clues to understanding the republican period of 1902–1958, the bridge between Spanish colony and revolutionary government. Nationalism has tended to be examined within the context of the influence of the United States and the problems posed by a dependent economy. Less well understood is the relationship between education and nationalism in Cuba. That relationship is important because Cubans themselves used educational progress as a means of measuring the development, successful or otherwise, of their nation. As we shall see, secular public education and *Cuba Libre* came to be viewed as indivisible. Therefore, nationalist responses to the continued existence of private education require exploration. Nationalists proved unable to focus clearly or consistently on the connection between inequalities in the educational system and the larger problems besetting republican Cuba's political economy, because the nationalist vision of independence was open to interpretations from across the political spectrum. Yet it is overly simplistic to argue that nationalism inevitably hindered radical change or blocked incisive political analysis. The persistence of private education in republican Cuba became a source of nationalist anxiety and ultimately a focus of widespread perceptions of Cuban educational failure, and thus of national failure.

Under Spanish colonial rule, public education was so limited and under-resourced as to be effectively nonexistent. With very few exceptions, education was available only privately, to the wealthy. Private Catholic schools in Cuba attempted to suppress aspirations of national liberty by fostering the loyalty of the ruling male elite to crown and church. Crown and church in Cuba sought to deny the majority of Cubans an education, equating mass literacy with subversion and heresy. Republicans demanded the liberation of the Cuban educational system, through the eradication of the educational monopoly of Catholic schools and the spread of literacy. Nineteenth-century republican intellectuals argued that a system of free, universal, secular public education was essential to the establishment of *Cuba Libre*, the independent and democratic nation for which so many Cubans would fight and die. Influenced by Enlightenment ideals, a succession of Cuban intellectuals looked outside the church for ways of understanding conditions in Cuban society and the relationship between Cuba and Spain. In common with intellectuals throughout Latin America, where some rudimentary public educational systems were in the process of being established, Cuban *pensadores* rejected church scholasticism for liberal, rational thought. Educational methods, they argued, particularly learning by rote, teaching in Latin and emphasis on the abstract over the scientific and technical, worked to hinder both independent individual reasoning and the development of an independent and prosperous nation.

In advocating a nation-state, rather than the perpetuation of colonial ties, republicans understood the significance of secular, mass education differently from their colonial masters. Given the relationship between church and state in the colony, they insisted upon separation of the two as a prerequisite for independence; public instruction thus became inextricably bound with the drive toward secularism and a sovereign state. Improved levels of education, republicans argued, would increase economic capacity, facilitating the country's ability to compete on an international scale. In addition, mass education would enhance, rather than undermine, acceptance of state authority. Rather than being a dangerous vehicle for spreading revolution, universal education was seen as a critical means of forming productive citizens, loyal to the *patria*. It would be a vehicle for fostering *cubanidad*, or the collective consciousness of a unifying, unique heritage and identity, committed to a common progress, regardless of race or class. Thus, secular public education and Cuban independence became inseparable in Cuban nationalist consciousness, and this perception in turn became an incontestable ideological cornerstone of *Cuba Libre*.

SUPPORT FOR PRIVATE EDUCATION

It fell to the United States to lay the foundations for a public educational system in Cuba, during its military occupation of the island between 1899 and 1902. This led to a number of tensions that cannot be examined here. It is important, however, to bear in mind the following points. While Cubans resisted the "americanization" of education, they wholeheartedly supported the development of a national public educational system. Nonetheless, the new public schools did not replace private institutions. In fact, private education expanded as Protestant missionaries and U.S. business took advantage of the occupation to commence operations in Cuba. The military government initially chose not to regulate private schools in any way, although Spanish law provided a precedent to ensure satisfactory material conditions. However, public pressure led to regulations being imposed to ensure acceptable employment arrangements and teaching qualifications. The military government, although it had disestablished the church in Cuba, refused to go further and mount a direct challenge to religious private schools. To have done so would have meant to confront the growing influence of U.S. Protestant missionaries as well as alienating the wealthy Spaniards whom it believed to be natural allies and who showed a continued preference for private Catholic education. Nor did the 1901 Constitution take the issue of regulation any further.

Private schools in republican Cuba fell into different categories. A small number of private secular charitable schools existed; the *Sociedad Económica de Amigos del País*, for example, ran highly regarded schools founded by private benefactors for charitable purposes. Mutual societies, such as the Spanish Regional Association and other immigrant associations, particularly from different areas of Spain, frequently ran their own schools. Individuals founded private schools as commercial businesses. The most important private schools in terms of political influence, however, were those established by religious communities. Normally fee-paying but occasionally charitable, they were chiefly run by Catholic orders from Spain and Protestant orders from the United States.[1]

In the early years of the republic, in spite of popular and intellectual support for public education, educationalists reported that private schools multiplied "extraordinarily."[2] The growing numbers of private educational institutions in Cuba reflected the mounting lack of confidence in public education. Corruption, incompetence, and lack of political will, all ultimately consequences of Cuba's distorted and dependent political economy, took their toll on public schools, resulting in a chronic shortage of resources and abysmal conditions—poor hygiene, want of materials and space, high teacher turnover, and high absenteeism. Such conditions did not win parental confidence. Often children were sent to private schools in protest, in spite of warnings by educationalists that abandoning the public educational system would only lead to further decline.

Ethnic and religious influences and prejudices also guided parents in their choice of schools. Spanish immigrants often perceived themselves as distinct from native Cubans and consequently favored sending their children to schools run by fellow immigrants, alongside other children from their community. This feeling of distinctness lay behind the foundation of the very small number of Jewish schools in Cuba. Schools run by religious orders and business concerns from the United States were popular because parents believed that graduates stood a better chance of gaining entrance to U.S. schools for advanced study and subsequently of finding employment.[3] Parents were also motivated by the composition of the student body. Coeducation offended some, while others would not send their children to public schools attended by poor and/or black and mulatto children.[4]

Many Cubans retained the belief from colonial times that private education was superior to that offered by the state. While there is no evidence to support this assumption, private schools did appear to afford an easier, if more expensive, route to a better end. They provided qualifications in less time than state schools, and rumors abounded of university admissions made on the basis of school attended rather than academic ability. The newspaper *Heraldo de Cuba* reported that a private secondary school in Guanabacoa had printed final results one month before students took the final examination, an occurrence that failed to elicit protest from the public institution that authorized the degrees.[5] Two competing perceptions of private schools thus emerged: they were seen as institutions that provided superior education and opportunity, or places that, through corruption and unfair practice, fostered privilege.

THE DEBATE OVER PRIVATE EDUCATION: 1915

In 1909, the *Partido Independiente de Color*, a political party founded by black and mixed race Cubans, analyzed Cuba's educational system from the perspective of race. Private schools flourished, the party argued, because of the poor conditions in the public system, yet impoverished children and children of color did not normally have access to private schools, either because of lack of funds or direct discrimination. It attacked private education for frustrating the best aims of Cuban educators by using archaic methods, operating practices of racial discrimination, encouraging the formation of an elite group in Cuban society, and for anti-Cuban, antipatriotic teachings. The party demanded free obligatory education, both academic and vocational, up to and including university level, for all Cubans, in order to decrease reliance upon private education. In addition, it called for state regulation of private schools in order to ensure uniform education for all Cubans.[6]

In 1915, private education in Cuba became the subject of national debate. That year, the newspaper *Heraldo de Cuba* published a series of articles by school inspector Ismael Clark that described his experiences of private schools and examined the impact of private education on Cuban society. Developing many of the points raised by the *Partido Independiente de Color*, Clark's criticism of private institutions focused on three main themes. He accused them of maintaining unacceptable educational standards, of the perpetration of class and racial divisions in society and of holding antinationalist attitudes.

"Absolute pedagogical confusion exists in private schools in general and *above all in religious schools, principally in girls' schools*," charged Clark. "Most of the 'sisters' in charge of teaching are absolutely ignorant of method and even of the text intrinsic to the very subject which they are teaching."[7] With some honorable exceptions, private schools were "centres of opposition to modern pedagogy."[8] They continued to use teaching methods from colonial days. Many schools were staffed by teachers of dubious training and some were run, he alleged, by religious orders that had been expelled from other countries, particularly France and Spain.

Echoing the *Partido Independiente de Color*, Clark argued that private education exacerbated racism and class divisions in Cuban society. He cited fear of contact with "*gente sucia*"[9] in public schools as one of the reasons for patronizing private institutions. Private schools, he contended, fostered class differences in society, as well as notions of inferiority and superiority. They did so through their very existence and through what they taught, as well as by separating black from white and impoverished from wealthy. The latter practice in particular roused his ire. Some of the schools he described openly labeled children as rich or poor. "In consequence," he wrote, "children (and above all girls) are separated . . . forbidden to meet even in the street . . . and the parents of the poor children, because of vanity, because the school has a majestic name and their children wear a uniform, send their children there and consent to this humiliation!"[10]

In addition to class and race divisions, the lack of homogeneity and common history in the immigrant society of early twentieth-century Cuba troubled nationalists. Education, they believed, by fostering national solidarity, played an important part in fully incorporating immigrants into Cuban society. Nationalists argued that as long as immigrants and their children were educated in their own schools with their own curriculum, their only common interest with their new country would be economic, weakening Cuba's political development.

Clark condemned private schools for failing to foster nationalism in Cuba's children; he reserved particular vitriol for those that actively discouraged it. He protested that private schools failed to introduce children to the concept of *patria*, the child's relationship to it, the history of Cuba, or its patriots. They did not observe Cuban holidays and important days in the country's history. They acted as a "focus of denationalization."[11] Furthermore, "they use texts printed abroad, in which the subjects are not treated in accordance with scientific truth, nor a pedagogical plan, or in which Cuba is omitted, when it is not slandered."[12] As an example, Clark cited a college run by Jesuits in Cienfuegos. The text being used for moral and civic instruction taught, he claimed, "detrimental concepts" about Cuban sovereignty.[13] The Secretary of Public Instruction had ordered the college to modify the text or cease using it, but his instructions were ignored. Clark believed that such defiance provided sufficient cause to close a school.

Limited state secondary education in republican Cuba resulted in heavy reliance on private education at the secondary level. State regulation, such as it was, applied only to primary schools. As private institutions were frequently run by foreign religious orders, nationalists complained that secondary education had in effect become both private and religious, violating the principle of state secular education. It was most unlikely, they argued, that defeated Spanish colonialists and frustrated U.S. annexationists were teaching Cuban children the principles of *cubanidad*. "To claim," argued one newspaper column, "that foreigners teach Cuban youth of the glorious epics of 1868 and 1895, of heroes and martyrs, of the necessity to strengthen patriotic sentiment, of the great influence which the proximity of the United States has exercised over Cuba's destiny and, finally, of the vital necessity to create a potent and vigorous nationality, is to be out of touch with reality."[14]

The link between Cuba's economic and political problems and the availability of private education was pursued by educationalist Arturo Montori. He argued that poor pedagogical standards and antinationalism in private schools affected principally the wealthy, because it was they who attended these schools. Consequently,

Cuba's elite developed a low level of patriotism. As evidence of this assertion, Montori cited the large-scale sale of Cuban land and industry to foreign concerns, the preponderance of foreign businesses in Cuba and their influence on Cuban culture and society, and repeated Cuban requests for foreign, particularly U.S., experts to advise on Cuban problems, in spite of the fact that Cuba possessed professionals who could and did offer expertise.[15] Private schools, argued Montori, produced the badly trained and corrupt professionals and politicians who were such a feature of Cuban society. Private schools educated the class responsible for the frequent political disturbances experienced in Cuba.[16] "In truth, almost all the great collective problems from which this society suffers," he maintained, "stem from the defective education which this social class now receives."[17]

Clark's articles stirred nationalist sentiment, as nationalists recognized that a splintered educational system would lead to a splintered society at many different levels, undermining their aims of national development, *cubanidad*, and loyalty to the *patria*. The Fundación Luz Caballero, named for one of Cuba's renowned nineteenth century intellectuals, was formed to publicize the issues he raised. It argued that the state had both the right and the duty to mold a particular type of citizen, one who acted in accordance with "the economic, moral and political aspirations of society."[18] To overcome the perceived threat to this aim that private schools posed, nationalists argued not for the abolition of private education, but for its regulation, to ensure adherence to nationalist objectives. "I promise that I am not an enemy of private primary schools," Clark reassured his audience, "on the contrary I believe their disappearance would be a national calamity."[19] "Private schools cannot be prohibited because this would be an assault on freedom," he went on, "but as their existence is an assault on the Republic, it is necessary to submit them to the law: to regulate them."[20] The purpose of regulation would be to achieve what Clark identified as the theme of his campaign, the "cubanization" of private education.[21]

The proposed regulation aroused fierce opposition. The conservative newspaper *Diario de la Marina* ("naturally," wrote Clark) gave space to writers to attack Clark's position. Conservative educationalists maintained that the solution to unsatisfactory public education was a strong private system. They accused Clark of being antireligion, an accusation that Clark denied strenuously. Supporters of private education occasionally insisted that private religious schools did not teach antinationalist sentiments (Clark retorted that Belén may have produced some illustrious patriots, but they did not learn their patriotism at the school), but mainly focused their arguments on the issues of freedom of religion and education. Clark himself was personally attacked, anonymously threatened, and subjected to a stringent review of his previous six years of work in an effort to find grounds for his dismissal.

The conflict highlighted an ambiguity in the Constitution regarding private education. Clark's opponents argued that his proposals contravened Article 31, in particular the phrase that promised that "all persons may learn and teach freely any science, art or profession, and found or maintain establishments of education and instruction."[22] Clark, noting that the article also placed education "in the charge of the state," accused anyone who believed that regulation of private schools contravened the Constitution of being ignorant of its contents or unable to read.[23] Thus, the opposition to regulation was suspect. "If private religious schools," Clark wondered, "have the best buildings, the most educated teachers, the support of the best people, if their nature is almost deified, why evade the light of day, of what are they afraid?"[24]

The theme of cubanization resonated with many people. In 1917, in response to the debate and the work of the Fundación Luz Caballero, Fernando Ortiz submitted to the national legislature a proposal for the regulation of private schools. The proposal attempted to address the doubtful pedagogical credentials of many private institutions, and especially their alleged antinationalist teachings. Although this concern was not vocalized during the debate, it implicitly acknowledged the threat posed to the employment of Cuban teachers, particularly those educated in state normal schools, by the private school practice of hiring foreigners and Cubans trained in private schools. Supporters claimed that the proposal enjoyed wide public approval.

The proposed legislation asserted the state's right to inspect private schools, with inspectors hired for that specific purpose. It stipulated that only texts approved by the government-appointed Board of Superintendents should be used in the classroom and that the course of studies in private schools should match that of their public counterparts. The nationalist aspirations inherent in the position of Clark and his supporters were reinforced by the specifications that directors of private institutions should be Cuban-born; that the history of Cuba (not then taught in most private schools, or public secondary schools) and civics should be taught only by Cuban-born teachers; and that the Cuban flag should be placed prominently in all schools. It added that only those with qualifications recognized by the state should be entitled to employment. Public school teachers were to be forbidden to work in private schools at any time, an attempt to stop the practice of state employees supplementing their income by tutoring in private schools, resulting, it was alleged, in neglect of their duties.

Cuba's politicians refused to pass the legislation. Largely the products of private schools themselves, they also educated their children privately; they were therefore responsive to the vigorous and angry resistance of many private institutions and their supporters to the proposed regulation. The dispute continued to simmer, however, and reemerged on a national scale during the debates that surrounded the creation and implementation of the Constitution of 1940.

THE DEBATE OVER PRIVATE EDUCATION: 1941

The 1920s witnessed a growth of nationalism in Cuba, as the island's economic dependence and political impotence became the focus of national scrutiny. The political mobilization and divisions that followed, combined with the Depression, led to the crisis of the 1930s. Too complex to review here, it is nonetheless important to note two points. Firstly, government repression resulted in the virtual shutdown of public education, increasing reliance on the private sector by those who could afford it. Secondly, a new, progressive Constitution arose from the political settlement of the late 1930s. In spite of the hopes which the new Constitution excited, however, its achievements remained largely on paper. In many ways it served only to accentuate the contrast between nationalist conceits and Cuban reality, as the renewed debate over private education illustrated. The Constitution bestowed on the state a greatly expanded right to regulate private schools. However, the introduction of the required legislation by communist senator Juan Marinello in 1941 gave rise to ferocious opposition.

Education and its role in Cuban society featured prominently in the deliberations over the new Constitution. The Catholic church had lobbied for the introduction of religious instruction in public schools, a possibility resisted by Protestants, liberals, and communists defending the tradition of secular education in independent Cuba, who took the opportunity to raise again the themes of nationalism and education arising from Ismael Clark's reports in 1915. In addition to maintaining secular instruction in public schools, they argued in favor of restrictions on the nationality of teachers and regulations that would ensure that only those with qualifications recognized by the Cuban state would teach. "Almost all the teachers in private schools are foreigners, and religious foreigners," claimed one commentator. "The supervision of the foreign teacher is unacceptable for developing in children patriotic sentiment, the basis of a perfect national education."[25]

The Constitution encapsulated the nationalist aims of education around which the debate of 1915 had centered. "All instruction, public and private," it proclaimed, "shall be inspired by a spirit of *cubanidad* and human solidarity, forming in the minds of those being educated love of *patria*, its democratic institutions and all who have struggled for one or the other."[26] Indeed, the Constitution included many of the principles contained in the ill-fated legislation proposed by Fernando Ortiz almost twenty-five years earlier. Article 55 pronounced private institutions subject to regulation and inspection by the state. Article 56 insisted that civics, history, and geography of Cuba be taught by native-born Cubans, from books written by the same. Article 50 declared that only graduates of state normal schools could teach in primary schools in the public system.[27] Both private and religious education were protected by the Constitution, however. Article 54 confirmed that "official or private universities and any other institutions and centers of higher learning may be created." Article 55 pledged that, while official instruction must be secular, "in all cases the right shall be preserved of imparting, separate from technical instruction, the religious education that may be desired."[28]

The legislation that Juan Marinello proposed asserted the state's right to authorize and inspect private schools, to approve textbooks,[29] and to ensure that teachers held both Cuban citizenship and appropriate qualifications; and stipulated that any infractions of Article 20 of the Constitution, which declared illegal discrimination on the basis of sex, race, or class, be reported and punished.[30] Article 4 reiterated the right of schools to impart religious education. No aspect of the proposal contravened any of the Constitution's principles; Marinello argued that it provided the legislative framework within which to execute those principles. Each clause identified the clause of the Constitution to which it related, and in many cases the same wording was used.

Marinello's attempt to enforce the requirements of the Constitution revealed the limits of subordination to the state that conservative and religious, mainly Catholic, leaders would tolerate in private education. They objected strongly to the appointment of Marinello as head of the National Council of Education's committee for private education because of his membership in the Communist Party and because he had argued against the principle of private education in the Constitutional Convention. His opponents made unsuccessful efforts to expel Marinello from his position.[31] They directed their attention principally, however, to blocking the proposed legislation.

Early in May 1941, the conservative newspaper *Diario de la Marina* advertised a forthcoming meeting under the title "Por la Patria y por la Escuela." "Free Man," thundered the announcement, "liberty is the most precious treasure of man. Without freedom of teaching, Cuba in the future will be a nation of slaves. There are some who seek to interfere with the freedom to teach and to learn recognized in the Constitution. You must prevent this."[32] "Cuban Mother," a second announcement, on Mothers' Day, appealed, "on this day dedicated to you, a moment of meditation on the future of your children. . . . You can do something . . . in order that your children tomorrow will be free men, honorable and patriotic."[33] A separate appeal to fathers asked for their assistance in protecting "your freedom to teach your children where you want, so the conscience of your children will not be poisoned with foreign ideologies."[34]

Diario de la Marina published announcements, letters of protest against Marinello's position, and instructions for action every day, until the meeting took place on 25 May 1941. Thousands attended the gathering, held in the National Theater in Old Havana.[35] Seats were placed outside for those who could not fit into the theater, with the speeches broadcast through loudspeakers. The assembly attracted support from the *Asociación de Escuelas Privadas*, the *Asociación de Maestras Católicas*, alumni of private schools and some prominent Cubans. The British-owned private school St. George and the U.S.-owned Ruston Academy also supported the meeting.

The campaign declared its complete support for private education, asserting that Cuba's private schools were among the best in the world, and claiming, somewhat dubiously, that they provided benefits to all social classes, without regard to race.[36] One supporter argued that government attention should be focused on improving the public system, which bordered on chaos, rather than regulating private educational institutions; certainly private schools should not be placed under the care of the public authorities, which had proved themselves so much less competent than those who ran private institutions. Rather than regulating private education, he argued that the government should emulate private education in the public sector.[37]

Supporters maintained that endorsement of private education did not imply opposition to the Constitution. Nonetheless, they resisted every aspect of state control over private education granted by the charter. They warned that passage of Marinello's legislation would result in a communist (i.e., Marinello), not the state, regulating private schools and religious instruction. Such a situation, they claimed, would amount to religious persecution. They opposed standardization of teaching between public and private schools, maintaining that this would destroy freedom of teaching, and rejected state approval of textbooks on the grounds that approval equaled censorship and was therefore antidemocratic.

It was primarily the Catholic elite that felt threatened by Marinello's labors, although the *Diario de la Marina* denied that the movement represented an official Catholic position. It could not do otherwise, given the widespread adherence to the concept of a secular state and its long associations with nationalism and independence in Cuba. Nonetheless, the newspaper argued that Marinello's presence on the relevant committee of the National Council of Education represented an act of aggression against Catholics, and it made frequent references to the Catholic nature of the campaign. The day of the meeting, announced the newspaper, somewhat defensively, "was a great day, not only for Catholics, but for all Cubans."[38]

Marinello's proposed legislation was attacked on the grounds that it represented an attempt by communists to infiltrate education and to destroy the family. *Por la Patria y por la Escuela* supporters deemed it sufficient merely to make an accusation of communism to justify their position; they judged it unnecessary to explain why the proposals were communist or why communism should be opposed, other than to equate it with lack of freedom. "In a great demonstration of courtesy and patriotism," exhorted a *Diario de la Marina* headline, "the Cuban family must voice its most energetic rejection of communist interference in education and teaching."[39] The movement's manifesto concluded, "we oppose the participation of communism in the formation of the [Marinello] school law . . . because the law attempts to regulate freedom of teaching and communism, as a totalitarian tendency, is an enemy of free individuals and of democracy."[40] This point was repeated in the *Diario de la Marina* five days later.[41] Cuban democracy, institutions and national honor, freedom of teaching, and Christian morality must be defended against the onslaught of communism, supporters claimed. *The Havana Post* headlined its account of the meeting on 25 May, "Thousands support anti-communist movement," and recorded that the meeting's resolutions pledged to remove Marinello and to outlaw the Communist party, making no mention whatsoever of education.[42] As Fernando Ortiz later observed, *Por la patria y por la Escuela* subsumed all its arguments into the one argument of combatting communism.[43]

Supporters of the Constitution's provisions reacted swiftly. On 28 May, Emilio Roig de Leuchsenring placed an advertisement in the newspaper *El Mundo* warning that anti-Cuban and antinational elements were attempting to prevent the institutions and laws of the republic from discharging their functions.[44] He called for a meeting to be held at the National Theater on 22 June, the anniversary of the birth of José de la Luz y Caballero.[45] *Por la Escuela Cubana en Cuba Libre*, a coalition of liberal and left-wing groups, formed in response to his call. Thousands attended the June meeting, which also spilled into the park and streets outside the theater. Among other well-known Cubans, Fernando Ortiz, who had been prominent in the earlier debate over private education, joined Emilio Roig in the new campaign. Leading educationalists, many non-Catholic private schools, and public school students and their teachers voiced their support.

As did its opponents, *Por la Escuela Cubana en Cuba Libre* declared itself to be a nonpartisan movement, open to all without regard to race, class, or political affiliation. It affirmed its loyalty to the Constitution, in particular the undertaking in Article 51 that "all instruction, public and private shall be inspired by a spirit of *cubanidad* and human solidarity, forming in the minds of those being educated love of *patria*, its democratic institutions and all who have struggled for one or the other." "Cuba will have democratic education," declared Marinello, "not because a socialist senator wants it, but because the Constitution orders it."[46]

Por la Escuela Cubana en Cuba Libre pledged its support for public education, at all levels, urban and rural, academic and technical, and called on the government to end the tradition of neglect under which the system suffered. According to Emilio Roig, the decay of the public school system was linked to the fact that the politicians who had the means and the duty to improve it had themselves been educated in private schools, and in turn educated their children privately. He sought assurances that no government money would be granted to private institutions until public schools were judged satisfactory. At no time, however, did the movement attack either the principle of private education or the right to receive or impart religious instruction. Some members were quite explicit in declaring their acceptance of private education (many actively supported it), and their commitment to freedom of worship. The cause they championed was the continued separation of church and state, the provision of secular state education and state regulation of private education.

At one level, the battle for regulation was a battle for the economic improvement of less privileged sectors of Cuban society. The belief that all Cubans should be taught by Cubans, from textbooks written by Cubans, under the direction of the Cuban state, stemmed not only from nationalist pride but also from economic necessity. The claim that thousands of Cuban teachers remained unemployed while private schools hired foreign teachers, some with allegedly dubious qualifications, underpinned the insistence on the employment of Cuban teachers. Private schools were also accused of forcing staff to work long hours for low pay and in poor conditions. The stipulation that only graduates of state normal schools could work in public primary schools was designed to protect the poor teenagers who used normal schools as free secondary education and a route to future employment. In addition, the movement raised the issue of race and access to education, with Marinello arguing that black and mulatto Cubans faced prejudice in their quest for education and training, and later in finding jobs in education, and that these problems were compounded in the private sector.

Supporters of *Por la Escuela Cubana en Cuba Libre* declared that their opponents aroused fears of communism to divert attention from the presence of anti-Cuban foreigners, falangists, or Spanish fascists, and Jesuits in their opponents' ranks.[47] The movement warned of the dangers to Cuban independence of succumbing to church dogma. Juan Marinello argued that his concerns about the regressive aspects of church teaching came directly from José Martí.[48] Emilio Roig devoted part of his speech at a meeting on 1 June to demonstrating his belief that the Church remained anti-Cuba.[49] This accusation resonated on the island, where the Church had long been associated with Spain's attempts to prevent Cuban independence; radical opposition had deepened following its support of the fascists in the Spanish Civil War.

Claiming to be a nationalist coalition, the movement attacked its opponents for being "antinational." Picking up one of the important themes of 1915, *El Mundo* described the campaign as demanding the "nationalization and cubanization of teaching in our country."[50] It represented a positive affirmation of what its supporters believed to be the finest aims of Cuba's educational system: confirmation of the Cuban state's secularism; economic opportunities for Cubans, both students and teachers; respect for democracy; the fostering of a love of *patria* and a spirit of *cubanidad*. *Por la Patria y por la Escuela*, however, rejected the allegation that it was antinationalist. Supporters vigorously denied the charge that they had been organized by Spanish falangists (although the editor of the *Diario de la Marina* had connections with both falangists and Nazis). Their movement, they maintained, was organized by Cubans and open to Cubans of all races and classes; they opposed only communism, and communist interference in the educational sector.[51]

The debate between the two groups thus transformed itself into a battle to define nationalism in Cuba, and was frequently reduced to competing protestations of nationalist fervor. Part of the responsibility for this outcome lies with the liberal nationalists who focused the debate primarily, although not exclusively, on the consequences of private education for nationalism, rather than on the reasons why private education flourished in Cuba and its specific effects on the nation's political economy. Discussion of the deplorable state of public education led not to analyses of the way in which private education contributed to that state, but agreement that private education must continue in order to take pressure off the public system. The argument that private education put pressure *on* the public system was not adequately addressed. Conservative nationalists largely avoided the substantive issues raised and concentrated instead on inflaming fears of communism and destruction of family and nation; the liberal nationalist emphasis on nationalism allowed the conservatives to evade the issues unchallenged.

In the end, although liberal nationalists addressed themselves to the issues far more diligently and concretely, conservative nationalists won the struggle. Despite strenuous efforts by supporters, the proposed legislation was rejected. In practice the regulatory rights of the state remained substantially unchanged, although a new post of Inspector General of Private Schools was created. As before, the purpose of inspections was to assess the suitability of building and location, and to ensure the employment of qualified teachers. Conservative nationalists claimed victory, and liberal nationalists acknowledged defeat. "Schools run by foreigners," complained Roig, "continued, and will continue, enjoying privileges and protection decided by officials and the wealthy classes of the country."[52]

While private institutions officially recognized the authority of the state and the Minister of Education, in practice they could disregard the stipulations of the Constitution. It is arguable whether legislation would have increased observance, but certainly its absence was taken as a signal that the Constitution could be ignored. Even where the Constitution was quite specific, such as the requirement that teachers of certain subjects be Cuban-born, the possibility of punishment for infractions remained remote. The final defeat of Marinello's legislation in 1945 encouraged the *Confederación de Colegios Cubanos Católicos* to expand its efforts in favor of private education. It lobbied against catchment zones, state control over normal school education, and examiners who did not conform to "christian moral-ity," as well as campaigning for freedom from the slight pressure applied by school inspectors regarding curriculum and textbooks.

Enrollment in private schools continued to grow, as did their numbers. From 25,000 pupils in 1934, they educated 71,000 in 1943.[53] By 1949, 80,000 Cubans were enrolled in 580 authorized private schools, with perhaps another 10,000 in those operating without Ministry of Education approval.[54] The World Bank noted in its *Report on Cuba* of 1951 that private schools had "expanded very much more than public schools in the last quarter century."[55] In 1955, the Cuban government recorded 804 authorized private schools on the island.[56] The public school, claimed the World Bank, was "in danger of becoming a 'poor man's school.' This not only intensifies social class divisions. The public school also loses the interest and support of some of the most energetic segments of the community, and the process becomes a vicious circle."[57] It could certainly be argued that public schools were not "in danger of becoming" schools of the poor, but had already become so at the time the World Bank mission visited Cuba. Private institutions remained the domain of wealthy, white Cubans.

CONCLUSION

The association of secular public education with *Cuba Libre* was so strong in republican Cuba that support for public instruction became a vital component of nationalism. It is significant that when a leading educationalist warned of increasing illiteracy in 1910, he was pilloried not for inaccuracy, but for being *unpatriotic*. Yet, in spite of this old and powerful connection, limited regulation of private schools could not be enforced in republican Cuba, and the possibility of abolition could not even be raised. Although the growth of nationalism potentially involved a challenge to the political and economic order, competing claims to the nationalist vision meant that it also acted as a diversion.

The conflicts over private education highlight the limits of the nationalist response in identifying the causes of the problems in Cuba's educational system and thus in proposing strategies to overcome them. The general focus of anxiety was not private education per se but Catholic education, so closely associated with colonial subjugation. Consequently, rather than addressing how public and private education reflected power imbalances in Cuban society, the debates centered on the extent of nationalist expression within private schools; hence the proposed solution of regulation. Given the acceptance of the *principle* of private education, however, no amount of nationalist teaching or regulation could overcome the economic and racial divisions that private schools exemplified and propagated. Had Fernando Ortiz' bill, or the legislative framework to implement the provisions of the 1940 Constitution, been passed, and proved enforceable, the prejudice and privilege reinforced by private institutions would nonetheless have remained untouched. Regulation did not address the fact that in practice private schooling was open only to those who had the financial resources to purchase it. This condition alone conflicted directly with the establishment of the genuinely democratic educational system, and nation, promised by *Cuba Libre*.

The real issue in the debate over private education was not nationalism or the lack of it in private schools, but the abysmal conditions in the public system and why those who could afford to, and many who could not, opted out of it; why even bad private schools were regarded as preferable to education in the public system, and why the latter ultimately provided schools for working class and rural children only. To maintain, as did many nationalists, that the public system required good, regulated private schools as a complement, particularly in times of political and social upheaval, was to beg the question of why the public system needed complementing at all. The enthusiasm and commitment that went into the nationalist battle to regulate private schools, in spite of its good intentions, was in itself an excellent example of how private education diverted the energies of those best placed to pressure successfully for meaningful change in public education.

The clash over the state's right to regulate private schools was in effect a contest over who would become the country's future leaders, and who would control their education. It had little to do with implementing the vision of public education intrinsic to *Cuba Libre*. The resistance to regulation represented the determination by one class to retain its privilege. By locating the debate in private education, rather than the decay of state education, nationalists failed to address adequately the substantive conflicts and inequalities at the heart of the educational system, and consequently of their society. This failure, and the focus on nationalism in private education, allowed the fundamental issues involved in compromised sovereignty, its consequences for Cuba's educational system, and the impact on Cuban society to be deflected and contained.

In many ways, however, the dispute over private education presaged the national struggle between those who argued that the structure of republican Cuba was workable, but poorly implemented, and thus advocated reform, and those who decried the entire system, championing revolution. The repeated frustration of nationalist ambitions contributed to the revolutionary drive, and those frustrations were consistently evident in the debates over the role of private education in Cuban society. The failure of the public educational system to fulfill nationalist demands, the inequalities that the public/private educational split revealed so starkly, and the implacable resistance of powerful elements in Cuban society to any change, contributed to the general perception of the failure of reforms in the republic, and thus of the failure of the republic itself. The links between state secular education, educational opportunity for all, national development, *cubanidad*, and Cuban sovereignty were firmly fixed in the national imagination, and these were not issues over which the majority of Cubans were prepared to compromise indefinitely.

NOTES

1. The categories of private schools described here do not include *escuelitas*, which were little more than informal neighborhood daycare centers, or ad hoc arrangements made by parents, particularly in rural areas, to provide education for their children, such as hiring a teacher among several parents. For an example of the latter, see Lowry Nelson, *Rural Cuba* (New York: Octagon Books, 1970), pp. 229–30. It was also common for black Cubans, women's organizations and workers' associations to provide educational opportunities outside the state system.

2. Arturo Montori, "La educación en Cuba," *Cuba Contemporánea* 38:150 (June, 1925), p. 155. While the extent of the numerical growth of private schools is unclear, the perception of their growth was firmly fixed in the public mind.

3. Margaret E. Crahan, "Religious Penetration and Nationalism in Cuba: U.S. Methodist Activities 1898–1958," *Revista/Review Interamericana* 8:2 (Summer, 1978), p. 219.

4. Public schools were occasionally accused of separating white and black children, an accusation always denied by government.

5. *Heraldo de Cuba*, 25 July 1915, p. 6. Private schools could not independently bestow accreditation recognized by the state; they were therefore "incorporated" into public schools, which provided examiners for the private students.

6. Serafín Portuondo Linares, *Los independientes de color: Historia del Partido Independiente de Color* (La Habana: Ministerio de Educación, Dirección de Cultura, 1950), pp. 67, 72.

7. Ismael Clark, "Escuelas Privadas," *Heraldo de Cuba*, 9 July 1915, p. 5, emphasis in the original.

8. Ibid., p. 5.

9. Literally, "dirty people."

10. Clark, "Escuelas Privadas," p. 5. Although Clark clearly believed that private schools had particularly adverse effects on girls, he never accuses them of fostering gender divisions in society in addition to race and class divisions.

11. Ibid., p. 5.

12. Clark, quoted in Arturo Montori, *El problema de la educación nacional* (La Habana: Cuba Pedagógica, 1920), p. 28.

13. Arturo Montori, *Ponencia del Dr. A. Montori sobre reglamentación de las escuelas privadas* (La Habana: Aurelio Miranda, 1917), p. 14.

14. Julio Villoldo, "Voz de alarma," *La Discusión*, 25 March 1912, p. 8. He was referring in particular to Spanish orders.

15. Montori, *El problema de la educación nacional*, p. 9.

16. Ibid., p. 7; Montori, *Ponencia del Dr. A. Montori*, p. 20.

17. Montori, *El problema de la educación nacional*, p. 46.

18. Montori, *Ponencia del Dr. A. Montori*, p. 8.

19. *Heraldo de Cuba*, 23 July 1915, p. 8.

20. Clark, "Escuelas Privadas," p. 5.

21. See *Heraldo de Cuba*, 16 August 1915, p. 2 and 19 August 1915, p. 2.

22. Cuba, *Constitución de la República de Cuba* (La Habana: Rambla y Bouza, 1901), pp. 9–10.

23. Ibid., p. 9.

24. *Heraldo de Cuba*, 23 July 1915, p. 8.

25. María Corominas de Hernández, "La nacionalización de la enseñanza en Cuba," *Revista Bimestre Cubana* 37:1 (1936), p. 70. She originally argued this point in a speech during the Fiesta Intelectual de la Mujer in July 1935. Many commentators reported that most teachers in Catholic schools were Spanish, whereas those in Protestant schools were Cuban. See, for example, Ciro Espinosa y Rodríguez, *La crisis de la segunda enseñanza en Cuba y su posible solución* (La Habana: Cultural, 1942), pp. 42, 45.

26. "La Constitución de 1940," in Hortensia Pichardo, ed., *Documentos para la historia de Cuba*, 4, 2 ed. (La Habana: Editorial Pueblo y Educación, 1986), p. 341.

27. Ibid., pp. 341, 342.

28. Ibid., p. 342.

29. Textbooks did not have to be the *same* as those used in public schools, only approved by the ministry.

30. A copy of the proposed legislation may be found in Juan Marinello, *Por una enseñanza democratica* (La Habana: Editorial Páginas, 1945), pp. 20–24.

31. At the same time, some members of Congress were attempting to make the Communist party illegal.

32. *Diario de la Marina*, 9 May 1941, p. 3. See also *El Mundo* on 8 and 9 May.

33. Ibid., 11 May 1941, p. 3. See also *El Mundo* on 11 May.

34. Ibid., 14 May 1941, p. 3. See also *El Mundo* on 15 May.

35. Reports of attendance varied between 8,000 and 20,000.

36. *Diario de la Marina*, 28 May 1941, p. 3.

37. *Ponencia presentada por el Senador Marcelino Garriga a la Comisión de Derechos Constitucionales y reformas sociales del senado de la República sobre la proposición de Ley para reglamentar la enseñanza privada del Dr. Marinello*, (1945), passim.

38. *Diario de la Marina*, 25 May 1941, p. 4, and 27 May 1941, p. 4.

39. Ibid., 25 May 1941, p. 3.

40. Ibid., 15 June 1941, p. 5.

41. See ibid., 20 June 1941, p. 3.

42. *The Havana Post*, 27 May 1941, p. 1.

43. Fernando Ortiz Fernández, *Por la escuela cubana en Cuba Libre* (La Habana: n.p., c. 1941), p. 24.

44. *El Mundo*, 28 May 1941, p. 3.

45. José de la Luz y Caballero (1800–1862) was a renowned Cuban *pensador* and teacher.

46. Juan Marinello, *La reforma educacional en Inglaterra: La inspección de la enseñanza privada* (La Habana: n.p., 1945), p. 16.

47. Jesuits were accused of acting as agents for the Vatican in an attempt to intervene in Cuba's affairs.

48. Juan Marinello, *Por una enseñanza democratica* (La Habana: Editorial Páginas, 1945), p. 8.

49. "Por la escuela cubana en Cuba Libre: Trabajos, acuerdos y adhesiones de una campaña cívica y cultural." Pamphlet (La Habana, 1941), p. 33.

50. Quoted in Emilio Roig de Leuchsenring, *Males y vicios de Cuba republicana: sus causas y sus remedios* (La Habana: Oficina del Historiador de la Ciudad, 1959), p. 135.

51. *Diario de la Marina*, 21 June 1941, p. 3.

52. Roig de Leuchsenring, *Males,* p. 162.

53. República de Cuba, *Censo de 1943* (La Habana: P. Fernández, 1945), p. 484. Estimates of private school enrollment for the late 1930s vary between 30,000 and 40,000 pupils.

54. Mercedes García Tudurí, "La enseñanza en Cuba en los primeros cincuenta años de independencia," in Ramiro Guerra y Sánchez, *Historia de la nación cubana*, 10 (La Habana: Editorial Historia de la Nación Cubana, 1952), p. 142. She is using figures from the Inspección de Escuelas Privadas of the Ministry of Education. See the International Bank for Reconstruction and Development (IBRD), *Report on Cuba* (Baltimore: Johns Hopkins Press, 1951), p. 414 for the estimate of unauthorized enrollment.

55. IBRD, *Report on Cuba*, p. 414.

56. Cuba, Ministerio de Educación, *Estadística de la enseñanza oficial y privada, curso escolar 1954–55* (La Habana: Ministerio de Educación, 1955), p. 89.

57. IBRD, *Report on Cuba*, p. 414.

chapter 4

Intellectuals and the State in Spanish America: A Comparative Perspective

Nicola Miller

There is a common perception that modern Spanish American intellectuals have played a leading role in the politics of their nations. Closely related to this is the image of intellectuals as the bearers of a popular national identity. This chapter starts from the premise that this "tradition of the president-poet"[1] is—to use Hobsbawm and Ranger's famous phrase—an "invented tradition."[2] It has some basis in history, of course, as do all invented traditions, but was largely the creation of Spanish American intellectuals themselves during the first three decades of the twentieth century, particularly the 1920s, which was precisely the time when the intellectual sectors of these societies were being displaced from power by a newly emerging type of state committed to modernization. This tradition of the politically influential Spanish American intellectual was invented to buttress modern intellectuals' claims to national influence in the context of the interventionist state. In reality, as this chapter argues, twentieth-century intellectuals in Spanish America have enjoyed remarkably little political influence, particularly when compared with their nineteenth-century forebears.

Although modernizing Spanish American states denied modern intellectuals any significant involvement in public policy-making, these same states were obliged to accommodate intellectuals to some extent. This was partly because states needed them to satisfy the educational and cultural demands of their main immediate constituencies, the emerging middle classes, and partly because intellectuals appeared to be creating a putative role for themselves as mediators between the state and the masses. Likewise, the fate of intellectuals remained bound up with the modernizing state, even when they defined themselves in opposition to it, not only because they were often dependent upon it for employment, but also because it offered the only route to the realization of the intellectuals' visions. Thus, the tradition of the politically influential Spanish American intellectual was sustained alongside the modernizing state. It lasted, therefore, into the 1960s (when it was reinvented for the benefit of Western audiences during the literary "Boom"), but thenceforth became increasingly less plausible as the Spanish American project of state-led development collapsed into authoritarianism and debt.

Since the return to elected rule in the 1980s, a new conception of the state has been dominant in Spanish America, related to the adoption of neoliberal policies. Reduction of the state apparatus (more accurately, perhaps, its economic apparatus) has been the declared aim. Modernization is no longer thought of as the province of the state, but instead of the free market. Spanish American intellectuals have experienced a severe sense of disorientation (compounded for many by the collapse of communism in Eastern Europe) as a result of the decline of a modernizing state with which they could identify, however critically. As the modernizing state lost its link with the middle classes (or was reduced to reinforcing it by means of repression) in the 1960s and 1970s, so also its symbiotic relationship with the intellectuals weakened. At the structural level, private funding once again became a feature of intellectual life. This was evident in a variety of forms, ranging from the founding in 1958 of the Di Tella Institute in Buenos Aires by the sons of a prominent Argentine industrialist to the proliferation since the 1960s of social science research bodies funded by moneys from U.S. and European foundations, and indeed the Catholic church. These institutions provided a refuge for intellectuals excluded from universities subject to military intervention, and after the return to elected rule many have continued to be an alternative to state employment (although it should be pointed out that some of them have also received state grants). Apart from the often superior resources such organizations sometimes offer, they constitute a valuable, if still fragile, institutional basis for intellectual independence from the state. This possibility has been enhanced by the fact that since the 1960s, what can be termed, at least in relation to earlier decades, a mass market for books and magazines emerged in the region. It can be argued, however, that the role of the state in Spanish American intellectual life should not be underestimated even in the 1990s. But the main purpose here is not to pursue these debates, but simply to emphasize that from the 1980s onward the state and intellectuals in Spanish America had entered a qualitatively new relationship. The tradition of the Spanish American "president-poet" is much harder to sustain in this new context, although it certainly lingers on in residual form. This chapter focuses on the previous, crucial relationship between intellectuals and the interventionist state from the 1920s to the 1960s.

The argument draws on five case studies: Argentina, Chile, Cuba, Mexico, and Peru. These countries were chosen partly because they have all, at varying times, been important centers of intellectual activity in the region, and partly because their diversity of historical experience, political formation, and ethnic composition provides a broad basis for comparison. A case could always be made for the inclusion of other countries (especially Colombia and Uruguay). Brazil is not discussed on the grounds that it has a distinct intellectual tradition from the Spanish American countries, which is largely attributable to the late foundation (mainly in the 1930s) of Brazilian universities. For reasons of space, this chapter cannot treat all five case studies in depth and therefore sustains the argument at a comparative level, with illustrative examples.

Limitations of space also prevent any detailed discussion of the definitional minefields surrounding both the terms "the state" and "the intellectuals." Nevertheless, a few brief points should be made, firstly on the state. The term "state" (referring to the permanent institutions of government) is used on the basis that it cannot be reduced either to class/sectoral or to bureaucratic interests; it is neither monolithic nor necessarily consistent over time; and it must be defined relatively broadly in a Spanish American context, where institutions usually thought of in Europe as part of "civil society" (for example, trade unions or the media) have often been wholly or partly subsumed under the state umbrella.

This chapter's main analytical framework is the transition in Spanish America from what Whitehead calls the "oligarchic" state to the "modernizing" state.[3] This terminology is a useful adaptation to the Spanish American context of Gramsci's distinction between the "aristocratic" state, governed by a "closed caste," and the "bourgeois" state, which saw itself as "capable of absorbing the entire society, assimilating it to its own cultural and economic level."[4] In schematic terms, the main differences are as follows: the Spanish American oligarchic state was associated with the aristocracy, landed interests, export-led growth, European-dominated culture, and exclusionary nationalism; the modernizing state came to be associated with the middle classes, urban industrial interests, import-substitution-industrialization, and economic, cultural, and inclusionary popular nationalisms.

Whitehead dates the onset of the transformation of oligarchic states into modernizing states to the late 1920s, but there is a case for arguing that the process began earlier, at least in the five countries discussed here. Governments that sought their support base in modernizing coalitions came to power in 1916 in Argentina; 1920 in Mexico, Chile and Peru; and in Cuba in 1933. (Regarding Cuba, a case could even be made for 1925: it should not be forgotten that Machado was elected as the candidate of the emerging entrepreneurial and professional middle sectors, however quickly he lost patience with them once in office.[5]) Moreover, the 1920s were particularly important where cultural policy was concerned, because regimes that were unable (or unwilling) to challenge the economic or social power of the oligarchies bolstered their claims to modernizing legitimacy by giving prominence to issues of culture and education.

With respect to the question of definition of "the intellectuals," the following points should be borne in mind. Firstly, for the purposes of this argument, the noun "intellectual" is treated as a word with a history rather than a generic term. The idea of an intellectual first became current in Spanish America in the early twentieth century, soon after the Dreyfus Affair had popularized the term in France. However, although the Spanish Americans were certainly influenced by the French usage, they were operating in a very different context. In France, the term reflected a desire to break out of the ghetto of increasingly specialized knowledge and reclaim the universal moral and critical authority of the philosophes. In Spanish America, however, the word reflected the fact that the conditions for the professionalization of intellectual life were just beginning to be established, in other words, it was an idea dependent on a nascent modernity. The *pensadores* of the nineteenth century are not, therefore, considered as "intellectuals"; they were operating in very different conditions and had a wholly different conception of the relationship between power and knowledge. The heart of the distinction is as follows: the *pensadores* sought to have influence on specific issues because they were generally learned men; intellectuals, on the other hand, sought to establish a speciality and then use it to justify a bid for general influence.

Secondly, the term "intellectual" is used narrowly in this chapter, as it is most commonly used in Spanish America, that is, not (as in a sociological sense) to refer to virtually anybody who has received higher education (lawyers, doctors, academics, teachers, engineers) but rather to those people Enrique Krauze epitomized as "caudillos culturales"[6]: people who have won recognition as intellectual leaders of their society. The assumption here is that the process of becoming an intellectual is not simply a question of acquiring certain skills or attributes, but is one that requires the recognition of others. Being an intellectual requires constant reaffirmation and legitimation from at least two of the three following constituencies: other intellectuals, the intelligentsia, and the masses. The importance of the different constituencies varies with time and place, as do the criteria by which they grant recognition to an intellectual. Most of the people discussed in this chapter are creative writers, but this is not to accept the common assumption that "intellectual" is synonymous with "writer." Until World War II, it *was* almost exclusively writers who were thought of as intellectuals in Spanish America, but in the 1950s social scientists, particularly economists, began to be acknowledged as intellectuals. Analysis of such shifts in the criteria for being deemed "an intellectual" is perhaps more revealing about the relationship between power and knowledge than any attempt at categorical definition of the term.

Nevertheless, the position adopted here is not one of complete relativism: the following criteria determine who is included as "an intellectual" in this discussion. Firstly, they were national not local figures. Secondly, they were people who sought professional recognition for their intellectual work (therefore figures like Fidel Castro or Che Guevara, who were primarily interested in achieving political rather than intellectual authority, are excluded). Thirdly, they publicly intervened in debates on general social affairs, not confined themselves to their specialisms, and, fourthly, they maintained independence (at least as an aim) from both church and state. In brief, the term "intellectual" is used in what follows to designate an independent social critic.

The main argument of this chapter is that from the 1920s to the 1960s Spanish American states maintained conditions in which it was virtually impossible for intellectuals to establish independent critical communities that could have provided leadership to a civil society capable of challenging the legitimacy of the state. This was a result of deliberate policies on the part of modernizing states, which were remarkably uniform and consistent in their determination to curtail the power of intellectuals and relatively successful in so doing. Anti-intellectual policies were pursued by a wide range of regimes: democratic, authoritarian, populist. The means varied, but not the ends, which suggests that it was the nature of the state (modernizing) rather than the nature of the regime that was important in determining policies toward intellectuals. Sometimes states simply resorted to repression, imprisoning or exiling individuals they considered troublesome, and practicing censorship, most commonly of newspapers and periodicals, but also of literary and academic works. However, if states had only been repressive, they would not have been able to sustain a tacit alliance with intellectuals that was not broken until the 1960s and 1970s, precisely when the states in all five case studies did relapse into pure authoritarianism. The argument below therefore focuses on two other, more successful strategies adopted by states to contain the potential influence of intellectuals.

These were: (1) simultaneously denying intellectuals the opportunity to have any significant impact on public policy while keeping open the possibility of power or at least influence; and (2) establishing mechanisms of control, both direct and indirect, over the main institutions of intellectual life, most importantly, of course, the universities, but also intellectual honors (prizes, scholarships, and fellowships), prestigious appointments (such as director of the National Library), publishing and the press. In other words, states came to monopolize the routes by which Spanish American intellectuals were able to acquire what Bourdieu calls "cultural capital."[7]

INTELLECTUALS AND PUBLIC POLICY

Firstly, it is important to dispel the common myth that so-called intellectuals have maintained a constant relationship with the state since independence. In practice, this relationship underwent virtually a complete reversal as a result of the onset of modernization. During the nineteenth century, particularly when liberalism was dominant, certain distinguished men of letters (who either came from the elites or identified with them) occupied high offices of state or were influential advisers to government. Indeed, the tradition of Spanish American statesmen/intellectuals derives from this involvement in nineteenth-century liberal governments. However, this in itself is often overstated: the participation of men of letters in the executive branch of the state was mainly confined to Argentina and Mexico, although many did serve in the legislatures of other countries. At this time, the patronage of culture was undertaken mainly by members of the oligarchy acting in a private capacity. It was they who founded the major newspapers, hosted the literary soirees, and funded the Ateneos. The state's role in relation to culture during the nineteenth century was primarily that of censor.

In twentieth-century Spanish America, by contrast, intellectuals, who identified themselves on the basis of a claim to independence from the state have largely been excluded from public policy-making (as either executives or advisers), while from the 1920s onward states increasingly took steps to concentrate the direction of culture into their own hands, establishing bureaucracies to administer educational and cultural policy. This was one consequence of the transition from "oligarchic" to "modernizing" state discussed above. As part of a broad stand against the oligarchy, modernizing states redefined "culture" as no longer solely the high culture of the elites, but as part of a nation-building project directed in the first instance at the emerging middle classes, who were largely the creation of the modernizing state and became its main bulwark, and, in the longer term, at least in theory, at the masses. Both the initial emphasis on the middle sectors, themselves preoccupied with education, and the future concern for integration of the masses, required the nascent modernizing states of the 1920s to formulate specific policies toward the newly emerging "independent" intellectuals (most of them from bourgeois or petty-bourgeois backgrounds) who aspired to lead public opinion.

It is not difficult to gather evidence to show that the occupants of state office in twentieth-century Spanish America have for the most part despised and distrusted intellectuals. As has often been noted, military leaders have usually identified intellectuals as opponents to be defeated. However, for the purposes of this argument it is equally important to bear in mind that civilian leaders have frequently regarded intellectuals as rivals to be neutralized. Modernization did not only create the would-be professional intellectual; it also created the would-be professional politician. The intellectuals' claim to speak for the masses, to be the expression of a popular national identity, constituted a potential threat to those politicians and their own embryonic relationship with "the people." Politicians were wary of the inflammatory rhetoric of the intellectuals, particularly those—for example, Víctor Raúl Haya de la Torre or Julio Antonio Mella—who addressed themselves to the masses, and feared the possible social and electoral consequences of interaction between intellectuals and workers. The consequences of all this for the relationship between intellectuals and the state in Spanish America have been fourfold: (1) intellectuals have been systematically excluded from participation in high-level public policy-making but coopted into the lower levels of state bureaucracy; (2) exclusion and low-level co-optation have been masked by the granting of prestigious diplomatic appointments to a select minority of internationally renowned (or locally well-connected) intellectuals; (3) political challenges from charismatic individual intellectuals have been rapidly eliminated; and (4) state leaders have further undermined the position of intellectuals by appropriating cultural symbols to themselves. These points will be explored in turn below.

Even a rapid examination of the histories of these five countries from the 1920s until the 1960s reveals how rarely Spanish American intellectuals occupied executive office or were appointed as advisers on public policy. In this respect, there is little difference between countries where political parties have acted as channels between the state and civil society to a greater extent (Chile, Peru) and those where they have done so to a lesser extent (Argentina, Cuba, Mexico).

In Argentina, the only president from the 1920s to the 1960s who was prepared to seek the advice of intellectuals was Arturo Frondizi (1958–1962), and mutual disillusionment developed rapidly even in that case. In Cuba, intellectuals were regularly appointed to advise on education policy, and their advice just as routinely ignored. The essayist and poet, Juan Marinello, served as a minister in Batista's first government (1940–1944) but this was because of his role in the Communist party, not because of his stature as an intellectual. Since 1959, intellectuals have been firmly confined to administration of their own affairs (for example, the Writers' Union, UNEAC) and even that role was reduced in the 1970s, when party function-aries increasingly took over direction of the cultural bureaucracy. In Peru, although a number of intellectuals were elected to Congress, particularly for APRA, few achieved executive posts.

Even in Chile, where probably the most active party political system in the region functioned, the experience of active participation of intellectuals in the legislature and hardly any in the executive was repeated. The case of the poet, Pablo Neruda, is particularly revealing. Having resigned from the diplomatic service in 1943, Neruda returned to Chile and was recruited as Pedro González Videla's election campaign manager. Neruda was himself elected in 1945 as a senator representing a northern nitrate region, and joined the Chilean Communist party shortly after-ward. The immense popularity of Neruda's poetry readings among the workers not only in his own constituency but throughout Chile began to alarm the Popular Front coalition, but it was only when Neruda tried to play the role of the independent social critic that the government's patience finally snapped. Early in 1948 Neruda gave a speech to the senate denouncing González Videla, which he quite con-sciously gave "a Zola-like tone, titling it in his own handwriting, 'I Accuse' . . . [having] read the *Dreyfus Case* many times."[8] He was forced into exile shortly afterward.

Even postrevolutionary Mexico, so often held up as a state that has been prepared to accommodate, even cosset, intellectuals, is only a partial exception. The well-known appointment of José Vasconcelos as Minister of Education in 1920 was exceptional among both his own and subsequent generations. It is worth dwelling on Mexico, where the revolution (1910–1920) effected the earliest comprehensive transfer of power from oligarchy to bourgeoisie in Spanish America, and therefore offers the clearest example of the policies of a modernizing state toward its intellectuals.

The response of the postrevolutionary Mexican state to independent bids for political power by intellectuals has to be understood in the light of two factors: the role of educated men in nineteenth-century Mexican politics; and the role played by intellectuals in the revolution. The height of intellectual influence on Mexican political life was during the Restored Republic (1867–1876), when a generation of liberal men of letters was drafted in by Juárez to promote a national culture and a national history.[9] During the Porfiriato (1876–1910), Díaz, who was quite simply "allergic to anything intellectual,"[10] subordinated intellectual to military power by promoting a select group, the *científicos*, as advisers to his dictatorship. Their arguments that society should be administered by the best-educated, not governed by elected representatives, had an obvious appeal for Díaz, who not only gave this generation of intellectuals public posts, but encouraged them to enrich themselves to the extent that they had become the objects of intense popular loathing by the end of his rule. Other pretenders to intellectual influence were excluded: it was clearly difficult for emerging middle-class intellectuals to obtain a position in the Porfirian state.[11] By these means, Porfirio Díaz both contained and ultimately undermined intellectual influence.

Although Cockcroft asserts that intellectuals were "critically important" to the revolution,[12] there is little convincing evidence to support this, as several leading historians of Mexico have argued.[13] Many intellectuals backed Francisco Madero, with varying degrees of enthusiasm, but once mass uprising had broken out they adopted various means of retreat: exile, support for the repressive policies of Huerta, a romanticism about Villa, or apoliticism.[14] Few intellectuals supported Carranza, who, far from being anti-intellectual (like most of the revolutionary caudillos), "read the classics on campaign" and indeed believed that the "intellectual element" and not the illiterate masses should govern Mexico.[15] It was symptomatic of the declining role for intellectuals in the postrevolutionary order that they played very little part in the drafting of the 1917 Constitution.[16] As Vasconcelos acknowledged in his memoirs, Mexican intellectuals had been "belittled" by the inadequacy of their response to revolution,[17] and the Sonoran state was hardly likely to hold them in much regard.

Nevertheless, state leaders were mindful of the fact that intellectuals had been influential in the events leading up to the removal of Díaz. What also became clear fairly rapidly was that the Sonoran state saw itself as the exclusive arbiter of competing interests and "could not allow any criticism, any protest, any power apart from itself."[18] Intellectuals were therefore identified as potential rivals, but President Álvaro Obregón (1920–1924) also recognized that they could be useful in cultivating legitimacy for his initially beleaguered government both at home and abroad.[19] He sought to win the cultural elite's backing through the limited expedient of granting just one of their leading members a key role in the postrevolutionary order. Vasconcelos himself was unusual among intellectuals in that he had been involved in the revolution, at least until 1915. He was one of the few intellectuals that Obregón thought should not "retire to private life."[20] Obregón judged that Vasconcelos had the drive and the commitment to launch a postrevolutionary project of social engineering in education, which was one of the few policies upon which the divided revolutionary coalition could agree. By appointing Vasconcelos, the Obregón government succeeded in coopting a generation of independent intellectuals into supporting the revolutionary nation-building project, at a time when the university as an institution was a site of opposition. Once a more collaborative relationship had been established with the university after World War II, the state was able to attract generations of educated men who preferred the prestige and perks of political office to the meager rewards and recognition of the independent intellectual. Such men were trained as the specialists the industrializing Mexican state required, not as generalists. This institutional means of containing the emergence of independent intellectuals meant that from the 1940s onward the state had little need to offer any of them high political office and did not do so.

Meanwhile, in the 1920s and 1930s the Mexican state pursued a divide-and-rule policy toward intellectuals, displacing the traditionally central figure of the writer in favor of anthropologists and artists. Above all, the famous muralists, who were communist sympathizers, were permitted to play the role of flamboyant bohemian usually occupied in Spanish America by writers. The notoriety of Diego Rivera, in particular, with his radical politics and rumbustious love life, both appalled and fascinated the Mexican establishment. Rivera and the Mexican state played a game of political cat-and-mouse until his death in 1957, from which both derived advantages. It certainly suited the Mexican state to have the figure of the adversarial, communist intellectual incarnated in someone who was painting internationally acclaimed murals giving pictorial prominence to the role of workers and peasants in Mexican history. During the 1930s, the state succeeded in pitting the socialist realist commitment of the Mexican muralists against those intellectuals who, in trying to preserve their intellectual independence, adopted political positions that could be presented as right wing.[21] As Jean Meyer has argued, it was in the 1930s, especially during the presidency of Lázaro Cárdenas (1934–1940) that the eradication of intellectual dissent took place (most intellectuals were anti-Cárdenas at the time despite the fact that he became their hero in the late 1970s).[22] Calles' speech at the foundation of the PNR in 1930 had set the tone for the decade: he stated that he wanted the party to unite "workers from the countryside and the city, [workers] from the middle classes and the lower middle classes, and intellectuals *of good faith.*"[23] Those of bad faith—that is, those who rejected the state's project of national integration around the ideal of *mexicanidad* (such as the intellectuals loosely grouped around the journal *Contemporáneos*)—rapidly found themselves marginalized. By this stage, the state allowed no middle way between participation in its endeavors and the isolation of individual expression. This was the logical outcome of the acceptance by the postrevolutionary generation of intellectuals (led by Vasconcelos) of the Mexican state's monopoly over culture.

The Mexican Revolution resulted in the consolidation of a state that was fundamentally anti-intellectual, but acquired sufficient strength and flexibility to recognize that an accommodation with the intellectuals was in its best interests. Ironically enough, given that socioeconomic frustration had been one of the main causes for the intellectuals' support for Madero in 1910, the outcome of the revolution was ultimately to consolidate the hegemony of commercial values. Far from accommodating the universal intellectual, the postrevolutionary state has replicated the Porfirian tradition of specialists—administrators and technicians. Once revolutionary power had been institutionalized in Mexico, intellectuals have either had to accept full-time political positions, or they have been left on the margins of political power with largely ritual obeisance made to them. Thus, contrary to the common perception of Mexico as the country where intellectuals have enjoyed the most influence in politics, since the 1930s one of the strongest ideas in Mexican cultural life has been that "those who are genuine intellectuals must know how to keep their distance from power."[24] The postrevolutionary Mexican state has repeatedly proved resistant to the views of intellectuals. Even

Paz is ignored: his call for the election results of 1985 and 1991 to be respected fell on deaf ears.[25] Roderic Camp's research lends support to the argument that "any influence of the [twentieth-century Mexican] intellectual on public policy has been the exception rather than the rule."[26] Mexico is a clear example of a modernizing state that declined to accord the same degree of influence on public policy to its twentieth-century intellectuals as its oligarchic predecessor had conceded to nineteenth-century *letrado-políticos.*

Across Spanish America, the exclusion of intellectuals from high-level state policy-making occurred even in areas where they might have been expected to play a significant role, such as education. In Europe, education was one of the great nation-building crusades of what Gellner described as the "gardening" state,[27] and it dovetailed neatly with the ambitions of the philosophes and their counterparts to preach the gospel of reason to the common man. In Spanish America, by contrast, the modernizing state saw intellectuals as competitors for the allegiance of the people and, with the exception of Mexico, marginalized intellectuals from policy-making on elementary education during the 1920s and 1930s. Whereas the liberal positivists of the late nineteenth-century elites played a leading role in advising the oligarchic state on its education policies (for example, Domingo Sarmiento, Valentín Letelier, Justo Sierra, Francisco García Calderón), their twentieth-century counterparts had little impact on general education policy and were obliged to channel their reforming zeal into the universities (of which, more below). Once again, Mexico is only a partial exception. Vasconcelos was a crucial figure from 1920 until his resignation in 1924; Narciso Bassols served from 1931 to 1934 and instigated the notorious "socialist" education; but President Lázaro Cárdenas (1934–1940), who preferred to credit Obregón rather than Vasconcelos with the achievements of the early 1920s,[28] chose to enact his reforms without the participation of intellectuals.

Even in Cuba, where education was a persistent, indeed almost obsessional, theme in the writings of intellectuals from the early years of the republic until the 1950s, the state offered them remarkably few opportunities to put their ideas into practice. The modernizing state gave hardly any Cuban intellectuals executive posts in the Secretariat (later Ministry) of Education. The one possible exception was Machado's appointment of an isolated, conservative intellectual, Ramiro Guerra y Sánchez, to the nonpolitical post of Superintendent of Schools in the mid-1920s. Machado sought to appease the professional class by responding to their concerns about education, but Guerra achieved only minor reforms.

The attitude of Cuban politicians toward intellectuals has to be understood in the context of the fact that, had it had not been for a stray bullet in 1895, Cuba's first president might have been an intellectual, José Martí. Attempts by revolutionary students in the 1920s to appropriate the legacy of Martí to their own cause were countered in the aftermath of the "revolution" of 1933 by Batista. Given the importance attached to education in Cuba, where it became both a symbol of and a distraction from the nation's economic and political ills, it is hardly surprising that when Batista (operating at this stage behind the scenes) sought to consolidate power and promote legitimacy, particularly after the repression involved in ending the 1935 general strike (which was started by teachers), he turned to educational reform. The 1937 *Ley Docente* reorganized secondary and higher education, reopening the university, normal and secondary schools, which had effectively been closed since 1930. Batista extended bureaucratic control over education, authorizing the formation of a *Consejo Nacional de Educación y Cultura* to oversee the technical aspects of educational reform. But most of his reforming zeal was related to the need to pacify the rural areas. Batista realized that, politically, he could kill two birds with one stone with a program of rural education, which would provide a mechanism for controlling rural social unrest, and at the same time would meet intellectual and popular criticisms of the Cuban education system. In February 1936, Law 620 aimed to establish a network of primary schools in rural areas and to implement a program of what became known as "civic-military-rural education." In other words, Batista sent as teachers sergeants, who were answerable only to his army command instead of to the Secretary of Education. In short, education was militarized. Payment of the military teachers was funded by a new sugar tax imposed in December 1936; and by doing so, Batista secured funds to expand the army under the guise of extending education.[29] Batista added insult to injury as far as intellectuals were concerned by introducing the Flor Martiana (a white artificial pansy flower awarded as a badge of merit) in a crude attempt to reappropriate Martí and the tradition of *Cuba Libre*.[30] Throughout the pre-1959 period, intellectuals were drafted for tasks that sounded significant but ultimately had negligible impact, for example, rewriting the curriculum—when few teachers and fewer resources were available to implement the recommended changes.

Many of the examples often cited by those who propagate the idea of Spanish American intellectuals being highly politically influential (Mario Vargas Llosa's campaign to be elected president of Peru in 1989; Ernesto Sábato's heading of Alfonsin's human rights' commission) have occurred in the changed conditions of the 1980s and were a product of them. It is precisely the opportunity for intellectuals to maintain a real, rather than a rhetorical, distance from the state that has enabled them to act as more effective critics. With reference to the decades before the 1980s, however, the evidence does suggest that it is difficult to dispute Vargas Llosa's assertion that the twentieth-century Spanish American intellectual has rarely been granted a seat at the table of power.[31] The sole example of an intellectual-president is Venezuela's Rómulo Gallegos, who served in 1948 for just nine months before being overthrown by a military coup. To be sure, many intellectuals served as minor functionaries in state bureaucracies, and a significant proportion were congressmen, but few of them were truly influential.

The extent to which Spanish American intellectuals have acted as ambassadors for their nations has also been greatly exaggerated. Relatively few governments have adopted this policy, which has usually been designed to add a veneer of prestige to the exile of a potentially troublesome voice from the local political scene; only a minority of intellectuals (mostly those who already enjoyed international renown) have been its beneficiaries. In Mexico, for example, the strategy has been skillfully applied to selected famous intellectuals at sensitive times. The most notable example is Octavio Paz, who has made a particular point of emphasizing his position of critical independence. Paz joined the Mexican diplomatic corps in the 1930s and was posted as ambassador to India in 1962, at a time when intellectuals were actively organizing in opposition to the regime. Given that their emphasis was on democracy, Paz might well have been persuaded to join. Paz always vehemently denied that his position as a diplomat compromised his role as a writer. But in the eyes of many his independence was tarnished, notwithstanding his resignation after the massacre of Tlatelolco in 1968, and the state knew this all too well.

In general, the oppositional militancy of twentieth-century Spanish American intellectuals has largely been confined to small, left-wing parties or movements that posed little threat because of their lack of a mass base. This was partly because states, by promoting a few chosen intellectuals into posts that carried prestige if not power, succeeded in persuading many others that the potential for public influence was there. However, on the rare occasions when intellectuals did succeed in attracting widespread mass support, the state clamped down quickly. For example, the postrevolutionary Mexican state may have been prepared to give Vasconcelos a platform while he was willing to administer its goals, but as soon as he tried to establish an independent political position, the state quickly mobilized its resources to neutralize his challenge. In the crucial election of 1929, Vasconcelos stood as an independent presidential candidate, having refused to found a political party.[32] Pledging honest government, he traveled throughout Mexico on the campaign trail and, according to Jean Meyer, this "triumphal tour took on the glamour of a plebiscite."[33] Once Vasconcelos had taken the step of making contact with the Cristero forces in January 1929, President Emilio Portes Gil and his *eminence grise* Calles were prepared to enlist the services of the U.S. ambassador, Dwight Morrow, to intimidate the Cristeros into a peace settlement and undermine the intellectual's bid for power. After a manifestly fraudulent election, Vasconcelos fled the country. Similarly, at another important conjuncture, as the postwar institutionalization of the revolution in favor of business interests proceeded apace, the federal state made it quite clear that it would not tolerate victory by Vicente Lombardo Toledano's *Partido Popular* (which was supported by a few worker and peasant groups) in the state elections of 1949. Lombardo's presidential candidacy in 1952 foundered amidst official propaganda that he was a closet communist.

Lastly, one further way in which those occupying state power undermined the influence of the intellectuals at the policy level was by their own appropriation of cultural symbols. Here, the sense of rivalry felt by political leaders toward intellectuals is clearly revealed. As a general rule, the more a political leader was inclined to adopt anti-intellectual policies, the stronger his tendency to indulge in public displays of erudition, invoking the authority of intellectuals to legitimate his actions or statements. For example, Juan Perón, who branded most of Argentina's intellectuals as accomplices of the *vendepatria* oligarchy whose power he challenged, and treated some of them accordingly, nevertheless adopted the pen-name "Descartes" and littered his speeches with intellectual references. In a speech to the first national congress of philosophy, held in 1949, Perón attempted to demonstrate that he was no philistine military man by mentioning virtually every leading Western philosopher from Hesiod to Heidegger.[34] Similarly, in Fidel Castro's speech at his trial in 1953, "History will absolve me," his references ranged from characters in Balzac to Dante's hell, with a four-page litany of heroic resistance to tyranny down the ages, including such intellectual luminaries as Thomas Aquinas, Martin Luther, John Knox, John Milton, Jean-Jacques Rousseau, and Thomas Paine.[35] In Spanish America, state leaders, particularly those who are aware that their authoritarianism is unlikely to win the support of intellectuals, have rarely hesitated to appropriate to themselves the prestige surrounding culture.

THE STATE AND THE INSTITUTIONS OF INTELLECTUAL LIFE

The reality of underdevelopment has meant that during the period under discussion the intellectuals' main source of status and power was the state, rather than any particular class or social sector, because of the lack of a mass reading public who could provide a market and an audience for their work. From the 1920s onward, states made explicit their policy of assuming control over not only education but also culture; in several countries, these aims were embodied in new constitutions. See, for example, the Cuban Constitution of 1940, introduced under Batista's first elected presidency, which had a whole second section devoted to "Culture" and one article (no. 47) stating that "Culture, in all its manifestations, constitutes a primary interest of the state."[36]

In their quest to dominate the acquisition of cultural capital, states established networks of prizes and scholarships for intellectuals. In some states, publishing houses were founded; for example, Cárdenas established the Fondo de Cultura Económica in 1934, which remained the main Mexican imprint for academic works until the 1960s. Everywhere, ways were found to keep a relatively tight rein on the press. Official advertising was a crucial source of revenue for many newspapers and periodicals; and state agencies often controlled the distribution of paper, newsprint, or the newspapers themselves. As a result, most of the means for an intellectual to earn a living led ultimately back to the state. Unless they possessed a private income, intellectuals were almost invariably obliged to accept employment in an institution directly or indirectly controlled by the state. This in itself had obvious implications for the potential independence of intellectuals, especially since distinctions between the state and the government have rarely been upheld in Spanish America. The Argentine writer, Ezequiel Martínez Estrada (himself an autodidact, who worked in the post office), painted a bitter but not inaccurate portrait of the state of affairs that persisted from the 1930s until the 1960s in Spanish American countries:

It is true that there are in Buenos Aires what could be called specific structures dealing with science, art, and the liberal professions, but they are . . . all . . . ultimately sponsored or subsidized—somewhat secretly—by the government. If the intellectual wishes to clear a path in the jungle of interests mobilized by politics, he is obliged to offer his talent to the only bidders: journalism or public administration. Unable to derive benefit or joy from his work—which no one reads—he claims a subsidy, which automatically defeats him: he is but a collaborator. . . . Newspapers, universities, and salons maintain themselves by a complex system of interlocking interests; they protect each other, and throughout the entire chain flows only one blood and only one vital fluid: politics.[37]

The argument now turns to the most important of intellectual institutions, the university. This was the earliest arena for the struggle for control over intellectual life between modernizing states and the intellectuals, and it was to prove a crucial element in the key role that the state played in intellectuals' lives and development. A few general points should be made about the famous University Reform Movement, launched in Cordoba in 1918, and that subsequently spread to Peru, Chile, Cuba, Colombia, Guatemala, and Uruguay. The University Reform, which resulted in the granting of autonomy to universities, was believed at the time to represent a significant advance in the intellectual community's bid to increase its independence from the state. The popular image of Spanish American universities from the 1920s to the 1960s, particularly the huge national institutions in the capital cities, which attracted over half of the student population, was that these self-proclaimed "ideal republics" were, as some commentators have argued "in active, articulate, and sometimes militant opposition to the state."[38] As with other standard views of Spanish American intellectual life, this one bears some relation to reality. Moreover, as Néstor García Canclini points out, the Reform Movement achieved a lay university that had a framework of democratic organization at an earlier stage than many European societies.[39] But the idea that the University Reform Movement led to "increased university autonomy, student and faculty participation in the designation of administrators, [and] academic freedom [becoming] mainstays of Latin American universities" needs careful reexamination.[40] So, too, does the argument that "the university community in LA . . . has throughout this century been a leading force in the fight for democracy and freedom."[41]

The first point to make is that University Reform was not so much won by the reformists as *bestowed* by early modernizing states representing antioligarchic interests. By the 1920s, higher education had become an issue in all five countries, largely because of the emergence of a middle class that clamored for access to education as a route to social mobility. As David Rock has argued, Hipólito Yrigoyen's radical government saw reform as a means of simultaneously defeating their own conservative enemies in the struggle for cultural hegemony and coopting the support of the middle classes.[42] The same can be said of Peru's Augusto Leguía and Cuba's Ramón Grau San Martín. In Mexico, Emilio Portes Gil's granting of partial autonomy in 1929 is now generally interpreted as a move designed to sow confusion among the student support base of independent presidential candidate Vasconcelos.[43] Throughout the region, the removal of many university staff who were wedded to out-of-date teaching methods and curricula enabled antioligarchic governments to defeat at least some of the forces of cultural reaction. The introduction of more modern curricula enabled them to start training the professionals they believed that they needed in order to extend the state's role in economic development. It is also worth remembering that in countries where governments were not trying to appeal to the middle classes, movements for university reform were simply repressed (for example, Venezuela, Bolivia, and Paraguay).

The second point to be raised is that historians of the Reform Movement have argued that states were in a better position to exercise control over the universities after the reform than they had been before.[44] Of course, the existence of formal autonomy proved no deterrent to intervention by authoritarian states, and military occupations of university campuses have been a regular feature of university life in most Spanish American countries. But even when autonomy was formally observed, the state had simply traded direct channels of control for more indirect mechanisms. The increased financial dependence on the state resulting from the abolition of tuition fees is only the most obvious example of those indirect mechanisms.

Equally important was the question of the politicization of the universities. On this issue, states took advantage of the fact that reformists had far more coherent ideas about what the universities should not be than they did about what they should be.[45] The students' initial rebellion in 1918 was against the retention of incompetent and old-fashioned staff and inadequate teaching methods. Ultimately, however, the University Reform took its aims far beyond the rectification of inadequate university practices: it claimed to be a national regeneration movement, linking university democratization with a broad platform of anticlericalism, anti-imperialism, hispanoamericanism, and an ill-defined idea of social justice. As a result of this, as Daniel Levy has argued, "student politics became inextricably linked with national politics and often served as a conduit to national office."[46] Adopting the students' own definition of the universities as the crucible of the nation enabled states to turn them into nationalist institutions that were essential for aspirants to public office to attend.

Granting autonomy to the universities at a time when they were highly politicized meant that there was little danger they would take advantage of that autonomy to pursue independent, critical intellectual activity. Instead, the modernizing states established universities as institutions in which youthful radicalism could run its course while those same radicals were making the social and political connections necessary for future advancement within the elite. states quickly stamped on the most threatening outcome of the University Reform, which were the Popular Universities.[47] Again, their concern was to prevent the intellectuals' identification with the masses from developing beyond the rhetorical.

At a point when the state universities seemed to be in danger of becoming too radical after World War II, some states simply changed tack and began to encourage the foundation of private universities to dilute the political impact of the leading public universities. This dovetailed neatly with the need to meet growing middle-class demand for an expansion of higher education. Such initiatives were backed by the United States, particularly after 1960, and many of the new institutions were organized along U.S. lines. By and large, however, Spanish American states were willing to allow their educated youth a few years of radicalism which, until the polarization of the 1960s, was easily containable. Thus, the state took the lead, and the university communities acquiesced, in the creation of a university ethos that attached more importance to power than to knowledge. The universities may have been centers of political resistance to the state, but they failed to act as a focus for the establishment of a civil society capable of challenging the legitimacy of the state.

CONCLUSION

The Mexican anthropologist, Roger Bartra, wrote recently:

Political power finds it inconvenient to deal with thinking intellectuals, restless, unstable people, who are always testing this or proving that. It is better and safer to deal with established professionals . . . that is, with trustworthy people who practice but do not believe, who accumulate information but not knowledge, who record but fail to understand.[48]

Ultimately, Spanish American states found it preferable to coopt those who were prepared to become professionals and repress the militants than to tolerate the emergence of a critical intellectual community. This was true across a broad range of regimes in countries with varying social and political formations.

Even Chile, as in other respects, is only an apparent exception. Chile is distinctive in terms of its intellectual tradition in which conservatism rather than liberalism was dominant for most of the nineteenth century, its institutional continuity (virtually unbroken democratic rule until 1973), and the vitality of its party political system, particularly its apparent capacity to tolerate the activities of Marxist parties. Nevertheless, when political consensus broke down during the 1960s, Chilean intellectuals proved as unable to sustain an independent role as their counterparts in other Spanish American countries that lacked corresponding political traditions. They, too, abandoned their intellectual authority in the quest for direct political power. The events of the 1960s and 1970s revealed just how fragile was the division of power between the oligarchy and the middle sectors on which the most stable democracy in Latin America had rested. Those events also demonstrated that the existence of active political parties and a tradition of respect for freedom of speech had obscured the fact that in Chile, as elsewhere in Spanish America, little separation between culture and politics had taken place. Barrios and Brunner have argued that, until the 1980s, Chile lacked a cultural tradition that made a distinction between scientific and political practice.[49]

This lack can be explained in terms of the fact that when the modernizing state emerged in Chile in the 1920s, like its counterparts in other Spanish American countries, it also developed a strategy to ensure that an independent intellectual community did not cohere. But, because of Chile's comparatively successful history of institutional stability, the Chilean state could afford to be more tolerant toward intellectuals while ultimately pursuing the same aims as in Mexico, Peru, or

Argentina. What the modernizing Chilean state did do from an early stage was to take an entrepreneurial role in the creation of a technocracy, so that the route to public office was perceived to be linked to expertise, in other words, the opposite of the intellectual's claim to universal judgment. This was a constant policy pursued by a succession of governments of highly varied ideological complexion: Carlos Ibáñez (1927–1931) promoted an engineering and administrative technocracy; CORFO, the Chilean Development Corporation was created by the Popular Front in 1939; President Alessandri (1958–1964) launched what became known as the "managerial revolution."[50] From about 1960 onward, the state began to sponsor the development of modern social science. By the early 1960s, the concept of technocracy was under attack from Christian Democrats and left-wing parties, but a long-term perspective suggests that the *intelectual comprometido* (committed intellectual) of the 1960s and 1970s should be seen as an exception in twentieth-century Chile. The Chilean modernizing state was in a position to move earlier than any other in Spanish America (including the Mexican, which waited until it had consolidated its position in the 1940s) to create a technocracy which, by its very existence, undermined the role of the independent intellectual by making specialism rather than universalism the route to public influence.

Symptomatic of the relative success of state containment of intellectuals is the fact that the concept of "civil society" did not acquire currency in Spanish America until the 1970s, once the full coercive power of the state had been unleashed by the military dictatorships. Jorge Castañeda has drawn attention to the irony that the idea of civil society began to be discussed in Latin America at about the same time as poststructuralist thinkers in the developed world were questioning the possibility of making any meaningful distinction between state and civil forms of power. The late emergence of the term "civil society" is also indicative of the extent to which Spanish American intellectuals fulfilled the ideological role prescribed for them by the state rather than trying to create an analytical role. In this sense, Castañeda's image (drawn from Carlos Fuentes) of the intellectual as an *involuntary* substitute for the structures of civil society has to be revised.[51]

From the 1920s until the 1960s, Spanish American states succeeded in creating a situation in which intellectuals were preoccupied with power rather than knowledge. A precursor of the twentieth-century relationship between intellectuals and the state occurred when Domingo Faustino Sarmiento became President of Argentina in 1868: his own draft inauguration speech was replaced by a version written by the politician, Nicolás Avellaneda, on the grounds that only an experienced politician was capable of manipulating the language of power. As the Argentine writer, Ricardo Piglia, has suggested, this is "an apt metaphor" for the continual displacement of culture by politics that has taken place throughout twentieth-century Spanish America. [52]

NOTES

1. José Donoso, in Doris Meyer (ed.), *Lives on the Line* (Berkeley: University of California Press, 1988), p. 184.

2. Eric Hobsbawm and Terence Ranger (eds.), *The Invention of Tradition* (Cambridge: Cambridge University Press, 1983).

3. Laurence Whitehead, "State organization in Latin America since 1930," *Cambridge History of Latin America* Leslie Bethell (ed.), vol. VI, part 2 (Cambridge: Cambridge University Press, 1995), pp. 3–95. The term "modernizing" is used without the ideological connotations of U.S. modernization theory of the 1950s.

4. Antonio Gramsci, *Selections from the Prison Notebooks*, Quintin Hoare and Geoffrey Nowell Smith (ed. and trans.) (London: Lawrence and Wishart, 1971), p. 260.

5. Louis A. Pérez, Jr., *Cuba under the Platt Amendment 1902–1934* (Pittsburgh: University of Pittsburgh Press, 1986), pp. 236–57.

6. Enrique Krauze, *Caudillos Culturales en la Revolución Mexicana* (Mexico City: Editorial Siglo XXI, 1985).

7. Pierre Bourdieu, *Distinction: A Social Critique of the Judgement of Taste*, Richard Nice (trans.) (London: Routledge and Kegan Paul, 1984), pp. 114–15.

8. Volodia Teitelboim, *Neruda: An Intimate Biography*, Beverley J. DeLong Tonelli (trans.) (Austin: University of Texas Press, 1991), p. 291. Echoing Zola, Neruda's speech consisted of a series of specific accusations. It was later published as a pamphlet entitled "Yo Acuso."

9. See David R. Maciel, "Los orígenes de la cultura oficial en Mexico: Los intelectuales y el estado en la república restaurada," Roderic A. Camp, Charles A.Hale and Josefina Zoraida Vázquez (eds.), *Los Intelectuales y el Poder en México* (Mexico City: El Colegio de Mexico/UCLA Latin American Center Publications, 1991), pp. 569–82.

10. Daniel Cosío Villegas, "L'intellectuel mexicain et la politique" (1966) in GRAL Institut d'Etudes Mexicaines-Perpignan, *Intellectuels et Etat au Mexique au Xxe Siecle* (Paris: Editions du CNRS, 1979), pp. 9–17.

11. James D. Cockcroft, *Intellectual Precursors of the Mexican Revolution, 1900–1913* (Austin: University of Texas Press, 1968), p. 45.

12. Ibid., p. 233.

13. Knight summarizes the arguments in "Intellectuals in the Mexican Revolution," in Camp, Hale and Zoraida Vázquez, *Los Intelectuales*, pp. 141–72.

14. Ibid., p. 167.

15. Ibid., p. 142.

16. The Congress at Querétaro was primarily made up of middle-class professionals, most of whom were keen to recite the litany of the *licenciado* (university graduate), displaying their knowledge of "the American Constitution, the French Revolution, Rousseau and Spencer, Hugo and Zola." See Alan Knight, *The Mexican Revolution*, vol. 2 (Cambridge: Cambridge University Press, 1986), pp. 473–75. But few of these people would have been identified as intellectuals in the sense used in this chapter. One possible exception is the liberal-positivist, Andrés Molina Enríquez, who drafted Article 27. Compare the far greater contribution of men of letters to the constitutions of 1824 and 1857. See Jaime E. Rodriguez, "Intellectuals and the Mexican Constitution of 1824," in Camp, Hale and Zoraida Vázquez, *Los Intelectuales*, pp. 63–74.

17. J. Vasconcelos, "Intelectuales y políticos," in *Memorias* (Mexico City: Fondo de Cultura Económica, 1982), p. 840.

18. Jean Meyer, "Revolution and reconstruction in the 1920s," in Leslie Bethell (ed.), *Mexico since Independence* (Cambridge: Cambridge University Press, 1991), pp. 201–40.

19. The intellectuals were more than willing to play their part. In 1921, for example, Daniel Cosío Villegas organized a congress of students that promoted recognition of

Obregón's government from an international cultural elite. Gabriel Zaid, *De los libros al poder* (Mexico City: Editorial Grijalbo, 1988), p. 67.

20. Vasconcelos, *Memorias*, p. 945.

21. Carlos Monsivais, in GRAL Institut d'Etudes Mexicaines-Perpignan, *Champs de Pouvoir et de Savoir au Mexique* (Paris: Editions de CNRS, 1982), pp. 83–107.

22. Meyer, "Introduction," in GRAL Institut, *Intellectuels et Etat*, p. 7.

23. Louis Panabiere, "Les intellectuels et l'etat au mexique (1930–1940)—Le cas de dissidence des Contemporaneos," in GRAL Institut, *Intellectuels et Etat*, pp. 77–112. My emphasis. All translations by the author unless otherwise stated.

24. Xavier Rodríguez Ledesma, "El poder como espejo de los intelectuales," *Revista Mexicana de Ciencias Políticas y Sociales* XXXIX:158 (Oct.–Dec. 1994), pp. 67–91.

25. Ibid., p. 90.

26. Roderic Camp, *Intellectuals and the State in Twentieth-Century Mexico* (Austin: University of Texas Press, 1985), p. 231.

27. Ernest Gellner, *Nations and Nationalism* (Oxford: Blackwell, 1983).

28. William Cameron Townsend, *Lázaro Cárdenas: Mexican Democrat* (Ann Arbor: George Wahr Publishing Company, 1952), p. 63.

29. Laurie Johnston, *"Por la escuela Cubana en Cuba libre:* Themes in the history of primary and secondary education in Cuba, 1899–1958." Ph.D. diss., University of London, 1996, p. 182.

30. Ibid., 179.

31. Mario Vargas Llosa, "El intelectual barato" [1979], in *Contra viento y marea* (Barcelona: Editorial Seix Barral, 1986), vol. II, pp. 143–55.

32. Enrique Krauze, *Textos Heréticos* (Mexico City: Editorial Grijalbo, 1992), p. 116. Krauze sees this as a lost opportunity to establish "a broad civic front."

33. Meyer, in Bethell, *Mexico since Indepedence*, p. 215.

34. *Conferencia del excmo. senor presidente de la nación argentina Gral. Juan Perón pronunciada en el acto de clausura del primer congreso nacional de filosofía*, Mendoza, 9 de abril de 1949.

35. "History will absolve me," in Fidel Castro/Regis Debray, *On Trial* (London: Lorrimer Publishing, 1968), pp. 33, 42, and 62–65. My thanks go to Walter Little for drawing this point to my attention.

36. Constitución de la República de Cuba (1940), in Hortensia Pichardo, *Documentos para la Historia de Cuba*, vol. 4, part 2 (La Habana: Editorial de Ciencias Sociales, 1980), pp. 329–418.

37. Ezequiel Martínez Estrada, *X-Ray of the Pampa* [1933], trans. Alain Swietlicki (Austin: University of Texas Press, 1971), pp. 285–86.

38. Joseph Maier and Richard W. Weatherhead (eds.), *The Latin American University* (Albuquerque: University of New Mexico Press, 1979), p. 6.

39. Néstor García Canclini, *Culturas Hibridas: Estrategias Para Entrar y Salir de la Modernidad* (Buenos Aires: Editorial Sudamericana, 1992), p. 72.

40. Jorge Castañeda, *Utopia Unarmed: The Latin American Left after the Cold War* (New York: Knopf, 1993), p. 175.

41. Orlando Albornoz, *Education and Society in Latin America* (Basingstoke: Macmillan/St. Antony's, 1993), p. 13.

42. David Rock, "From the First World War to 1930," in Leslie Bethell (ed.), *Argentina since Independence* (Cambridge: Cambridge University Press, 1993), pp. 139–72.

43. Francisco López Cámara, "La UNAM en la política mexicana," *Revista Universidad de Mexico* (Sept. 1992), pp. 19–23; and Daniel C. Levy, *University and Government in Mexico: Autonomy in an Authoritarian System* (New York: Praeger, 1980), p. 26.

44. Rock, "First World War"; Daniel Levy, Higher Education and the *State in Latin America: Private Challenges to Public Dominance* (Chicago: University of Chicago Press, 1986).

45. José Luis Romero, "University Reform," in Maier and Weatherhead, *Latin American University*, p. 136.

46. Levy, *Higher Education*, p. 48.

47. In Cuba, the Universidad Popular José Martí, founded in 1923, was closed by Machado in 1927. Mexico's Universidad Popular, which antedated the reform and had been operating since 1912, was closed down in 1922. In Peru, the Universidad Popular lasted just three years, from 1921 until 1924.

48. Roger Bartra, "Luis Villoro piensa en Mexico," *La Gaceta del Fondo de Cultura Económica*, no. 301, enero 1996, pp. 47–49.

49. Alicia Barrios and José Joaquín Brunner, *La Sociología en Chile* (Santiago: FLACSO, 1988).

50. Patricio Silva, "Intellectuals, technocrats and social change in Chile: Past, present and future perspectives." Unpublished paper, n.d., pp. 200–201.

51. Castañeda, *Utopia Unarmed*, p. 182.

52. Ricardo Piglia, "Los pensadores ventrílocuos," in Raquel Angel (ed.), *Rebeldes y Domesticados: Los Intelectuales Frente al Poder* (Buenos Aires: Ediciones El Cielo por Asalto, 1992), pp. 27–35.

chapter 5

Ideology and Populism in Latin America: A Gendered Overview

Marta Zabaleta
Translated by Caroline Fowler and Mike Gatehouse

INTRODUCTION: THE "FORGOTTEN DECADES"

The relationship between populism and women is one of the least studied but, at the same time, one of the most misrepresented phenomenons of Latin American history. This means that we still lack a complete and systematic understanding of the political role of Latin American women (including those of Central America and the Caribbean) over long periods of time and in several of the continent's countries. This lack of knowledge applies to governments motivated by diverse ideological discourses, ranging from the left and center to the right. The political projects which they have promoted can be classified as either radical popular nationalist , as in the case of Sandinismo; bourgeois popular nationalist, as in the case of Peronism, Varguismo and Freismo, or workers' democratic populism, as in Chile's Allendismo.[1] This has several consequences, some of which are mentioned below.

Firstly, as has been pointed out by other authors whose work we are attempting to continue and complement, it becomes very difficult to effect a

sufficiently rigorous evaluation . . . of the phenomenon of the 1970s, which were marked by the appearance of women on the Latin American political scene . . . [because we do not . . . know whether the extent and the form of activity which we see today were original to this period, or whether they were a reworking of the experiences of a previous period. [Its]. . . most immediate antecedent, which is still present in our historical memory, were the struggles and mobilizations which took place in various different countries between the 1930s and the mid-1950s, when [women] gained political rights on an equal footing with men.[2]

This study aims to cover these two topics, and attempts to show that the gap to which Barbieri and Oliveira so rightly refer has unfortunately not prevented the interpretative void of the many "forgotten decades" from being frequently filled with descriptions molded to fit the paradigms of the day, descriptions that have frequently distorted the phenomenons they are trying to explain, as I have discussed previously.[3] This, in turn, creates additional problems, such as sometimes producing angry, emotional responses, in which we native women express our frustration in critical attacks, on occasion slipping into possibly over-personalized observations.[4] This chapter, conversely, endeavors to draw attention to issues relating to ideology that currently deserve a greater concentration of energy. This is precisely the case with the need to produce diversified feminist discourses that facilitate the task of arousing the consciousness of members of society of different genders, and also of all politicians, planners and academics with an interest in social justice on the Latin American continent.

The chapter is in two parts. The first, which is intended to identify some of the frequent inaccuracies in the study of women in Latin American politics, specifies some of their consequences. The second endeavors to summarize the advantages derived from the application of a Marxist and feminist methodology to the study of one ideology in particular, and its discourses, in the context of the specific physical conditions of the production, circulation, and consumption of those discourses: Peronism (Argentina, 1943–1955). This will allow us not only to interpret the political behavior of Eva Perón and other Peronist women, but also to understand the reasons for the success of the Peronist discourse in a context in which other populist ideologies failed. This chapter defends/pleads the case for a reevaluation of Latin American history from which no social group should be once again excluded, and adopts a methodology that may be considered to be feminist, populist, and revolutionary.

PART ONE: INACCURACIES IN THE STUDY OF WOMEN IN LATIN AMERICAN POLITICS

The inaccuracies that accompanied the appearance of the pioneering works to which I wish specifically to refer, and which were reiterated in different conceptual garbs in the recent bibliography on women in Latin American politics, are related to three misconceptions that, implicitly or explicitly, are connected to the ideology and political conduct of Latin American women.

These misconceptions are as follows: firstly, the assertion that Latin American women have tended to be more conservative than men historically, which is an over-generalization; secondly, that women's support for populism in general, and Peronism in particular, is proof of their traditional conservatism; and finally, that the women of Latin America appear to be less feminist than their European or North American counterparts.

These assumptions take for granted, among other things, the following: (1) that the political conduct of men is the norm by which women are to be judged; (2) that "populism" is, by definition, reactionary; and (3) that "feminism" is something foreign to the female Latin American idiosyncrasy, wrapped for more than 500 years in the ideological cloak of marianismo and machismo.

The aforementioned is often associated with the name and the political activities of Eva Perón, in the same way that the protests by right-wing women against the populist governments of Goulart (social democratic) and Allende (socialist) were previously used as a typical example to illustrate the astonishing preference of Latin American women for right-wing ideologies. These conclusions do not take into account, among other things:

1. that, to date, no systematic study, feminist or otherwise, of the political conduct of Peronist women in general, or of Eva Perón in particular, has been published, so far as I am concerned;

2. that the true behavior of Eva Perón in principle bears no relation to that attributed to her by Chaney, which is often quoted in order to generalize the political role of Latin American women—that of a supermother, a concept originally coined by Chaney,[5] and later repeated insistently by herself and others right up to the present day;[6]

3. that there is, for instance, an enormous difference between the bourgeois populist proposal of Goulart and the possibility of a worker-peasant populism that arose in Chile as a result of the triumph of *Unidad Popular* in 1970, an example that gives an idea of the inaccuracies to be stumbled into when one generalizes about political movements and ideologies;[7] and

4. that the men of left-wing groups or parties are frequently condemned for their negative attitude toward the political participation of women in their quest for social change. Even more frequently, within the left, feminism is accused of dividing the popular forces, or of being by definition an ideology of middle and upper class women in Latin America. In contrast, little exists resembling a systematic discussion of the shortsightedness regarding gender, class, and/or race apparent in diverse ideological trends and political practices that are generally regarded as progressive.[8]

These are some of the important stereotypes, myths, or omissions that must be confronted in undertaking a study of the ideologies and ideologues in Latin America, if it is done from a gendered perspective. Regarding this, in the following pages we will attempt to set the discussion of women and populism in a somewhat unusual analytical framework, and one that is, in its turn, more compatible with a new style of academic work.[9]

Bearing all this in mind, another warning needs to be given: we will only give here a few bibliographical examples that apply to our theme, that have been selected with a view to offering a certain historical perspective on the persistence of certain problems, and for their vast and significant influence on studies relating to women in Latin America for over more than two decades.

This neither explains nor justifies, however, the condensed form of this study, or the logical omissions and weaknesses this has given rise to, which an attentive reader will observe.

Pioneers Studies On Women, Sex, And Class In Latin America

In Peru and Argentina, the franchise was extended to women by "populist" leaders whose regimes were based on increasing participation within the traditional social framework rather than on radical structural and institutional change. More recently, female conservatism has received considerable attention because of the role played by women in bringing down the *radical* [!] government of Salvador Allende in Chile.[10]

On the assumption that Latin American women have more power within the family than women in other parts of the world, and are therefore more inclined to exploit their "feminine resources" in the political arena, it has been asserted that this "may provide an explanation for the spectacular success of certain female politicians in Latin America who have gained national and even international prominence . . . the *populist* patrona parlaying personal charisma and patronage to create bases of support among the urban poor. . . . Eva Perón of Argentina is the most obvious example, but María Eugenia Rojas de Morena of Colombia and María Delgado de Odría of Peru also come to mind."[11]

The Chilean and Peruvian women who secured posts in the APRA government in Peru (Belaunde, 1963–1968) and in the government of the Christian Democrats party in Chile (late E. Frei, 1964–1968), were added to the long list of female conservative maternalists in Latin American politics partially as a result of quotations—sometimes second- or third-hand quotations—from the influential, interesting, but often contradictory book by Elsa Chaney.[12] From the point of view of this study, it is worth pointing out that the two governments mentioned above each offer a different model of populism in power. However, it is not easy to deduce this from this book's handling of their discourse strategies. To be fair, I think that it is possible to deduce from the contents of the book that the author herself was aware of the limitations implicit in her work, which in my opinion derive from an excessive methodological adherence—unconscious or otherwise—to the developmentalist prism that reigned supreme in the 1960s in social studies about Latin America. In any case, although Chaney later tried to modify her analysis, she does not seem to have regained the same acceptance.[13]

Unquestionably, the study by M. Mattelart[14] contributed enormously to shaping a pattern for interpreting the conservatism of Latin American women. She is an author from whom one would have hoped for greater analytical sophistication, given that she later dedicated herself to revealing the ideological function of soap operas in the acceptance of the gender-defined roles assigned to women in the capitalist countries of the center and of the peripheries of Latin America.[15] Mattelart, who worked as an adviser of Salvador Allende's government in the state editorial, the publishing group Quimantú, was quick to propose a somewhat schematic ideological explanation of the extreme right's securing of the support of large female sectors of society during the reformist left-wing government in Chile. She also affirmed the existence of a "rapport between the women and the state in a capitalist society." Chilean women, according to this influential author, would have felt unprotected because the state was changing its virile character—in other words, changing hands and threatening to escape the control of the bourgeoisie. So they went out into the streets, to demand the restoration of manly power, the ideological synonym of order for these women. It so happens that for middle-class women, Mattelart tells us, the state is men's business.[16]

Having said this, where do the women who were not coopted by the male-oriented ideologies of the Chilean right fit in? Even today, little is known of the vast quantity of Chilean women who backed the *Unión Popular* (UP) and who mobilized themselves en masse in their support, and Mattelart pays them very little attention. But on this subject, Chaney does exert herself to say: "It is significant that in Chile (in 1960) the figures for abstentionism amongst women were constantly lower than those amongst men, sometimes by as much as five or six per cent, a fact which challenges the stereotyped idea of less political activism amongst women."[17] She also points out that everything seems to indicate that women of the working classes were one of the most important factors in Allende's victory, and that everything seems to indicate that in the 1971 elections, they voted in even greater proportions for UP.[18] These women were socialists, communists, Miristas, Trotskyists, Christians, and so on, and many of us, as distressing as it may be for everybody, and continue to ignore us though they may, were feminists. But Mattelart was not about to concern herself with feminist practice in Chile under the government of the UP, given that she considered it, at the time, to be a deformation that weakens the union of the working classes. In other words, feminism was apparently for her a degeneration of the movement of the masses, in line with Jacquette's specification.[19] Jacquette, in her turn, has continued to absorb new lessons, derived today from the women's mobilizations against the dictatorships of the Southern Cone.[20] This development is similar to that experienced by Mattelart when, in 1977, she assigned herself the task of reconsidering the relationship between women and "fascism" in Latin America, and wrote:

The relationship between women and fascism is not one which has been established once and for all. It is subject to the concrete historical circumstances in which authoritarian regimes arise. In the fascist countries of Latin America today, women no longer take to the street to acclaim the natural leader that a *duce* or *führer* aspires to be. The recruitment of women in Montevideo has nothing now of the pomp and crowd ritual of European fascisms. This is because, in Uruguay, as in Chile, the history of the last years—especially for women—has been that of a deception which can no longer be hidden.[21]

Or, alternatively, because the author of this assertion began to listen to the other side of female history?

Feminist Revolutionary Struggles: "One Doesn't Talk about That" ("De Eso No Se Habla")

Where do we feminists of the left fit in? We were women who had read the classic texts of Simone de Beauvoir, including the prologue dedicated to the anticolonialist struggle of Algerian women; who knew of the important role played by women in the Russian Revolution of 1917 and of the tradition of anarchism in Argentina; for whom the classic texts of Engels and Marx, Lenin, Trotsky, and Gramsci were more than just a superficial presence on the library shelves; who read with renewed anxiety the poetic works of Alfonsina Storni and the works of Virginia Woolf (translated into Spanish by the feminist Victoria Ocampo) in search of inspiration; who assiduously read socialist publications from the rest of the world and who knew that domestic work *is* work; who articulated feminist popular demands in our writings and who later went out into the streets and the fields to attempt to implement them. Although there were never more than a few hundred of us, we were not just cafe or desk revolutionaries. We tried to be active participants in our own history, not just subjects of the investigations that haunted us, or militant members of a specific political party and therefore enemies of women who were militant in other parties. Some of us grouped together to form the Revolutionary Women's Front (FMR).[22]

We were women who were not afraid of the "change of hands" of the bourgeois state. But we also knew that the Chilean left was not offering any differentiated gender options to the working masses, except for an extremely traditional one, both patronymic and maternalistic.[23] From the perspective of my personal experience, I can add that the double fact of being women and of being conscious of being women, prepared to fight in order to change the social formation that determined our subordinated social situation, actually marginalized us within the left, both before and after the UP gained access to the control of part of the state and its apparatuses in 1970. But at least the "change of hands" opened up to us a new avenue of action. The UP, formed of seven Chilean left-wing and center-left parties or movements, held little appeal to those who might espouse its policies qua woman, and even Fidel Castro—not exactly pro-feminist—noticed the absence of attention to the "Woman's Question," and pointed it out publicly during his visit. However, it was precisely to revolutionary feminist women that reformism offered a new chance: "a new way of doing politics." This was done in the midst of permanent negotiations, often tense and troubled, between men and women of different classes, races, marital status, religions, ideologies, and even nationalities. But within the party structures, sex was never formally discussed.

The strategy of feminist revolutionary women was adapted to the priorities of different sectors of the masses whose mobilization was vital, in order precisely to change the bourgeois nature of the state. In our group in particular, we saw the UP government as extremely *machista*, led by a socialist reformist, doctor, and mason, Salvador Allende, an honest patriarch. We sought to permeate the ancestral Chilean patriarchism and to help the government to radicalize its decisions for the benefit of the members of our gender, until the day when the most macho of all, led by Pinochet, wrenched the petals from the flower of Latin American socialism, on 11 September, 1973.

Even though our gendered demands were weighed down by the dominant (hetero)sexual model, inherited from our cultural dependence on the progressive

European, American, and Asian (Vietnamese, North Korean, Chinese) ideologies, the state never supported us in the methods we used to achieve them. For example, the land seizures of the settlers in order to build houses; the seizures of workshops where women worked; the seizures of estates where owners were refusing to accept the implementation of the new agrarian reform law; the marches for more grants and for help to avoid clandestine abortions amongst secondary-school and university students; the distribution of food and fuel in accordance with the number of people in each household; the resolution of the financial and family necessities of members of the JPAS (*Juntas de Abastecimiento y Precios*); the temporary expropriation (and free transport) of buses and minibuses on days when the owners of the means of transport were on strike; in order to guarantee access to work for the working population; sexual and political education, including the discussion of a national document of petitions (*Pliego Nacional de Peticiones*), for the members of the domestic workers' unions; the production and dictation of political education classes on the nature of women's work for the workers of the new nationalized factories in the Concepción area; discussion about domestic violence and workplace discipline in the nationalized factories and mines; these are some of the examples that come to mind.

Feeding on the ideas of the different groups of women mobilized in defense of their specific group interests, we often denounced bureaucracy and state inefficiency. Our methods were mainly those of persuasion, and always genuine and exploratory; with no historical role to emulate, our new "femininity" was often confused and/or abused by our male comrades, and very infrequently understood and respected by the majority of them as a rational expression of our militant political commitment. This was particularly the case in universities, where the left in power never dreamed of offering equal opportunities. Not, at least, to those of us who constituted its critical conscience.

Our work, which we began in the year 1971, was basically centered on the city of Concepción, 500 kilometers south of the capital, and extended to the center and the south of the country, especially during the summer of 1972–1973, the time of student vacations. Obviously, we also had to confront the problem of different ethnic origins in the FMR, given that our membership encompassed various different races, such as Araucanian Indians and their descendants, together with Creole Chileans; and we even had a few foreigners, Creole Latin American and European women. I do not believe that we managed to find any major practical solutions in this respect either; given, in particular, the strict rigidity of the social division of work in Chilean society in the period of "the transition to socialism," organized as it was around clear gender boundaries, particularly—but not only—at the level of the poorest classes. And this is where Indian women abounded. Badly paid, badly dressed, frequently sexually abused by fathers and brothers brutalized by centuries of white domination, they were just as interested in feminist ideas as other women, especially if they were single and had no children to look after. These were women for whom written history seems to have no ears. In any case, many of these women are now dead because of their courage, and their testimony will never be heard.

For us, in conclusion, the main enemies were neither men qua men, nor the state in itself; nor were they even the dramatic protests by right-wing women shrouded in black and clattering saucepans. As a result of our daily practice, we were used to seeing power spread into and infiltrate every aspect of our lives: our sexual relationships, our homes, the party, the economy, culture, the armed forces, and the police; the interests of the multinationals and the local bourgeoisie; the obstruction or bureaucratic indifference of the people (mainly men) in charge of the Economic Apparatus of the State; the lack of democracy within the political parties; the discrimination against women experienced in educational establishments; women's magazines, including those published by Quimantú; and so on. *There was no ideology that fully represented us, except the modest discourse that we ourselves were interweaving.* Then, as now, we were feminists. And socialists. And as a consequence of having had the privilege of participating in a period of a relative degree of ideological questioning regarding the bourgeois state and its apparatuses, many of us paid the price with loss of freedom, exile, and a whole range of indignities, and many paid with disappearance and their lives for the wonderful experience of *belonging and doing*.[24]

"New Social Subjects and New Forms of Political Behavior"

According to Barbieri and Oliveira, with the appearance of the feminist movements of the 1970s significant changes have occurred in the content and the implementation of the political and social tasks of women in the different Latin American countries. The pattern of female participation in the political scene since then is characterized by great diversity and heterogeneity, because women take on gender subordination and permanently change their demands toward other social forces and the states. The authors identify ten new forms of political behavior.[25]

Some of these have captured the attention of researchers, and have given rise to publications that have undoubtedly increased the number of readers interested in Latin American politics, as is the intention of their authors, and from which we have all benefited. However, it is possible to see here the schematism of endeavoring to synthesize the relationship between women and populism in a kind of straitjacket, especially, but not only, when Peronism and Eva Perón are referred to. The introduction to the study by S. Radcliffe and S. Westwood offers an example of this.[26]

This is a shame, given that the editors proposed, as is stated in the introduction, to emphasize the diversity of identities that exist among the women of Latin America, and argued for the consideration of distinguishing factors such as race, ethnic origin, class, age, and provenance in the formation of female identity. This was an important and ambitious task, which in practice was more often than not reduced to the analysis of class issues, according to the just criticism by Safa and Lebon.[27]

In *Viva*, and under the heading of authoritarian populism, the cases of Peronism in Argentina and of Vargas in Brazil are grouped together, in contrast to the (truly) popular populism "mobilised during the 1980s across the states of Latin America."

A new variant of authoritarian populism would, according to this work, be the continuing authority granted to *gauchero* figures in Argentinian politics, with the election in 1989 of Carlos Menem.[28] Eva appears once again in the guise of supermother.[29] This type of reference is reminiscent of academic stages that we believed to have been overcome forever, regarding populism in Latin America.[30]

At the same time, however, new practices have developed that have permitted increasingly rich communication between academics and activists. For example, the feminist encounters in Latin America, the growing number of women's networks in different Latin American countries, and the struggle to open up new fields of academic analysis related to art, literature, science and history produced by women, in all of which is expressed the discursive diversity of the women of the continent, of which this chapter is just one example.[31] Like these last authors, and to sum up, I have consistently focused on the significance of memory and writing in the creation of oppositional agency; assuming that gender and race are relational terms that foreground a relationship—and often a hierarchy—between races and genders; and finally, that there is an interdependent relationship between theory, history, and struggle.[32]

Feminist analysis has always recognized the centrality of rewriting and remembering history and the need to produce our own understanding. This does not mean that we are not also seeking to establish a permanent dialogue with the so-called "white western middle-class feminists." On the contrary, I believe that it is only and precisely through the dialogic relationship between different practices within international feminism that different native consciousnesses can be nourished.[33] That is, a consciousness that bears no relation to the postmodernist consciousness (or identity). It is a stance that postulates: "I write, they write, we write; we read, they read, you read us. We are the authors of our own time."

Therefore, it is not true that the author has died; from his grave rises a ghost: that of the female authors; no longer the actors in a refrain written by men, as, in some ways, Eva Perón was.[34] Now we want to write the librettos. It is also a consciousness that unites with the Foucaultian desire to see man removed from his place in the center of social sciences, but which does not seek to replace him with "Woman." It is a consciousness, in the case of the writer of this chapter, of a political subject with a multifaceted reality, who seeks to collectivize the primitive challenge of having been put in prison for the first time during the government of General Perón, in 1954, in Argentina, for not having wanted to espouse his popular nationalist vision of bourgeois democracy.

PART TWO: TOWARD A FEMINIST THEORY OF POPULISM

In 1976, I was a victim of Latin American history again: the dictatorship of General Videla in Argentina, and thanks to the enormous support of men and women across the world, I arrived to exile in the United Kingdom. I was convinced that something was innately wrong with me, so I decided to explore my political past from the very beginning. I started gendering Argentina's history in a study on the populist Peronism case.[35] By revealing the crucial role played by ideology in the political behavior of Peronist women, the study served to question the assumption that women can be considered a priori a social sector endowed with age-old conservatism when it comes to political activity.

While more than enough evidence emerged of the singular characteristics of the Peronist case, it also became clear that it shares a number of common traits with other Latin American political movements. Some of them are hardly ever thought of as variants of populism: not surprisingly, since in most Western minds of different ideological persuasions, Peronism has simply and wrongly been automatically assimilated to fascism. From my feminist standpoint, on the contrary, Peronism in its populist stage, for all its peculiarities, was not in itself an exceptional phenomenon, but a typical case of Latin American populism. The following are some of the lessons to be learned from it.

The Type of Feminine Social Consciousness That Peronism Helped to Construct

As Molyneux has stated, because women are positioned within their societies through a variety of different social relations—among them class, ethnicity and gender—the interests they have as a group are similarly shaped in complex and sometimes conflicting ways. One of the corollaries of this is that the way in which the gender interests of women are conceptualized is crucial for an understanding of women's consciousness.[36] Moreover, the way in which their interests are represented and are articulated is crucial to define the nature of their specific discourses. Accordingly, I have outlined elsewhere[37] a classification of the types of female social consciousness. However, before examining these issues in the context of the Peronist case, it is essential to clarify three basic assumptions upon which the classification is based.

The first is that when referring to women our study was referring not to *all the women* of Argentina, but specifically to those who were constituted as the subjects of Peronism. Secondly, although the study did not extend to non-Peronist women, it is reasonable to assume that many of them also found their interests advanced by Peronism. Others on the contrary found their strategic gender interests deferred (for example, the feminist socialists) and/or part or all of their privileges sacrificed to the redistributive policies attempted by Peronism (typically the case of the women of the 200 richest families of the country). The third assumption, which is obviously implicit in Molyneux's proposition as well as in mine, is that when we refer to feminism, we are not thinking of a set of demands that is international in character, timeless, and inflexible. On the contrary, feminist demands must *always* be considered in the context of the specific conditions of their production and existence in a particular historical context.

That said, neither the consciousness exhibited by Peronist women in general, nor that of Eva Perón in particular, support in our view the notion that women are conservative by nature, nor that they are more conservative than the men of the same social class as themselves. Nor was this, as Hollander sustains, a case of support for a "conservative feminism."[38] The majority of the women who supported Peronism did so because they possessed a class perception of the vital problems confronting them in everyday life. In my study I have shown how Peronism took steps to resolve these problems in the period before taking power through the Secretariat of Labor and Welfare, and once it was in government by implementing a series of specific measures. These helped to satisfy the needs women themselves prioritized as some of their more pressing economic and financial gender needs: paid work; housing; a healthy diet; clothing; access to education for themselves and for their children; paid holidays; improvements in their working conditions to cover all aspects of job security, including wages closer to the levels paid to men and/or family allowances sufficient for their basic subsistence and in proportion of the number of dependent children; benefits in the field of health, including a comprehensive system of preventive medicine that led to the eradication of various endemic and venereal diseases and easy access to contraceptives; and so on.

It is true that these formal benefits were acquired wholly or partially through the male members of the family, except for that percentage of women who were in paid work or the ones helped directly by the Eva Perón Foundation and the Peronist Feminine Party (PPF)[39] And of course this whole range of policies was perceived as beneficial by the men of the working classes as well. Nevertheless, the benefits accrued to women of the popular classes through a process of social transformations, in the course of which they themselves acquired a collective political identity and perceived themselves as making up a social group distinct from that of men. The Peronist women felt themselves to be members of a specific social group that was a part of the coalition that sustained the national government in power, and they were conscious that their support was of considerable importance in order to maintain the situation.

This acquisition of social consciousness by women was in no small part the result of their having won a series of civil rights that placed them on a more equal footing with men, and in particular the right to vote, to elect, and to be elected to public office. Their formal participation in government in 1952 was the highest in the history of Latin America, and the informal even more impressive, as it is shown in the case of Evita. Her name was proposed for the post of deputy-president by the most powerful trade union movement of the whole history of Latin America, the General Confederation of Workers (CGT) and by the only other women's front as powerful as the Cuban Women Federation (*Federación de Mujeres Cubanas*), in numerical terms at least: the Peronist Feminine party, with nearly 4,000,000 supporters. Had she been elected, Eva Perón would have been the first woman allowed to occupy high office in the world. Another crucial element in the development by Peronist women of their new political identity was the fact that they were called upon as women to take political action; that a specifically feminine discourse was directed at them; that they obtained their own meeting places, their own literature and their own forms of organization and representation in the state. All of this, moreover, occurred in the midst of a process of social transformations through which women obtained a revaluation of their social importance and public recognition of their new status by the sectors that were hegemonic in society as a whole.

Peronist women recognized that they had a community of gender interests and showed signs of intra-gender solidarity among themselves. They adopted a militant posture to defend these interests and did so in great measure under the inspiration of a female leader, Eva Perón, who created in politics a new model of femininity that was, pace those who regard her as an example of the Supermother, completely at variance with the patterns traditional in Argentina. Women's camps were built in the streets to lobby the government and support Evita's nomination to the deputy-presidency of the nation.

It is fair to conclude that Peronism helped to construct a reformist or economist type of consciousness among its female supporters, just as it did within the labor movement. Through exercising this consciousness these women could ensure the satisfaction of their immediate and medium-term gender interests. However, in return for the satisfaction of their most immediate needs, and certain additional benefits such as access to secondary and university education, protective labor legislation, eligibility for public office, equality among the children born in or out of the marriage contract, a divorce law, and so on, Peronist women defended a government of which they themselves were only a subordinated part.

In the course of constructing the reformist consciousness of its women supporters, Peronism did indeed provide women of the popular classes with a more advanced understanding of their situation, but not enough for them to realize that they themselves were potentially capable of radically changing that situation, and taking action to effect such change. Thus, to say that Peronism did not facilitate the acquisition by its women supporters of a feminist or revolutionary consciousness is to assert the diametric opposite of Hollander's conclusion, which denies these women their political potential, and describes them as passive, submissive, dependent, and infantile.[40]

Ideology and the Acceptance of Gender Subordination

By showing the type of consciousness possessed by women as the outcome of a specific historical process, it has been possible to clarify the crucial role played by ideologies in the perception women have of political participation. Peronism represented a process of moderate but progressive social transformations, in the course of which gender relations were reformulated so as to benefit women. Nevertheless, neither Peronist ideology nor Peronist discourses questioned the existing gender social division of labor and the traditional role of women within that division. This demonstrates, therefore, that as important as the existence of a basically unjust assignment of *social tasks and functions* is the way in which that assignment *is represented ideologically*.

By studying how Peronist ideology functioned, and doing so from a feminist popular perspective, I have been able to establish that, for those women who as supporters of Peronism were constituted as its social subjects, the type of consciousness they acquired was determined by the class and masculine-gendered character of that ideology. In the present case that amounted to the acceptance by Peronist women of their, albeit reformulated, social subordination.

This acceptance was achieved principally through social institutions that acted in effect as Ideological State Apparatuses, notably the family system, the ruling political party and especially the branch called the Peronist Feminine party. There is no question that Peronism "politicized" the family and the feminine roles derived from women's membership of the family. But it did so in such a way as to reinforce the most traditional values. For example, in glorifying the maternal Catholic role of women, Peronism managed to create the idea that playing this role was essential not just for women to feel themselves fulfilled as individuals but as the expression of their political commitment to Perón and his government. The crucial role of women in the economy was revalued by Peronism, but unequally, with women's contribution to production being minimized in contrast to the exaltation of their domestic roles in the traditional sense. These, moreover, were valued rhetorically, but never assigned a monetary reward, as had been promised, except where they were performed by persons outside the family, in other words the women (and a minority of men) in domestic service. Nor was there even a mention of tasks within the home being shared with men.

I proceed then to examine the type of party membership Peronism promoted among women, and its decisive role in inducing them to accept the new political implications of their traditional ascriptive roles. Especially after the establishment of separate membership, women were trained to obey the party rules, to acquiesce in being represented by men, and themselves to have no say in the formulation of party policy as a whole. They had to accept that a handful of women chosen in the most autocratic fashion would be in charge of every aspect of politics for women, and that the decisions of even this group could be vetoed by Perón, although it is not known whether he exercised that veto directly. Given the events surrounding the candidacy of Eva Perón for the vice-presidency, it is reasonable to assume that he did.[41] In any case, one constant in Peronist discourses for women and men was the contrast drawn between, on the one hand, the honorable, frugal, and hard-working father and head of family, aloof from vice, disciplined member of the (male) party, and on the other, the new housewife. The housewife must be honorable, clean, neat, a consumer but a careful one, in charge of the budgeting for the family and responsible for the proper socialization of the children in the manner expected by the party and the government. For single women as well as for married ones, Peronism deployed the image of Eva Perón as the feminine ideal and exemplary housewife, active in politics, challenging, but loyal to orders given from above, and especially loyal to the figure and to the commands of Perón. In short, here were the new fathers and heads of family and the new housewives required by the new model of capital accumulation.

Not surprisingly, membership in a family was, *for members of both genders*, almost a prerequisite for being a "good Peronist." As far as we know there was no mass opposition to this idea either from men or from women. It is clear, however, that Peronist women found it difficult to draw a line between party and family obligations, not least because so many of the tasks assigned by the party were concerned with social welfare work. Nor is it surprising, all things considered, that women Peronists accepted the new political tasks that confronted them during the period 1946–1955 with rational satisfaction and a considerable sense of their own importance. Besides, none of the opposition political forces had anything very different to offer, and what they did propose were merely partial reforms, and not a fundamental change in Argentine society. In the Argentina of Perón, a country divided between the social forces that supported him and those that spent their energies in opposition, social revolution in any of its variants was simply not on the agenda.

The bourgeois character of Peronist ideology imposed its hegemony with staggering efficiency upon *women and men* of the popular classes alike. In 1945 the political forces of the subordinate classes lost the historic opportunity to create the possibility of a worker's populism in Argentina. The majority of Argentinean women—and men—are left with the burden.

NOTES

This chapter has been developed from a paper prepared for the Conference of the Society for Latin American Studies (SLAS), University of Leeds, 1996. I would very much like to thank Will Fowler for the encouragement he gave me in working on the original version of the paper. Additional support for the present version came from thought and discussion over the years with Mike Gatehouse and Kate Young, and the renewed challenge provided by my students of "Latin America: Gender, Culture and Society" at Middlesex University. The final result is therefore a collective effort.

1. On this, see the works of Emilio de Ipola, particularly *Ideología y discurso populista* (Mexico City: Folios Ediciones, 1982), pp.116–17; E. Dore and J. Weeks, *The Red and the Black* (London: University of London, 1992). Within this scheme of ideas, the government of the *Unidad Popular* in Chile can be thought of as an example of worker's populism, although the use of the term in this context is my sole responsibility.

2. Teresita de Barbieri and Orlandina de Oliveira (eds.), *Presencia política de las mujeres* (San José: FLACSO, 1991), Cuaderno de Ciencias Sociales, no. 40, p. 9.

3. Marta Zabaleta, "Research on Latin American Women: In Search of Our Political Independence" *Bulletin of Latin American Research* 5:2 (1986), pp. 97–103.

4. María Theresa Alves, *Viva-fying the Other* (London: Kala Press, 1994).

5. Elsa Chaney, *Supermadre* (Mexico City: Fondo de Cultura Económica, 1983), p. 39.

6. Chaney explains in her book that she used descriptions that came from Talcott Parsons when she characterized current male and female roles, which assign to women the task of nurturing and giving affection even in their public duties, in contrast to what was expected of men in such positions: aggressiveness, authoritarianism and keeping on course for success. (Chaney, *Supermadre*, p. 38). She concluded from this that women in Chile and Peru (in 1967 and 1972) were overwhelmingly in agreement with the aforementioned political role. Then, taking a quotation from Eva Perón's autobiography completely out of context, she

concluded: "Eva Perón, who was perhaps the most formidable woman that Latin America has produced, thus explained her public role in terms of the eternal feminine tasks of women," (Chaney, *Supermadre*, p. 39). In any case, nobody denies that many female Latin American politicians are not ashamed to fulfil, both efficiently and with joy, the tasks of motherhood; and many of them are feminists (Marta Zabaleta, "On the Process of Construction of a Feminine Social Consciousness. The Peronist Case (Argentina, 1943–55)." Unpublished Ph.D. thesis, University of Sussex, 1989, p. 87).

7. In *Concepción*, Paul Sweezy and Bobbye Suckle Ortiz (Monthly Review Press), who were invited by Allende to his presidential investiture, admitted, in an interview at which I was present with several of my Political Economy students from the local university, that UP's program contained only embryonic socialist measures.

8. We do not have the space to refer to this in depth; it would need a separate chapter. But unlike those who talk about a "despotism of the male left," as Mota does on the subject of the Dominican Republic, or as when Chaney quotes her (Mota, 1980 in Chaney, *Supermadre*, p. 134), I am inclined to think that this is a result of their ideology. Those men are the subjects of male-oriented ideologies. Nor is this a biological problem of the left-wing male: many women also adhere to this shortsightedness. Examples can even be found in the testimonies of leaders of the left, indigenous women such as Domitila and Rigoberta Menchú, in prejudices that are inherited from the academic world, or vice versa; in the work of researchers of the center, like the Mattelarts, who considered feminism as an imperialist weapon (see Jacquette in note 10, below). All of which proves, in my judgment, that it is not a question of any lack based on sex or ethnic origin, but rather a result of hackneyed discourses that are either male or female oriented, sexist and racist, *machistas* or *hembristas*, depending on the case.

9. For example, the activities promoted in *Passages: A Journal of Transnational and Transcultural Studies*, by the Department of Sociology, University of Massachusetts; the Women's Studies Network (U.K.); Women's International Studies Europe (WISE); the results of the research of authors such as Torres, Ann Russo and Juanita Ramos; Mary Maynard and June Purvis; Louise Morley, Val Walsh and Liz Stanley; and many of the new feminist or womanist practices that have developed in Latin America.

10. Jane Jacquette, "Female Political Participation in Latin America," in J. Nash and H. Safa (eds.), *Sex and Class in Latin America* (New York: Gergins, 1980), pp. 228–29. My emphasis.

11. Ibid., p. 241. My emphasis.

12. Chaney, *Supermadre*.

13. For more details, see Chaney, "Supermother Revisited: Is Feminine Politics Equal to Eolitics?" Paper delivered at the V Interdisciplinary International Congress on Women, University of Costa Rica (February, 1993); Marta Zabaleta, "Mujeres y hombres en América Latina: Representaciones genéricas y formas de resistencia." Paper delivered at aforementioned congress.

14. Michele Mattelart, "Chile: The Feminine Version of the Coup d'Etat," in Nash and Safa, *Sex and Class*, pp. 279–301.

15. Mattelart, *Women, Media, Crisis* (London: Comedia Publishing Group, 1986), pp. 57–113.

16. Mattelart, "Chile: The Feminine Version," p. 295.

17. Chaney, *Supermadre*, p. 144.

18. Ibid., pp. 162–63.

19. Jacquette, "Female Political Participation," p. 234.

20. See Jane Jacquette (ed.), *The Women's Movement in Latin America* (Boston: Unwin Hyman, 1989).

21. Mattelart, *Women, Media, Crisis*, pp. 109–10.

22. Marta Zabaleta, *La organización de las mujeres para el proceso de Reforma Agraria* (Santiago: El Rebelde, 1972).

23. See Batya Weinbaum, *The Curious Courtship of Women's Liberationism and Socialism* (York: South End Press, 1978); Diana Kay, *Chileans in Exile* (Basingstoke: Macmillan, 1987); and Bobbye Suckle Ortiz, "Changing Consciousness of Central American Women" *Economic and Political Weekly* 20:17 (India, 1985), pp. 2–8.

24. In her excellent study Ximena Bunster describes many of the experiences that we suffered as political prisoners of Chile's military regime. Quoting at random, when she says: "the agonising impact of the sobbing and crying of other women being raped in an adjacent room or a few feet away"; "the false news of the death of family members and/or by the threats of having a loved one disappear"; "when a woman political prisoner, with a revolver against her forehead, listens to her torturer shouting: 'Talk, talk, for once and for all, because you are going to be executed and you will never see your small daughter again,' " (Ximena Bunster-Burotto, "Surviving beyond Fear," in J. Nash and H. Safa (eds.), *Women and Change in Latin America* (South Hadley, MA: Bergin & Garvey, 1986), p. 313); once again one listens, one does not cry, one tries to forget who one/she/he is; you feel once again guilty, even after twenty-three years. See Carmen Castillo, *In a Time of Betrayal* (Global Image, Channel 4, London, 13 June 1994); and Bunster-Burotto, "Surviving beyond fear," pp. 297–325.

25. Barbieri and Oliveira, *Presencia política*, p. 15.

26. Sarah Radcliffe and S. Westwood, *Viva: Women and Popular Protest in Latin America* (New York: Routledge, 1993). For a revised introduction and a more comprehensive criticism, see H. Safa and N. Lebon, "Book Review," *Gender and Society* 9:3 (June 1995), pp. 382–84.

27. Safa and Lebon, "Book Review," p. 383.

28. Radcliffe and Westwood, *Viva*, pp. 10–11.

29. Ibid., p. 12.

30. For a full discussion of the best known theories of Latin American populism and how they differ from a feminist and Marxist interpretation, see Zabaleta, "On the Process of Construction," chapter 2.

31. Chandra Mohanty, Anna Russo, and Lourdes Torres (eds.), *Third World Women and the Politics of Feminism* (Indianapolis: Indiana University Press, 1991).

32. Ibid., pp. 13–14.

33. See Barbara Harlow, "The Grammar of the Death Penalty." Paper delivered at the Conference on Gender, Culture and Colonialism, University College Galway, Ireland, June 1995; and Marta Zabaleta, "Women and Men in Argentina: From Modern Nation to Multinational Haven (1880–1996)" *New Left Review* (in press).

34. Marta Zabaleta, " 'We Women Are the Actors in the Drama of Our Times.' An Analysis of the Speeches of Eva Perón" in Mary Bucholtz et al. (eds.), *Cultural Performances* (Berkeley: University of California Press, 1994), pp. 787–800.

35. Zabaleta, "On the Process of Construction."

36. M. Molyneux, "Mobolization without Emancipation?" *Feminist Review* 11:2 (1985), pp. 227–54.

37. Zabaleta, "On the Process of Construction," p. 94.

38. N. C. Hollander, "The Peronist Women's Movement Reconsidered," undated, mimeo.

39. Zabaleta, "Women and Men in Argentina."

40. N. C. Hollander, "The Peronist Women's Movement," p. 10.

41. Abel Posse, *La pasión según Eva* (Barcelona: Planeta, 1995).

chapter 6

Ideology and the Cuban Revolution: Myth, Icon, and Identity

Antoni Kapcia

Whereas a persistent theme of early studies of what was the largely unexpected and often incomprehensible revolution in Cuba was its apparently "ideology-free" nature, the by-now voluminous literature on the post-1959 system has tended to move away from such questionable premises.[1] Although recent studies still seem surprisingly stuck in this ideological time warp, the issue of the revolution's "ideology" seems less controversial than before.[2]

This can be attributed to two developments. Firstly, the term itself is now more broadly used than before and the narrower approaches to the issue of ideology that underlay many of the early studies of Cuba have been superseded by an academic and political debate that now allows for more complex meaning.[3]

The second factor in the shift has been the more widespread acceptance among students of Cuba that there was in fact a definable ideology within the revolution in 1959, with a clear historical pedigree and a relatively clear set of implicit policies. Whether one refers to this ideology as *cubanismo*, nationalism, or populism, Cuba by 1959 boasted a coherent tradition of dissidence that looked back to the social nationalism of the two wars of independence (1868–1878, 1895–1898), developing through the subsequent phases of dissent.[4] It developed above all through the principal leader and ideologue of the second rebellion, José Martí and then through the student protest of the 1920s that looked to his ideas.[5] Equally, the post-1931 challenge to the dictator Machado, resulting in the unusual revolution of 1933–1934, was inspired by and proposed policies that reflected that same tradition; the radical nationalist platform that briefly characterized that revolution was *cubanista* to the core.[6] Finally, the various groups who challenged Batista in 1952–1953, after his coup, all reflected that same set of principles and that same tradition, whatever ideological veneer may have distinguished them otherwise.[7] By 1958, the common codes of that *cubanismo* included a belief in history as both past and destiny, in equality, the liberating effect of culture, agrarianism, community, heroic action, the responsibility of a benevolent state, and, overall, a faith in nationalism.

Clearly, however, whatever the present academic consensus, the coherence of this perspective depends on a particular understanding of ideology and of the mechanisms by which this may function in any given society. It should therefore be made clear that this study is based on a particular set of definitions that sees ideology as a shared set of codes (themselves a mixture of beliefs, myths, symbols, values, and—perhaps least importantly in their inculcation but most visibly in their exposition—intellectual ideas); that to a greater or lesser degree, depending on circumstance, shows sufficient coherence to be seen as the collective world view of a given social group (class, region, nation, etc.); that is able, or willing, to identify itself collectively and cohesively as different from other groups, classes, or nations. In this context, such a perspective can be taken as a world view—and therefore an ideology—since it is used, consciously and subconsciously, by that particular group to express its preferred and shared view of the world as it has been (its collective perceived history), as it is (its present situation, seen either negatively as "dilemma" or positively as vantage point), and as it should be (its perceived destiny, rather than likely future).

Such an ideology therefore necessarily both explains the group's context (its "world")—explaining its "success," dominance, marginalization or oppression—and posits an ideal future based on one of three outcomes: the maintenance of that world (if it is seen as unproblematic and if the group exercises some sort of hegemony), its modification (if it contains sufficient acceptable elements with which the group can continue to identify), or its rejection and replacement by an alternative. The latter is necessarily modeled on the group's world view but also on certain critical elements of the now-rejected context, which are seen as organic to the group's identity and future. For any alternative ideology must necessarily be based on elements of the rejected society for that ideology to command popular support and present a viable, identifiable, and acceptable alternative; "revolution-ary" ideologies therefore seek both to conserve and to transform.

This is true also because ideologies can be either hegemonic or dissident, either reflecting, reinforcing and inculcating a hegemonic group's domination of a given society or, alternatively, existing as a cultural defense for collective self-identifica-tion of a dominated group. The latter's strength ultimately depends on a range of factors—economic, social, and political—but, within the narrow terms of ideology, on the existence or absence of alternatives to challenge the dissident ideology's claim to counterhegemony within the dominated group. The former's strength, besides depending on an equally wide range of complex factors, also varies according to the ability and willingness of the dominated group to accept the hegemonic ideology, either through ideological defeat, political and social dysjunc-ture, or a conscious acceptance of the dominant world view.

Returning to the specific situation of pre-1959 Cuba, two arguments can be sustained to propose the existence of a successful dissident ideology within the political culture of the 1934–1958 period. The first is that the particular features of dependency by the 1950s had created a social dysjuncture wherein weakened elites, weakened social institutions, and a degenerated and delegitimized political structure had conspired to produce a social, and therefore ideological, vacuum, where none of the conventional ideologies held much sway.[8]

The second argument is that the post-1934 realignment of U.S.-Cuban relations, whose features and limits were defined by the Reciprocity Treaty and the new quota system, produced a new politics characterized by a populism that claimed legitimacy from its roots in the 1933–1934 events (both in the case of Batista, who dominated from 1934 to 1944, and the succeeding *Auténticos*, who governed from 1944 to 1952), but which proved unable, or unwilling, to challenge the bases of the new situation.[9] Hence, its claim to be revolutionary, nationalist, and moral—all *cubanista* principles—proved hollow, since the first two were not permissible in the new relationship and the third was openly breached through rampant corruption.[10]

It was, in short, a flawed populism that, whatever its good intentions, could do no more than improve the superficial aspects of the "new Cuba" (which it did successfully in certain areas), given the new elite's fundamental lack of economic power. Mobilizing successfully, it proved unable to integrate and therefore control, and preferred recourse to political discourse, attempting to manipulate the language and myths of *cubanismo* as a means of obfuscation and distraction.

However, in the volatile context of the Cuba of 1934–1953, where many of the protagonists of 1933–1934 were still key actors (the Communist party was still industrially powerful until 1948 and the followers of the 1933–1934 minister of the interior, Antonio Guiteras, remained in radical politics) and where disillusion of a hitherto politically sophisticated, activist and radical population became a dangerous powderkeg, this manipulation proved counterproductive.[11] In the ideological vacuum (the ex-students being discredited by *Auténtico* corruption, the military radicals becoming Batista's Army, and the Communist party, having distanced itself from the main 1933–1934 rebellion, now having collaborated in the populist charade) the public flaunting of the *cubanista* platform and principles only served to remind the increasingly divergent and underground dissident constituency that the new politics was decidedly alienated from that tradition. Indeed, *cubanismo* became the cement that, in the absence of any other, bound an otherwise incoherent dissidence together.

It was, therefore, from this reservoir of radical dissidence that Castro's 26 July Movement came in 1953, and to which it appealed directly (in its various manifestos and above all in Castro's rallying call, "History will absolve me") and implicitly in both the shared codes and its decision to act decisively, heroically, and self-sacrificingly. The result was a close affinity between the rebellion and the popular desire for change.[12]

Whatever consensus there might be, however, about the 1953–1959 period, it is less widely accepted that this affinity continued after 1959. That implies clear and positive answers to a series of questions that go to the heart of the whole political and academic debate about the nature of the subsequent four decades of revolution, a debate often obscured by understandable a priori postures and judgments that reflect ideological or political agendas—questions about the depth of the pre-1959 reservoir of dissidence and the post-1959 process of political socialization, about the ideological role of the Partido Socialista Popular (PSP) after the victory, and about the possible evolution of *cubanismo*.

The evidence, however, seems to be that the reservoir did in fact prove to be not only deep and durable, but to be able to evolve and to play an active role. For the first two years of the revolution (1959–1961), while the internal battles were being fought within the ranks of the vanguards that vied for hegemony, and while the external pressures of the cold war began to make themselves felt on the internal dynamics, the atmosphere of ideological profusion and political confusion made the revolutionary process into an ideological battleground, but in a critical context of empirical radicalization. Thus the contending groups—two wings (urban and rural, Havana-based and Sierra-based) of the 26 July Movement, the PSP, the various liberals of the early government, the returning *Ortodoxos*—were fighting for ideological, as much as political control. Although Castro's popularity gave his movement a clear advantage; the legitimacy gained in the solitary struggle against Batista and reinforced by the successive *cubanista* manifestos and then policies made its position more immediately popular and stole a march on its ideological rivals.[13]

By 1961, with the rise of the PSP within the revolution (resulting from the political decisions of the revolutionary leadership to ally with the PSP's national structure, as well as the PSP's own opportunistic agenda), and also with the watershed of the victory of Playa Girón (the Bay of Pigs) and the break with the United States, the picture was politically less confusing and the direction ideologically more certain.

This arose from four factors. The first was the increasing sense of siege that characterized the new Cuba, isolated behind the U.S.-imposed embargo, expelled from the Organization of American States (OAS) and shunned by most regional governments. In the resulting siege mentality, the ideological shutters were put up, excluding external points of reference that might weaken the front and relying increasingly on internal, self-generated, criteria and traditions.

Secondly, as political crises internally (with the dispute between the 26 July Movement and the PSP erupting in 1962), and externally, after the Cuban Missile Crisis, forced the leadership to reexamine its new-found alliance with Soviet communism, the indigenous *cubanista* ideology began to regain any hegemony that it might briefly have lost in the two years of partial "Stalinization."[14]

Thirdly, as battle positions became clearer between Havana and Washington, and between liberals and radicals, a growing sense of revolutionary certainty began to replace the early confusion, with familiarity with known and accepted codes becoming more commonplace.

Lastly was the absence of a clear-cut national political structure. As the abortive Organization of Integrated Revolutionary Organizations (ORI) was replaced briefly by the somewhat meaningless Unified Revolutionary Socialist Party (PURS) and then, in 1965, by a Cuban Communist party that counted only 50,000 members and no party congress until 1975, a vacuum of control and coherent socialization was created. This meant that the only effective means for this task were empirical and the only effective agents were the various mass organizations that had sprung up—especially three: the Committees for the Defense of the Revolution (CDR), the Rebel army, and the militias, together with the seminal work carried out by the ubiquitous land reform agency, the National Institute of Agararian Reform (INRA), which virtually represented and effected the revolution's work in the radicalizing countryside.[15]

If these organizations and the experience of millions of Cubans active in them can be said to have replaced the potential socialization role of a leading party, the ideology that they inculcated was, unsurprisingly, *cubanismo*, not least because they were largely led or staffed by Cubans whose participation in the struggle of 1953–1958 or in the defense work of 1959–1962 legitimized both them and the nationalist ideological framework in which they developed and worked. By 1962 most Cubans, and certainly most in the vanguard, had little faith in imported political, economic, or ideological models and preferred to rely on known refer- ences. The critical combination of empirical radicalization and recourse to the *cubanista* tradition reinforced the latter's hegemony.

Moreover, by 1963, that *cubanismo* had added new elements that largely enhanced the central core of codes constituting the ideology, emphasizing, for example, its implicit agrarianism in ways unexpected by the guerrilla rebels themselves in 1959. Similarly, the siege experience, enhancing the underlying sense of isolation, embattlement, and self-righteousness, also strengthened nationalism, while the collective work, defense, debate, and suffering reinforced the existing *cubanista* elements of "communalism" (based on old social and industrial struggles and religious identities).

Evolving and adapting, *cubanismo* thus linked a perceived heroic past, a suffer- ing present, and a hoped-for glorious future, not just among a highly politicized vanguard (whose size and close-knit nature enhanced the intensity of that politici- zation) but also among the population at large, which, rejecting the opportunity to leave, had effectively voted to participate in the collective task of building some sort of shared vision of a radical future.

The key question, however, that has to be asked refers to the mechanisms by which this inculcation-reinforcement actually worked, in making the perceived and recognized ideology concrete, active and internalized on a mass scale. Although much work remains to be done on many of the mechanisms suggested, it seems likely that the process of internalization depended on a complex range of factors and experiences. The most obvious but least provable was the actual collective experience of revolution, which had a distinctly radicalizing effect on those who participated in and benefited from it; the experience of social reform, sacrifice, economic austerity, siege, defense, mobilization, and debate—all new, dramatic and, in their own way, perceived as empowering—created a sense of community. In this atmosphere of heightened tension, excitement, pressure and empirical learning, the inclination of each Cuban who more or less sided with the revolution was to view his or her contribution as vital to the collective good, defense, or survival, as well as cultivating an enhanced sense of collective self-belief and therefore of an ideological self-reliance to match the mood of political and economic self-reliance that became the norm between 1963 and 1970. In such a context, those recently educated or politicized, lacking the leading role of an ideologically certain party to guide the process of socialization, tended to fall back easily on the known, trusted forums of debate and community—especially the CDRs and unions—and the equally established and familiar sources of ideological certainty, namely the now radicalized *cubanista* tradition. The collective auto-radicalization that took place within hundreds of CDRs denied any ideological guidance from party cadres was a deep and lasting experience.[16]

Beyond this basic factor were a range of different mechanisms that individually and collectively reinforced both the existing *cubanismo* and the new radicalism. The first was education, which saw a vast and impressive expansion in its formally structured provision and a continuing expansion via campaigns such as the 1961 Literacy Campaign—which, in its mixture of the educational, political, and social, was the archetypal radicalizing experience—and via the various mass organizations.[17] For "conscientization"—deliberate and incidental—characterized the educational experience of the 1961 campaign, the militia manuals, the Rebel army's political education program, all of which used overtly political primers as part of the drive to achieve their educational objectives.[18] Given the sense of gratitude that education often produced in its beneficiaries, this political message was more easily, because willingly and uncritically, absorbed. Even the more politically sophisticated activists within the 26 July Movement and PPS were exposed to overt politicization in their educational experience within the briefly existing Schools of Revolutionary Instruction (EIR), which used both Marxist and *cubanista* texts and were staffed by PSP and 26 July cadres.[19]

The second obvious mechanism was the growing and ubiquitous presence of street and media propaganda, through ever more impressive and effective posters, newspaper headlines and cartoons, and revisions of Cuban history in the ever-more political press and the new cinema.

Equally, the expansion of culture and its emphasis on participation radicalized many, especially as much of the new literature, cinema, and drama was both politically committed and essentially liberating in its effect, as hitherto "uncultured" proletarians and peasants became exposed to and involved in poetry, theater, magazine short-stories, and other active cultural experiences. The emphasis on cultural self-reliance that resulted simply paralleled and strengthened the accompanying ideological ethos.[20] Language—especially rhetoric—was another such mechanism.

The final, and perhaps most crucial, factor for the process of internalization was myth. The term used in this study is taken to refer to the coherent set of values expressed in a symbol or figure, which, collectively, is perceived by a given social group to express the essence of its ideology in simple, symbolic, or human—and therefore comprehensible—form; it is therefore also seen to reflect a group's, a society's, or a nation's, basic beliefs and self-image. It is, essentially, the distillation of what is otherwise a complex, and usually contradictory, system of beliefs, which is identified with readily by the group to which it belongs because it is most commonly expressed in either a value with which that group identifies itself (e.g., self-sacrifice, suffering, superiority) or a real, fictitious, or legendary person (e.g., national hero, liberator, patron saint).

Hence, myth as used here should not be obscured by unhelpful reality/illusion dichotomies, for it should not be measured by objective truth but rather by group belief and perception. The myth may not express reality, but if the group, society, nation feels it to be real, then it exists.

The essential nature of social myth, however, lies in its roots in the society to which it belongs, in other words, its organic nature. But what factors guarantee that organicity? The first is the existence, as the essence of the myth, of a basic storyline or plot, whose essentials remain largely unchanged, but whose form, precise detail, and particular interpretation must vary, often considerably, according to the needs of the time; the historical, social, or religious context; and the interpeters or the group to which it is being interpreted. It follows, therefore, that myth must be reinterpretable, with a meaning or relevance that, alongside the form, is capable of being adapted and reexplained and also that the plot must necessarily encapsulate the underlying and perceived meaning of the myth and, with it, the perceived essence of the ideology it represents and expresses.

The second factor in guaranteeing organicity is the need for myth to be seen to be born out of a given collective experience of its host group. Whether real or invented, it is essential that this initial experience is seen to have lasting relevance for the group.

The third factor is the need for interpreters, who must necessarily enjoy a degree of acceptability, respect, or honor in the group, entitling them to claim the right to be the high priests of the myth, the ones best placed and most legitimate to interpret the myth for others. These might typically be shamans, priests, or oracles, but, in secular terms, could equally be historians, political leaders, writers, poets, or musicians.

Historically, societies have tended to adopt two sorts of myth. Where the hegemonic ideology is essentially religious, God, gods, or saints play the role of myth figures or symbols, as the comprehensible expression of the myth, not least through the convention of identifying a given value, or values, with a particular god or saint. However, since such religious mythification necessarily talks in terms of deities and the supernatural, the inherent theism of the myth alienates its essential meaning from common experience and concerns. Consequently, the myth survives as a perfect, but essentially unattainable, ideal designed to inspire. In other words, these myths tend, over time, to be become iconized.

The concepts of icon and iconization are fundamental to the historical significance of myth. For, while myth necessarily has a storyline and an evolving, living, nature, icons are static, alienated versions of myth, lacking the basic storyline. While both are essentially idealized and unattainable, myths are projected models for real action but icons are alienated models for perfect being, whose purpose is veneration. Icons are myth made sanctified; for a myth must be identified with by a social group in order to be believed in and acted upon, while an icon must be distanced from that group in order to be venerated. For icon is also a concrete codification of a truth, a symbol of a myth, and an embedding of its basic storyline.[21] This, of course, raises the question of the process of iconization, which can be either accidental—if the myth ceases to be organic or relevant but remains of value in the group—or deliberate, for the purposes of obfuscation and ideological control, by elites but necessarily through a priesthood that no longer interprets alone but also creates the ritual for veneration.

In more secular societies, however, religious myth tends to give way to historical, popular, myth, focused on and manifested in the figures of a real or fictitious person with a storyline, or representing a storyline, which, in its essentials, is seen to express the social, spiritual, and political needs and self-image of a given society at a given moment but which then becomes established as a national myth, reflecting that society's self-image, perceived past, and destiny. Such myths exercise power precisely because, unlike religious myth, they are embodied in human form, in a person with whom the myth's adherents can identify, however idealized that representation might be. They are also powerful because mythic status is created by actions at moments of significance for the group's self-image and history, thereby enabling the myth to become the rallying point for a society in need of mobilization or of a coherent self-image set against external attempts to deny it. Here, the myth's storyline is all-important, since its essential changeability and adaptability makes it readily reinterpetable as the society changes, either naturally or under pressure.

Organicity also depends on the willingness of key groups to accept the myth, for, even if it is deliberately created or fostered, as artifact myth, by a hegemonic group, to cement its hegemony and ensure quiescence, it can only function successfully if the subordinated groups adopt it as reflecting their past, their essence, their destiny, and their hopes. Such myth-making, therefore, implies a tension, in that an organic popular myth has a limited capacity to be a mechanism of control and, conversely, a great potential to be appropriated by subordinated groups as a means of collective self-identification and defense.[22]

In pre-1959 Cuba, historical myths were integral to the fabric and sustenance of the political culture. In particular, three were important. The first was the storyline implicit in the Platt Amendment—of a frustrated, betrayed independence—which dominated nationalist discourse from the inaugural moment of a questionable independence, in which it became a symbol of Cuba's perceived prostration. It was a myth that saw Cuba essentially as the object of its own history, and Platt as the denial of identity.[23]

The second was the concept of generations, with its messages of renewal, continuity, and change.[24] In societies whose self-image is one of revolutionary legitimacy or denial of identity, where the concept of renewal is fundamental to collective self-belief or sense of destiny, generational myths have a motive power and clear function, justifying both the idea of change (implying future hope that the next generation will correct the failures of previous generations) and the idea of continuity with an essential past, seeing each succeeding generation as the torch-bearer of the national soul. Generationalism, therefore, could be both optimistic and pessimistic, revolutionary and traditional.

The third myth overlapped with these two and remained more inherently powerful—the myth of José Martí. For, while Martí was central to the reality of the independence struggle of the 1890s—as political organizer, propagandist, and leader—he became, after his death in 1895 and the end of the war in 1898, critical to the collective self-image of the assailed nationalist constituency and, therefore, critical to the growing dissident tradition.[25] Until the 1920s, his image was subject to a steady, organic mythification, with the essential storyline of his life—*lucha, muerte, traición* (struggle, death, betrayal), framed within an evidently "pure" life—being seen increasingly as the representation of Cuba's history from 1868. To the significant subculture of a denied nationalism, within a corrupt pseudo republic, Martí encapsulated the evolving ideology.

It was, however, in the 1920s that the evolving myth found its integral priests, in the form of the rebel students who, by questioning public corruption, implicitly questioned the basis of the new republic. They became the myth's priests not just because of their actions—in taking up the fallen torch of a lost hero's struggle for independence, in challenging the new order, and in founding the political and cultural mechanisms to take that struggle forward—but also by rescuing Martí's ideas, popularizing them as the *ideario* of the new dissidence.[26] That same dissidence, armed with those same ideas, then challenged Machado's dictatorship and enacted the brief-lived revolution of 1933–1934. For that interlude reflected the *cubanista-martiano* tradition in its platform and its reforms, and, by the death of the leading priest, Mella, echoed Martí—adding fuel to the accompanying generational myth—and ensapsulated the storyline of the myth, of *lucha* (by the most recent generation of young patriots and by the priesthood itself), *muerte* (of the briefly reborn Cuba), and *traición* (by the renegade participants in the revolution, who had gone on to dominate post-1934 politics).

The post-1934 Cuba was, however, an illusion. While the particularities of the new U.S.-Cuban relationship removed the issue of the United States from the conscious nationalist agenda, allowing the new political elite to claim legitimacy (with the Platt Amendment repealed and many elements of the 1933 platform enacted as actual reforms by, first, Batista, and then the *Auténticos*), the underlying reality was that this elite was a pseudoelite, lacking an autonomous economic base.

The "re-Cubanization" that Batista proclaimed was either partial (especially where American interests had, anyway, withdrawn—notably sugar, small-scale manufacturing and finance) or cosmetic, since the basis of the new relationship was not capital but the sugar quota and the terms of the Reciprocity Treaty. Far from being a real national bourgeoisie, therefore, it remained an aspiring or putative elite, an elite by default.

More significantly, this pseudoelite increasingly lacked ideological legitimacy, with its unwillingness or inability to realize the goals of the *cubanista* tradition. The political elite, therefore, especially after 1944, with the election of Grau and the other veterans of 1933, resorted to the manipulation of that tradition in order to disguise the weakness of its claim. In particular, it appropriated the inherited and recently renewed myth of Martí, raising it to the level of sanctified, unthreatening, alienated icon, enshrining it as an object of veneration that would, in fact, give that elite vicarious legitimacy, not least in sharing the name of Martí's party.

Icons, however, also need a priesthood, because veneration and alienation demand initiated and acknowledged mediators to explain the inherently incomprehensible. Yet the potential priests' legitimacy was wearing thin. Not only were the veterans of 1933–1934 already discredited by corruption and betrayal, but the next student generation was also discredited by its degeneration into *bonchismo*.[27] The attempted iconization was, therefore, flawed and less successful than it needed to be, the underlying myth surviving in the subculture of dissent that outlived the post-1934 repression. Each attempt to reinforce iconization simply reinforced the longevity and power of the myth.

1953 saw the arrival of the next generation to interpret the myth, the newest priesthood, again identified with young students and heroic action. Coinciding with the celebration of a questionable independence and the centenary of Martí's birth—both raising deep questions about the basis of the republic—and reacting to Batista's coup, which had exposed the emptiness of the orthodox dissidence in its supine response to an outrageous assault on the democratic tradition, the young rebels were promptly labeled the *Generación del Centenario*. With their self-sacrificing action at Moncada, their youthful claim to be untainted by corruption, their roots in the *Ortodoxos* and their avowedly *martiano* platform, they immediately became the new priests of the myth, but, as in 1923, were strengthened in this claim by the coincidental revival of the actual writings of the hitherto symbolic *Apóstol*. Thus the reborn Martí myth remained the legitimating standard of the rebels throughout the insurrection (1953–1958) and into the early years after the victory.

From 1961, however, the myth became problematic, since its essential storyline (struggle, death, and betrayal) was for most Cubans no longer their collective self-image in the revolution, which was seen, instead, as the culmination of all preceding nationalist and radical struggles and not their betrayal. After the victory at Playa Girón, a myth recalling repeated, if heroic, defeats made little sense, although other elements of the myth still pertained in the new Cuba, corresponding to popular empirical perceptions: egalitarianism, heroism, dignity, self-sacrifice, and intellectual liberation. Given, therefore, that the myth's surface-level elements remained while the storyline became less relevant, a natural process of steady iconization began, as the living myth became converted into a more static icon. The continued public emphasis on Martí and on the revolution's *martiano* pedigree made sense under the circumstances, reflecting the revolution's ideological roots and traditions, but, given this natural iconization, this emphasis tended also to alienate the myth and raise it to the status of venerable object.

There were, however, other myths, either available in the *cubanista* tradition or newly developed or rediscovered, which were usable sources of mythic, and therefore ideological, inspiration. The most natural of these in the newly embattled enclave was the myth of Cuba as the biblical David.

It was natural because it expressed the collective self-image of heroic struggle leading to victory against a superior enemy, a myth made powerful because its recognizable human form was biblical, in a society where, despite the social weakness of organized religion, centuries of religious education and mythmaking, Protestant evangelization and the mythic emphasis of *santería* had created a fertile ground for fundamental familiar Judeo-Christian myths.[28] Moreover, it reinforced *martianismo,* given every Cuban's familiarity with Martí's words, "mi honda es la de David."[29] In a sense, therefore, the Martí myth regained vitality through this new, morally righteous myth, which retained the historicist justification of the old and, despite the current siege and suffering, offered real hope of redemption.[30]

1967, however, brought a moment of deep ideological crisis for Cuba, for in that year, at a time of growing isolation from both the hemisphere and Cuba's new socialist allies, Che Guevara was killed in Bolivia.[31]

It is difficult now, in the face of speculation, propaganda, and historical revisionism, to appreciate the impact on Cuba of Guevara's death. He was, after all, never as popular as Fidel Castro, was not Cuban, was never an orator in the Castro mold and was generally less visible than other Cuban leaders; he also had the reputation of intellectual, emotional coldness and of an ideological certainty. Whatever the truth to this reputation, however, he was clearly second only in importance to, and friend, confidant and ideological mentor of, Fidel Castro, and had been at the forefront of the revolution from the outset.[32] His departure in 1965 had been traumatic enough, but his brutal death now was a hammer-blow to the Cuban population, especially to the rebel vanguard, Che's old comrades-in-arms. Coming at a moment of isolation, economic stringency, and tension, it seemed to signal a collective loss of faith in the revolution's steady progress. Not only had the attempt to break the siege failed, but it had also taken one of the revolution's most important protagonists and most imaginative thinkers.[33]

In terms of myth, two interesting developments now occurred. The first, logically, was a process of mythification of the newly martyred hero, Che, who, after 1968 was named *Año del Guerrillero Heróico*, and whose image became universalized, especially dominating the Plaza de la Revolución, and whose words were reproduced voluminously. However deliberate this process, it clearly responded to both the vanguard's and the average Cuban's genuine sense of personal loss.

Linked to this Che myth, however, was an upsurge in the popularity, frequency, and use of the myth of the "New Man." This had been part of the revolutionary political culture since the early days of the victory and had its roots in two traditions—the indigenous *cubanista* tradition, especially with its codes of renewal, generationalism, and heroism—and the newer Marxist tradition (as opposed to what was already part of *cubanismo*), especially the version that filtered through the highly unorthodox interpretations and writings of Guevara. To those dual origins, however, was now added the collective ethos that was evolving empirically out of the shared struggle and out of the experience of social development, together with the post-1966 economic policies that reflected a fusion of ideological preferences and practical imperatives.[34] This newly forged myth, part-organic and part-artifact, now became a publicly adopted myth, reflecting both the new ethos of the economic, political, and external struggle and the popular identification with Guevara's image and storyline; for, effectively, the myth found a natural, and hence more powerful, manifestation in the figure, the writings, the image, and the storyline of Che—a storyline, essentially, of self-sacrifice and dedication to the collective good. The Che myth thus benefited through being intellectualized in the New Man, while the New Man myth benefited through popular identification with the real Che. These two myths, in addition to the existing ones of Martí and David, found a fertile soil in a Cuba ever more isolated (and in need of ideological self-sustenance), with morale declining and even the most recent certainties now fundamentally questioned. Given that any revolutionary process inevitably bewilders, animates, and potentially disconcerts, the experience of Cuba between 1966 and 1970 exaggerated that tendency and increased the need for myth.

After 1970, however, the revolutionary process, and, with it, its structure, ethos, and leadership, changed once again. The radicalism, voluntarism, and bewildering pace and change of the 1960s, together with the "moral economy" and the peculiarly Cuban definition of revolution gave way to a more stolid process of orthodox institutionalization and the Economic Planification and Development System (SDPE), economic policies based on the once-rejected criteria and more acceptable to a Moscow willing to grant conditional aid to the crippled Cuban economy. With orthodoxy came a greater role for the formerly discredited ex-PSP leadership and cadres in a revived Communist party.[35]

In a climate of greater consumerization and more measured social improvements (now financed by an improving economy and advantageous trading links with communist economies [COMECON]), pressure for mobilization was also reduced and the sense of permanent crisis dissipated. In these circumstances, as ideology again underwent reappraisal, the 1960s myths also underwent changes. The most useful, and even organic, myths were now the David myth (celebrating survival and even greater external acceptance)—although Cuba was demonstrably less alone than in the days of the siege—and the New Man, since, although the myth of the 1960s had focused on an essentially heroic, self-sacrificing, and unremittingly revolutionary figure and message, the 1970s version was an educated, politically conscious servant of the communal good. In a sense, however, these two myths were already being iconized, given their less natural affinity with the perceived reality than in the 1960s. Equally, the renewed use of the Martí myth after 1970 lacked a degree of organicity and threatened even greater iconization, especially as the new emphasis of the revolution was less on its Cuban past than on its renewed affinity with Soviet-defined socialism.

It was, however, the Che myth that became most iconized. Post-1975 Cuba was led, and defined, not by the old guerrillas but by a mixture of old-PSP leaders and new, Moscow-trained, technocrats, espousing ideas defeated in the Great Debate but now apparently hegemonic, implying the rejection of those that were espoused by, and identified with, Guevara. This new vanguard clearly needed to legitimize its authority and claim to hegemony; in this, it had natural recourse to the useful myths of David, the New Man, and Martí, but also even more usefully, to the Che myth—an established, popular, and once organic myth, which, despite its identification with a figure of unmistakably revolutionary stamp (in contrast to the new, apparently unrevolutionary, patterns), could not challenge the new orthodoxy. For, although the new leaders were those defeated by Guevara's arguments in 1965 and associated with a definition of socialism that he had increasingly rejected, they had also been his political allies and contemporaries and the whole process was clearly still being led by Guevara's closest *compañero*, Fidel Castro. The further away from Guevara's ideas the new process moved, the more Che was iconized by those who led that distancing. Throughout the 1970s, therefore, images of Che abounded, with selected phrases legitimizing the new direction; but few of his writings were now published and those associated with him and his ideas were demoted within academic and political circles.[36]

At two levels, however, the Che myth survived as myth. Most powerfully it survived at the popular level, based on what was obviously still a lingering, genuine affection for the memory of a respected hero, but also, curiously, as a means of maintaining a link with the shared experience of what was perhaps seen as a heroic, if now distant, past. Many Cubans now, while welcoming the present material rewards of past sacrifice, seemed to cling to memories of a period that, for all its hardships, had brought with it a sense of community, heroism, and even spirituality.[37] In preserving the Che myth, these ordinary Cubans were in fact preserving a memory of, and belief in, what they still saw as the essence of a revolution that was now less recognizable. The enthusiasm that greeted Cuba's new internationalism in the late 1970s can partly be explained by ideological commitment, giving the opportunity to relive the myths of the New Man and Che.[38]

The second level where the myth survived was in the ranks of what we might call the "dissident" leadership, those ex-guerrillas (including Castro himself) who had been relatively marginalized by the new developments but who remained in the structure, either in the higher organs of power (albeit with little influence) or in the lower ranks of the party. To these, the survival of the Che myth was both natural (given their evident affinity with their recently dead comrade) and useful, as it legitimized their continuing presence and their claim to ideological hegemony. The more that Che was iconized (in a system whose public policies so often differed from his actual ideas), the more legitimacy was conferred on those who were still publicly identified with him. So long as Che remained in popular consciousness, these "dissidents" had no need to formulate political arguments; the continuing myth argued for them anyway.

It should, of course, be said that as Cuban society evolved, becoming especially younger, a range of new myths arose at different levels, notably those around womanhood, youth, and an Afro-Cuban identity, past, and culture. In the 1970s, however, these were largely myths in formation, unused politically in the same way as the Martí, Che, or New Man myths; moreover, as the new orthodoxy tended to iconize the 1960s myths, these tended to be replaced by myths focusing on values rather than people—heroism, equality, unity, and struggle (but mostly the struggle of the insurrection and the 1960s, especially Girón). Above all, history became a myth in itself, like all the other values legitimizing and explaining the present in the context of the past and positing a future based on the enhancement of tradition. The new historiography that blossomed in academic circles and in the popular press both revised the past in the light of a confident present and consciously presented Cuba as the subject of its own history, as opposed to the old history and myths that had seen Cuba as victim and object. The traditional "history as destiny" ethos of *cubanismo* now saw Cuban history in a new light and used it to forge and legitimize the new identity.[39]

Thus, when, by the end of the 1980s, the revolution was plunged into a new, but dangerous, crisis, the political system cried out for new, or renewed, myths.[40] Moreover, the internal struggles that underlay and resulted from that crisis, reinforced that need, for, from 1985, but especially after the 1986 Party Congress, the once marginalized "outs" of the vanguard—mostly the ex-guerrillas of the 1960s—had returned to center-stage, increasing their hold over economic direction and ideological patterns.[41] Now, without both Soviet protection and the constraints of the Soviet links, and with new challenges facing the embattled leadership, a new direction was demanded in economic policy, political definition, and therefore ideology. Indeed, rectification had stressed something of a return to the values and economic policies of the 1960s—not least the old emphasis on indigenous resources, criteria and solutions, and a reinforcement of the traditional revolutionary mobilization ethos. Although the new measures were practical, designed to prepare the population for the rigors of an untold misery and to batten down the hatches for the coming economic storm, there was also a sense in which this strategy harked back to the survival strategies of the days of the siege.

One major characteristic of this new emphasis, indicative of its ideological underpinning, was the increased emphasis on the writings of Guevara. The once marginalized leader's works were revived, from 1987, and greater attention was again paid to the ideas that he had offered in the 1960s, partly to lay claim to the revolutionary legitimacy that they offered and partly to seek revolutionary ways of dealing with a crisis that, increasingly, demanded the ending of old taboos, an opening to once disregarded foreign trade and capital, and turning a blind eye to all manner of black market and once illegal trading.

However, while the restored leadership, in a revolutionary system being shaken to its foundations, looked to Guevara for practical motivations and encouraged the study of his ideas, the myth of Che was reawakened in an unusual manner. For, although there was some deliberate fostering of the existing myth, to restore revolutionary legitimacy to a system whose credibility was now under threat, the myth itself was increasingly taken up by young Cubans for different reasons.

Steadily throughout the 1980s and 1990s, the growing youth population of Cuba had become partially alienated from a system that seemed to restrain its creativity, at a time of exciting change in the once stolid Soviet Union (after 1985), bewildering and disconcerting change in the old socialist world and the end of a cold war that had done so much to shape, and even misshape, Cuba's revolution. While this alienation was rarely problematic, it did signal a need to restore legitimacy, a fact recognized by the attention paid to the *Unión de Juventud Comunista*. Two underlying problems caused this alienation—the mismatch between the official myth of youth and the reality of the aging leadership, still in power after three decades, and the expectations created by social and educational improvements that, after 1984, could not be met easily.

Hence, by 1989, many young Cubans were speaking a different language from the vanguard and showing a declining respect for the once inviolate leaders; in 1994, this emerged with a vengeance as youth discontent in parts of Havana erupted in street violence and eventually mass exodus in the remarkable *balsero* flotilla of August.[42] Whatever specific causes there may have been of this episode, there can be little doubt that one underlying cause was a sense of alienation among sectors of Havana youth.

It was therefore remarkable that it should be young Cubans who most readily took up the myth of Che at the time of crisis, almost adopting the symbol of the old revolution as part of their statement against the present one; young Cubans in search of a more Western lifestyle, at least superficially, seemed to have gravitated toward the myth of someone who, by dying young, could not be blamed for any of the events of either the orthodox 1970s or the harder 1980s and 1990s, someone who also represented an age of revolutionary innocence that now began to attract their attention.

All of this brings us back again to the underlying themes of myth and ideology. For there can be little doubt that the developments of the 1990s have meant, and will continue to mean, a deep ideological crisis for the revolution. Quite simply, the leadership cannot expect a rapid liberalization of economic policies, structures, and values to be unleashed without some political effect; it cannot expect the influx of foreign tourists, dollars, and carpetbaggers to leave social and moral values unaffected. A revolution that for decades has stressed equality, nationalism, moralism, community, and heroism, cannot easily retain its essential features in the face of the growing social inequality created by access to the dollar, the growing willingness to cede rights to foreign capital, the growing problems of prostitution and petty crime, the growing individualistic drive for personal economic survival in the informal sector and the unheroic dash for survival at all costs. Moreover, for the first time in the revolution's history, economic policy-making and issues have become separated from politics, from the process of revolutionary transformation. One thing that made myths powerful, organic, and usable in the 1960s, and even the 1970s, was the total integral coherence of economic, political, and social structures, change, and decisions; myths in those circumstances had a totality that made them identifiable. The revolution's new search for revolutionary identity, in the face of crisis, change, and a totally new world therefore necessarily involves a search for a new, or perhaps rediscovered, ideology, but also, if that is to have effect, a new, or rediscovered, set of organic myths.

NOTES

1. There were several variations of this perspective, most notably those seeing the process as a "revolution betrayed," arguing either for the existence of a hidden communism within the rebel movement or a subsequent inposition of Marxism-Leninism on an otherwise nonideological or liberal rebellion. The most outstanding of these studies included Theodore Draper, *Castro's Revolution: Myths and Realities* (New York: Frederick A. Praeger, 1962) and *Castroism: Theory and Practice* (New York: Frederick A. Praeger, 1965).

2. Two recent works, in particular, have tended to see the process in the older perspective, the collection edited by Enrique A. Baloyra and James A. Morris, *Conflict and Change in Cuba* (Albuquerque: University of New Mexico Press, 1993), and the study by Julie Marie Bunck, *Fidel Castro and the Quest for a Revolutionary n Culture in Cuba* (State College: The Pennsylvania State University Press, 1994). It seems clear that these, and much of the journalistic coverage of the post-1989 crisis in Cuba, were based on an expectation that, as in Eastern Europe, an ideological conflict between populace and leadership was leading inevitably toward collapse.

3. This debate has, in particular, been transformed by the reappraisal of the writings of the Italian Marxist Antonio Gramsci, but also by the work of, and debates around, Louis Althusser and structuralism.

4. The term *cubanismo* has been used by this author in many studies of the revolution. See especially, Antoni Kapcia, "Martí, Marx and Morality: the Evolution of an Ideology of Revolution," in Richard Gillespie (ed.), *Cuba after Thirty Years: Rectification and Revolution* (London: Frank Cass, 1990), pp. 161–183.

5. The student protest began in 1923 with the manifesto by thirteen intellectuals (*Protesta de los Trece*) against university corruption, then rapidly broadened into a wider, and more radical, protest against the whole political system. For further discussion, see Antoni Kapcia, "Cuban Populism and the Birth of the Myth of Martí," in Christopher Abel and Nissa Torrents (eds.), *José Martí, Revolutionary Democrat* (London: The Athlone Press, 1988), pp. 32–64.

6. The Revolution of 1933–1934 grew out of the student movement against the increasinbly dictatorial rule of Gerardo Machado (1925–1933) and resulted in the alliance of students (the DEU) and rebel sergeants (led by Fulgencio Batista), which came to power between September 1933 and January 1934. For further discussion of this episode, see especially Luis E. Aguilar, *Cuba 1933: Prologue to Revolution* (Ithaca: Cornell University Press, 1972) and Lionel Soto, *La Revolución del 33* (Havana: Editorial Pueblo y Educación, 1977).

7. In 1952, Batista returned to power in a coup, preempting an almost certain election of the opposition *Ortodoxo* party (see footnote 12). Although Castro's 26 July Movement was

the largest and, ultimately, most successful of the groups challenging Batista, there were other smaller resistance groups, mostly growing out of the *Ortodoxo* Youth movement or student groups. The most important were the MNR and the *Directorio Revolucionario Estudiantil* (which was fused with the 26 July Movement after 1961).

8. Here, by "dependency," I refer both to the specific nature of Cuba's economic dependence on the United States and to the condition defined by the more general theories of dependency of the 1960s and 1970s, which talked especially of the distorting social effects of Latin America's structural dependency on the world metropolitan economies. In the Cuban case, the outstanding study of this distortion is still Robin Blackburn's seminal article from 1970, "Prologue to the Cuban Revolution," in *New Left Review*, 21 (October 1963), pp. 52–91.

9. In 1934, Batista's post-revolutionary government signed a Reciprocity Treaty with Washington (replacing its 1903 predecessor), which, in response to the Depression, guaranteed the continuing entry into the American market of Cuban sugar, on reduced but still preferential terms, in exchange for the privileged entry into the Cuban market of American manufactured goods. Locking Cuba further into an economic role as producer of raw sugar for one market and captive market for U.S. goods, it tended to petrify economic development while, momentarily, ensuring security. Critically, it also linked with the new quotas for countries exporting sugar to the American market, quotas determined by the Department of Agriculture on an annual basis. The Revolution of 1933–1934 was followed by six years of governments dominated by Batista, by constitutional rule by Batista following the 1940 Constitution and elections, and then, between 1944 and 1952, by the rule of the *Partido Revolucionario Cubano* (known as the *Auténticos*), who were led by and were largely the student rebels of 1933–1934 (the PRC had also been the name of José Martí's party in the 1892–1898 period).

10. Corruption became rampant after 1934, just as it had been between 1902 and 1933. In particular, Batista left office in 1944 some $40 million richer, while Grau San Martín (ex-leader of 1933–1934 and president from 1944 to 1948) and his successor Prío Socarrás oversaw a vast expansion of peculation and personal enrichment by officials.

11. The Communist party (having changed its name in 1944 to *Partido Socialista Popular*, as part of its drive to respectability and moves toward Batista, to form the populist alliance, *Coalición Democrática Socialista*, in 1938) was partly driven underground in 1948, when its preeminence in the CTC trade union confederation, was replaced by *Auténtico*-linked leaders. Guiteras had been a heterodox leftist within Grau's 1933–1934 government, commanding enormous popularity. In 1935, he led a broad general strike against Batista, and was asassinated in that year. His followers tended to gather in the new *Joven Cuba* organization.

12. The 26 July Movement was founded in the aftermath of the assault on the Moncada barracks in Santiago de Cuba on 26 July 1953, led by Castro (then a student leader); his defense speech, ending with the words "Condemn me. It does not matter. History will absolve me." (Fidel Castro, *History Will Absolve Me* (London: Jonathan Cape, 1967, p. 104). This became the first manifesto of the movement. The composition of the original rebel group was mixed but included many (including Castro) from the youth wing of the *Partido del Pueblo Cubano* (known as the *Ortodoxos*), an offshoot of the *Auténticos* founded in 1947 to challenge the latter's corruption and led, until his public suicide in 1951, by Eddy Chibás, a veteran of 1933–1934 and, many had assumed until Prío's selection, the heir apparent to Grau. For some time, adherents of the movement referred to it as "armed Chibasismo."

13. From 1956, the rebellion had had two foci, Havana (often called the *Llano*—Plain) and the Sierra, a division that became accentuated as the guerrilla struggle radicalized its participants. In large part, this division became the basis of the evolving radical-liberal divisions within the rebellion and the early Revolutionary government. The PSP, having opposed the rebellion in 1953 and again in 1956, chose to support it in 1958, becoming part of the post-1959 alliance (with the 26 July Movement and the DRE).

14. In 1961, Aníbal Escalante, a leader of the PSP, had been entrusted with the task of constructing a single party organization to unite the three then in alliance; he set up the ORI (*Organizaciones Revolucionarias Integradas*), but with a central committee with excessive PSP membership. Consequently, he was removed, the ORI disbanded, and the PSP relegated. October 1962 also saw the Cuban Missile Crisis, when the angry Cuban response to both the Soviet climbdown and Soviet insensitivity to Cuban feelings gave rise to a considerable cooling of relations.

15. The CDRs had been set up in 1960 in response to the growing threat of Miami-based invasion; in 1961, they played a key role in defeating the invasion at Playa Girón, after which they multiplied and became the main agent locally for political socialization and for effecting the social, political, and economic work of the revolutionary transformation. INRA (*Instituto Nacional de Reforma Agraria*) enacted the two major land reforms (1959 and 1963), and, with close supervision by both Castro and Guevara, it rapidly became the revolution's agent, and even government, in rural Cuba, broadening its remit from land to social and educational issues.

16. In this respect, the radicalization effect of "unsupervised" socialization might be likened to that which, according to some observers, took place in the 1960s and 1970s, within sectors of the Catholic church in Latin America, once the radicalizing Church Base Communities were allowed to develop in the absence of priests.

17. For details of this Campaign, see Richard R. Fagen, *The Transformation of Political Culture in Cuba* (Stanford: Stanford University Press, 1969), pp. 33–68.

18. The term "conscientization" refers to the theories of education through consciousness in the work of the Brazilian educationalist, Paulo Freire, whose ideas were influential in the Cuban education reforms of the 1960s.

19. For discussion of the EIR, see also Fagen, *Transformation*, pp. 104–137.

20. Self-reliance became something of a watchword in the academic and intellectual debate that developed in the 1960s in Cuba. One outstanding contribution to this debate came in the collection of essays by Edmundo Desnoes, *Punto de Vista* (Havana: Instituto del Libro, 1967).

21. I am indebted for the development of these ideas to the help given in discussions with my colleague, Jean Gilkison.

22. What is referred to here is a process akin to what occurred over centuries in Latin American religious "syncretism," whereby dominated cultures adopted the forms of the hegemonic religious beliefs but maintained their indigenous belief system beneath the surface.

23. The Platt Amendment was passed by the U.S. Congress, which obliged the new Cuban Constituent Convention to incorporate it in the Constitution of the new Republic; it allowed for effective and legal control of Cuba by the United States, controlling external treaties, permitting American military intervention, and obliging the perpetual lease of military bases. The new republic, defined by Platt, became known by nationalists as the "pseudorepublic."

24. Cuba was not unique in the Hispanic world in extolling generations, but the Cuban generational experience seemed particularly significant and identifiable, recycling itself

every twenty or thirty years: the 1868–1878 rebellion, the 1895–1898 rebellion, the 1923–1933 protests and revolution, and, finally, the 1953 rebellion.

25. As a journalist, Martí traveled widely throughout Latin America and the United States, propagandizing, writing, and mobilizing Cuban émigrés. In 1892 he founded the *Partido Revolucionario Cubano* and in 1895 organized the invasion of eastern Cuba, which set off the second War of Independence, a war in which he lost his life within days of the invasion.

26. Above all, it was the student leader, Julio Antonio Mella who popularized Martí's ideas, with his "Glosas al Pensamiento de Martí" in 1927, then went on to cofound both the Universidad Popular José Martí (a worker-oriented educational institution), and, in 1925, the Communist party.

27. The *Bonche Universitario* was set up in 1934 by the *Auténticos* to challenge leftist influence in student politics and the unions. By the early 1940s, *bonchismo* was the term for all the different student groups that had moved from political activism to open gangsterism in the university. Despite their nomenclatures and their association with veterans of 1933, 1935, and the Spanish Civil War, they had ceased to be political.

28. Because of the relative weakness of Spanish colonialism, especially in the nineteenth century, the Catholic church in Cuba remained largely white, urban, and either aristocratic or middle-class; these characteristics remained after independence, as a result of which, by the 1950s, the hold of Catholicism was more tenuous in Cuba than most other parts of the continent. On the other hand, certain Protestant churches, especially the Baptist communities, did enjoy support in rural Cuba, and the Afro-Cuban religions that collectively went under the name of *santería*, remained popular in urban Afro-Cuban communities.

29. From Martí's letter to Manuel Mercado (written on the day of Martí's death), immediately following the most quoted of Martí's words, usually translated as "I have lived in the bowels of the monster and I know him well, and my sling is David's." From José Martí, *Paginas Escogidas* (Buenos Aires: Espasa Calpe, 1954), p. 183.

30. It is interesting to note here that, at that time, many Cubans publicly equated their situation, their isolation and their struggle with Britain at war (1939–1945), but also with Israel—a society with which, before 1967, it was possible to see certain parallels, notably the sense of righteous struggle against a hostile siege, a history of emigration, suffering, and denial that seemed to lead to a destiny now being realized, to be defended by an armed citizenry and a collectivist mood for solidarity.

31. Isolation from the socialist allies was created by the growing ideological and political divorce between Havana and Moscow over definitions of revolution and policies in Latin America; by 1967, relations were often bitter, and erupted vicariously in a bitter war of words between Castro and the loyalist Venezuelan Communist party.

32. On 1 January 1959, Guevara, having led the column that spearheaded the rebels' westward march, entered Havana. Thereafter, he took charge of the Cabaña fortress, from where he helped control resistance in the capital, became head of the Industrial Department of INRA (1959), led many overseas visits to establish links with the socialist and Third World countries, became Director of the National Bank (1959–1961), and Minister of Industry (1961–1965), and, throughout, remained part of the inner group that formulated the revolution's basic policies.

33. Although there were broader motivations for the Bolivian *foco* being set up, the Cuban leadership clearly also saw it, and the whole insurrectionary strategy of Latin American policy, as a beans of ending Cuba's regional isolation. The author's interviews with many of

Guevara's colleagues of that time have confirmed the significance of his death within the small, cohesive, and tightly knit group of ex-guerrillas and activists.

34. In 1962, Castro sanctioned an extensive debate (conducted in the pages of the party and academic journals between 1962 and 1965), between a "radical" perspective, championed by Guevara, and an "orthodox" perspective (representing in particular the views of the PSP theoreticians, and certain Western and Eastern European economists). At the end of the Great Debate, economic policy from 1966 was established as a compromise between the two positions, with a sugar-based future (mostly the orthodox view)—geared toward the production of 10 million tons in 1970—and a commitment to central planning and "moral" rather than material incentives (the radical view).

35. The failure of the 10-million-ton *zafra* meant a thorough reappraisal of policies, not least at the insistence of Moscow. This led to the restitution of the party and, within it, of many of the old PSP cadres and leaders, and a new economic strategy, enshrined in the SDPE (*Sistema de Desarrollo y Planificación Económico*). This process was closely tied to Cuba's entry into the Council for Mutual Economic Assistance (CMEA) (COMECON) in 1972 and the institutionalization of the political structure, in the First Party Congress (1975), and the Constitution and the Popular Power electoral system (1976).

36. One example of this demotion was the fate of the group around the Guevarista *Pensamiento Crítico* magazine of the late 1960s who fell from favor in the new order.

37. This slightly contradictory nostalgia reflected the process seen in Britain in the more materialist and consumerist 1950s–1970s, when veterans of the wartime experience—of a shared sacrifice, struggle, and shortage   began to look back from their more comfortable standards to regret the passing of less materialist values.

38. "Internationalism" was the term given to the program of aid to over forty Third World countries from the mid-1970s; this aid was mostly human, and involved sending experts in education, health, engineering, and other sciences to serve abroad. The military aid to Angola (from 1975) and Ethiopia (from 1978) should also be included in this, not least because, although it served the leadership's wider political purposes (in gaining leverage within Cuba, against pro-Moscow elements, and in the Third World, against the Soviet Union) and although those volunteering for service gained materially from their experience, the rate of volunteering initially reflected something more. Indeed, the official myth around Angola of the *retorno de los esclavos* (return of the slaves) struck a popular chord.

39. Many of these new myths, however—based on values—seemed not to be so effective as those focused on people, perhaps because of the identification potential of the latter; indeed, a process of personalization of the "value" myths was discernible, as in the case of the equation of heroism with the literacy worker, Conrado Benítez.

40. This crisis was the trauma that resulted from the sequential collapse of the Eastern Bloc (1989), COMECON (1990), and the Soviet Union (1991), followed by the tightening of the U.S. embargo in 1992. The knowledge that this crisis was unfolding stimulated the creation of the Special Period in Peacetime strategy, which sought effectively to place Cuba on a war footing economically, reducing consumption, encouraging mobilization and alternative methods, supplies and ideas, and taking the necessary crisis management measures to deal both economically and politically with the collapse that ensued.

41. From the late 1970s a partial re-Fidelization of the political leadership was discernible; this emerged more clearly in the early 1980s, with demotions and promotions within the structure, and was codified in the 1986 Party Congress which, besides initiating a thorough overhaul of the party, launched the "Rectification (of Past Errors and Negative Tendencies)" process, seeking to streamline, restore ideological criteria and correct the

"errors" of the 1970s (an overimitative dependence on Eastern Bloc criteria, trade, definitions, and policies).

42. Following rising tensions in a commodity-starved Havana and also measures in May 1994 to reduce the growing black market, discontent came to the surface in parts of Old Havana, leading to some violence and a spate of hijackings of boats and invasions of embassies. Finally, in August, the government tolerated the mass exodus of, as it turned out, over 34,000 Cubans (mostly young, mostly Havanans) who left on all manner of craft to cross the sea to Florida. The move proved to be skillful political management, as the American response was to seek to end the exodus, to begin talks with Havana on a new migration accord and to end certain anomalies in relations with Cuba.

chapter 7

U.S. Ideology and Central American Revolutions in the Cold War

David Ryan

Much of what ideologies say is true, and would be ineffectual if they were not; but ideologies also contain a good many propositions which are flagrantly false, and do so less because of some inherent quality than because of the distortions into which they are commonly forced in their attempts to ratify and legitimate unjust, oppressive political systems.

Terry Eagleton, *Ideology,* p. 222

To examine the interaction of the United States with various Central American "revolutionary" regimes and their attendant ideologies in terms of the cold war is to drastically narrow the focus and to perhaps miss the broader reasons for U.S. hostility. The specific response to various revolutions or movements for change was characterized by cold war conditions or assumptions, but U.S. responses before the Cold War were not that significantly different. To demonstrate this it is necessary to contextualize some aspects of the Inter-American relationship with a broader temporal perspective to facilitate the identification of long-running tensions between U.S. hegemony and pluralism; between revolution and U.S. ideas on self-determination; between freedom, democracy, and the U.S. operation of a sphere of influence. These tensions largely bring ideological concepts into conflict with the requirements of power.

While there may appear to be tension between these concepts (which are not just abstract when understood in relation to the lives of so many people in Central America), the ideology that motivates and characterizes the U.S. reaction to revolution or alternate ideologies seem to find some harmony between the tensions by reference to some higher purpose. This can only be understood through the various cultural assumptions associated with the ideas on manifest destiny, U.S. exceptionalism, and nationalism. These terms remain vague despite considerable work having been done on them, but the components of these terms exercise a potent force in U.S. foreign relations that cannot be ignored in systemic approaches to the subject. Within the documentation on U.S. foreign relations there are both constant references to systemic imperatives and to the higher or longer term purposes of the United States in the world. Within the cold war context references were made to such abstract concepts as the supposed "threat of communism," to "national security"; or in the broader context, the Manichean tendencies of the Monroe Doctrine (1823) posit a threat from old world ideologies or powers, which was extended at the turn of the century in the "progressive" and "civilizing" rhetoric of the Roosevelt Corollary (1904–1905).[1] The official U.S. rhetoric and orthodox histories of the inter-American relationship constantly suggested some benevolent purpose in U.S. action. But there is a greater need to examine the relationship of language and power in the historical record, and as Michael Hunt suggests there is a need to encourage historians to examine the wider cultural context to give the archival documentation greater meaning.[2] Edward Said suggests the discourse on "American specialness" has been so influential that the concept of U.S. imperialism has only "rarely and recently" found its way into accounts of U.S. foreign relations. "But," Said argues, "the connection between imperial politics and culture is astonishingly direct. American attitudes to American 'greatness,' to hierarchies of race, to the perils of other revolutions . . . have remained constant, have dictated, have obscured, the realities of empire, while apologists for overseas American interests have insisted on American innocence, doing good, fighting for freedom."[3]

Even though the various Central American ideologies or revolutions have been formed partly in opposition to either direct U.S. intervention in, or influence over elites within the countries, or in reaction to the consequences of the international economic system, and the concurrent national inequalities, Washington, as a generalization, has had the tendency to downplay the importance of socioeconomic conditions as causes for instability or revolution and instead it has focused on the extent to which communism was involved in the revolutions.[4] Within the cultural and ideological context of the cold war it was thus assumed that the instability or the threat was either directed or influenced from "outside." U.S. ideological imperatives, which played on this dualistic or Manichean world view, constructed cultural and diplomatic assumptions that constantly perceived an external threat, facilitating the reconciliation of the use of hegemonic power with the idea of a benevolent mission or disposition. In the late nineteenth and throughout the twentieth century, the United States tried to maintain a hegemonic position within the inter-American system. The cold war altered the sense of urgency, reinterpreted some ideological assumptions, and changed the political discourse to accommodate the "new" communist threat in the ongoing regional efforts to alter hemispheric relationships.

U.S. IDEOLOGY: THE COLD WAR AND BEFORE

While it is neither logical nor necessary to exclusively define ideology, it is necessary and valuable to explain the sense in which the term is used in this analysis. Ideology as used here is not a reference to the systematic exposition of ideas; but used in the more inclusive sense Hunt derives from Clifford Geertz, as an "integrated and coherent systems of symbols, values, and beliefs [which arise from] 'socially established structures of meaning' associated with culture."[5] In this broader use of the word there is a rejection of the rationalistic and the somewhat deterministic functions of ideology, though it still provides for an understanding of how the world ought to be. Perhaps with Althusser's interpretation of ideology, it can allude to an unconscious relationship with the world, and "to the ways in which we are pre-reflectively bound up in social reality." In this sense ideology reflects a nostalgia and expresses a hope, rather than describing a reality. It is a matter, as Terry Eagleton explains, "of fearing and denouncing, reverencing and reviling, all of which then sometimes gets coded into a discourse which looks as though it is describing the way things actually are." Eagleton argues that ideologies must be more than "imposed illusions" and with all the internal inconsistencies an ideology must still provide a version of reality that is credible to the society. In this sense, a coherent identity can be created from the ideology, and individuals can form the basis for their motivations for translating ideas into effective action.[6] Ideology presents a tacitly coherent picture of the existing condition of the world and its desired shape. The gap between the two, according to Peter Novik, throws up three responses: an individual belonging to the dominant ideology would hardly identify any divergence between the actuality and the aspiration; while accommodationists identify a gap, but are generally happy with the system and are willing to work with it to close the gap (normally progressives and liberals); finally the oppositionist response to ideology does not see the gap, between things as they are and as they should be, closing. When using the cultural interpretation of ideology, the reference is by and large to either the dominant ideology or the accommodationists. The debate in making U.S. foreign policy similarly reflects this position; there is little overt ideological opposition in the United States at the levels involved in policy making. Thus, Geertz contends "ideology bridges the gap between things as they are and as one would have them be, thus insuring the performance of roles that might otherwise be abandoned in despair or apathy." It does this by denying the gap or through legitimating it through references to some higher purpose.[7] The function of ideology in U.S. foreign relations is to identify for the recipient culture their place in the world, and tends to provide a basis for moral action to "shape a better future."[8]

With the construction of an identity and a purpose in the world the U.S. culture and, to a lesser extent, that of the policy makers tends to reduce a heterogenous and complex world to limited, finite, and comprehensible terms. The ideology that operates in tandem with this reductionist understanding of the world ultimately suggests "appropriate ways of dealing with . . . reality."[9] Throughout the cold war as well as the longer history of the inter-American relationship there has been a tendency to regard the supposed opponent or the apparent threat through a reductive and essentialist perspective, seeing or presenting this threat as homogenous. The consequences have often been tragic. Of course in the cold war the complexities of the world were reduced to the bipolar understanding, as exemplified in the Truman Doctrine, containment, and then militarized and globalized in the 1950 crusading policy document NSC-68. Peoples and nations around the world were characterized and then categorized according to this Manichean approach. There were, by presidential assertion, only two ways of life and a choice had to be made. In the early cold war with the greater homogenization of the enemy or the "other," any type of social change in Central America was regarded as communist; almost anything anti-American was assumed to be communist inspired. The process of categorization, according to Richard Immerman, was in a sense a strategy for managing information overload, and again providing a clear direction for U.S. foreign policy. Complexity was reduced through categorization, which facilitated the process of making simple judgments. So by the end of the 1950s, everyone knew that: "Egypt's Gamal Abdel Nasser is another Adolf Hitler. Guatemala's Jacobo Arbenz must be a Communist. If it looks like a duck and acts like a duck, it is a duck." [10] And with the word communist associated with any government or movement one axiomatically assumed the duck was fed by the Kremlin. It should be noted that the U.S. public was far less willing to accept the characterization of the Sandinistas as Soviet-directed communists in the 1980s than the public was willing to assume these characteristics for Arévalo and Arbenz in the 1950s. Of course one of the orthodox lessons of Vietnam, that communism was not a monolithic bloc, punctuated the period between the overthrow of Arbenz and the attempted removal of the Sandinistas through subversion and low intensity conflict. It should also be noted that despite public wariness to this supposed threat posed by the Sandinistas, the Reagan administration continually presented its case in reductionist and ludicrously simple-minded terms. The avoidance of complexity in policy debates is in part an attempt to manufacture or maintain a consensus on U.S. policy goals. Consensus, however, needed to relate more to the ideological constructs rather than to the U.S. interests and power considerations.

Prior to the war in Vietnam there was a high degree of consensus in making U.S. foreign policy. There was an almost near absence of an oppositional ideology within the American political tradition, and the debates between the dominant ideology and the accommodationists were relatively trivial. Basically there was a high degree of agreement on the goals and objectives of U.S. foreign policy. The Vietnam War broke down this ideological consensus to some degree and gave rise to an "emotional alienation and intellectual distancing from Cold War constructs,"[11] which in part explains the greater resistance to Reagan's Central American policies from both the society in general, parts of Congress, and occasionally from within his own administration. The various administrations since Vietnam have tried to reconstruct an ideological consensus and have pursued different strategies for intervention in regional conflicts to facilitate this process. In many respects the process has been assisted by keeping the public in the dark and diminishing the role of Congress (undermining the system of checks and balances) through a restricted flow of information that has impeded the process of an intelligent debate on U.S. policy in Central America.[12]

The consensus based around ideological constructs was absolutely vital given the systemic motivations for U.S. foreign relations. In the early years of the cold war George Kennan, head of the Policy Planning Staff, identified key interests both in terms of global requirements and specifically in terms of hemispheric imperatives. Globally, Kennan explained that the United States had 50 percent of the world's wealth and only 6.3 percent of its population, and this "position of disparity" would have to be maintained "without positive detriment to our national security." In his Policy Planning Study 23 of 1948 he argued: "We need not deceive ourselves that we can afford today the luxury of altruism and world-benefaction. . . . We should cease to talk about vague and . . . unreal objectives such as human rights, the raising of living standards, and democratization." For Latin America, specifically, his primary consideration was the protection of and access to "our" raw materials,[13] that were inconveniently located in other countries. It is the contention here that the United States has consistently pursued such objectives in Central America throughout the twentieth century; though strategies changed quite often.

Michael Hunt has argued that ideology forces us, as no other approach does, to "focus on the consciousness of policymakers and the cultural values and patterns of privilege that shape that consciousness."[14] The U.S. response is more related to this consciousness and world view than any attempt at an objective analysis of the characteristics of the Central American revolutions or ideologies under consideration. The policy makers in Washington were more concerned with the extent to which any changes were compatible with or complementary to systemic imperatives, whether these were economic, ideological, or related to the self-defined U.S. credibility. The particular characteristics or ideologies of the Central American governments were largely irrelevant if they did not operate within the system or seek its alteration. Both aspects: the economic need to maintain order or opportunity, and the attempts to impose U.S. values were evident throughout the twentieth century (and perhaps since 1846–1848, in the prevalent historiography, and earlier in some analysis).[15] Perhaps pertinently and most clearly this sentiment and approach was put forward in the 1904 and 1905 Roosevelt Corollary to the Monroe Doctrine. "All this country desires is to see the neighboring countries stable, orderly, and prosperous," Theodore Roosevelt informed Congress, and "in the Western Hemisphere the adherence of the United States to the Monroe Doctrine may force the United States, however reluctantly, in flagrant cases of wrongdoing or impotence, to the exercise of an international police power." For Roosevelt and in the general thrust of the prevailing "progressive" foreign policies at the turn of the century, the idea of justice lay in the efficient use of resources, not in the social and distributive ideas associated with alternative ideologies. Roosevelt pointed out that Latin Americas "have great natural riches, and if within their borders the reign of law and justice obtains, prosperity is sure to come with them. While they thus obey the primary laws of civilized society they may rest assured that they will be treated by us in a spirit of cordial and helpful sympathy."[16] It was essential that Central America accepted the hemispheric system. The U.S. response to the revolutionary action in Central America during the first two decades of this century showed that Washington could not react in a friendly manner, because to some extent they contested U.S. visions of its greatness by challenging the system it created. The revolutionaries questioned the U.S. model, attempted to change internal sociopolitical structures, and crucially did not confine themselves solely to struggles for national independence.[17] It was this trend, this longer run challenge to U.S. imperialism, hegemony, dominance, or influence that Washington reacted against at different periods.

Finally in this section, before looking specifically at the U.S. reaction to two revolutions, it is necessary to briefly explore the relationship between ideology, exceptionalism, and nationalism to facilitate a more nuanced understanding of the issues. It is extremely difficult to credibly reconcile the more narrowly defined U.S. ideological objectives such as the encouragement of democracy and the promotion of self-determination around the world during the period of its expansion with the actual conduct of its foreign relations unless one makes reference to both U.S. nationalism and exceptionalism. Michael Hunt points out that the United States began the twentieth century "in possession of a coherent foreign-policy ideology validated by a remarkable string of successes." The power behind these foreign policy successes was bound up with the intimate connection between ideology and "American" nationalism. As Louis Hartz pointed out in his 1955 attempt to construct a consensus around the tradition of liberalism, there is a strange phenomenon of competing nationalisms in the United States. One is associated with the culturally understood ideals of the founding fathers and the other is associated with state or national security.[18] Hence, while the United States expanded, it did so in violation of its republican ideals by imposing its way of life on others without their consent. By mid-nineteenth century this was justified through references to a manifest destiny, and later in the century the "progressive" policies provided more secular justifications.[19] But there was a peculiar sense in which Americans did not view their expansion and position in the world as ideological; indeed it is especially evident that in the immediate aftermath of World War II the United States saw itself as opposed to ideological regimes.

The American consensus had worked on the idea that the twentieth century was, as Arthur Schlesinger wrote in 1963, "a record of the manifold ways in which humanity has been betrayed by ideology. . . . Surely the basic conflict of our times, the world civil war of our own day, is precisely the conflict . . . between ideology and democracy."[20] U.S.-style democracy was seen to be in opposition to ideology. Novik has linked the relative enthusiasm for the writings of Karl Popper in the early cold war period with its sharp anti-Marxist message, and the idea that it was providing an intellectual resistance to the ideologies associated with the recent experiences of totalitarianism and authoritarianism. Ideologies were, for Popper, the enemies of the book *Open Society*. While Hartz may have argued for the prevalence of a consensus, Daniel Boorstin took things further by claiming that Americans were united in their rejection of ideology, that there was no need for the United States to be concerned with such things because the American way of life was self-evidently exceptional and there was no need for ideological programs because "God seems to have had a thousand-year plan ready-made for us." For some sociologists in the 1950s, such as Daniel Bell, Seymour Martin Lipset, and Edward Shils, ideology had come to an end in the "American way of life" centered around ideas on liberty, egalitarianism, individualism, populism, and laissez faire economics. Toward the end of the 1980s a similar argument was pursued by Francis Fukuyama.[21] According to Novik, this tendency to denigrate ideology was "one of the most characteristic features of American culture in the Cold War era" and relates directly to the idea that Western thought patterns were not ideological but were empirical and objective. The denial that dominant thoughtways were ideological, that they were nothing else but common sense, was the greatest strength of ideology: the ability to subordinate intellect to power, according to Karl Mannheim. Similarly, Eagleton posits: "It is a choice irony that in seeking to replace an impassioned fanaticism with an austerely technocratic approach to social problems, the end of ideology theorists unwittingly re-enact the gesture of those who invented the term 'ideology' in the first place, the ideologues of the French Enlightenment."[22]

In this abstract and obtuse sense there is a close correlation between U.S. ideology, its nationalism, and its exceptionalism. The ideology was more or less seen to be embodied in the nationalisms of state security as well as the stated ideals of the society. These in turn were presented and deemed to be exceptional. A paradox emerged because the United States at once saw its development as "qualitatively different from other countries," that is, exceptional, but also consistently saw its society as a unique model for other nations to emulate. Ironically, as the United States sought to extend its model it also contributed to the demise of its uniqueness or its exceptionalism. As the United States arrogantly tried to extend its model it simultaneously considered that other peoples lacked the necessary character traits to successfully adopt U.S.-style democracy. The United States simultaneously insisted it was different but wanted others to be more like them. Serge Ricard argues that this

brand of republican messianism that was to be invoked to justify later territorial aggrandizements was derived from the . . . postulate of American uniqueness; but rested on an irreducible contradiction that would forever vitiate U.S. foreign policy: the basic incompatibility of the exceptionalist claim with political messianism, of singularity with universalism. This fundamental ambiguity largely accounts for the incoherence and the inconsistencies of the American diplomatic tradition.[23]

The cultural analysis of ideology provides for a more sophisticated approach to understanding U.S. motivations and perceptions of Central American revolutions and their associated ideologies. With the use of cultural analysis Clifford Geertz argues that all ways of thinking are ideological because it takes place within "webs of significance" that the culture has spun itself. In this sense ideology is derived from the "socially established structures of meaning" associated with various systems of symbols, values, and beliefs. Even if, as Ricard argues, it were an "extraordinary ideological cocktail" that was "concocted to assist an exceptional, and manifest, destiny," the core ideas associated with the ideology helped the nation forge an identity, a sense of purpose and a character. Hunt suggests this is especially important in the area of foreign policy, where the nation tends to unite in the face of a common enemy especially when the rhetoric of U.S. diplomacy presents the world in a dualistic manner. Furthermore, Hunt suggests, there is a close symbolic relationship between U.S. ideology and its concepts of nationalism, though concurrently there is an inclination to deny purely nationalistic motivations as again this is closely linked to millennial tendencies,[24] associated with both the end of ideology theorists and the more recent advocates of the end of history thesis.

THE SYSTEM CHALLENGED: GUATEMALA (1944–1954) AND NICARAGUA (1979–1990)[25]

The American way of life was not just an ideological construct knitting together its stated ideals and its symbols of nationalism and exceptionalism; it was also based on a world view and economic system that sustained this culture. Soviet-directed communism was presented as its principle threat to be "contained" or "rolled back" in Europe and other regional conflicts. In the Third World Washington policy planners were more concerned that governments subscribe to its preferred model of development. This was primarily centered around modernization theories that necessitated the increasing integration of these economies into a world system. Attempts to depart from or to significantly alter the preferred U.S. interpretation of the system was, in the prevailing Manichean outlook, seen as a threat from communism, axiomatically linked to the Soviet Union. In the absence of any real communist threat, social reform, nationalism, and political instability were linked to the anticommunist rationale of the early cold war period. In 1953 the National Security Council's top secret document NSC 144/1 considered that:

There is a trend in Latin America toward nationalist regimes maintained in large part by appeals to the masses of the population. Concurrently, there is an increasing popular demand for immediate improvement in the low living standards of the masses, with the result that most Latin American governments are under intense domestic political pressures to increase production and to diversify their economies. . . . A realistic and constructive approach to this need which recognizes the importance of bettering conditions for the general population, is essential to arrest the drift in the area toward radical and nationalistic regimes. The growth of nationalism is facilitated by historic anti-U.S. prejudices and exploited by Communists.

With these considerations an objective of U.S. foreign policy was to create "orderly political and economic development in Latin America so that the states in the area will be more effective members of the hemisphere system and increasingly important participants in the economic and political affairs of the free world."[26]

The particular ideology of either Arévalo, Arbenz, or later the Sandinistas is not the key to explaining the U.S. reaction to these revolutions, but an examination of these ideologies are important to demonstrate that the United States was not concerned with promoting democracy or self-determination along these alternative lines. As a hegemonic power, particularly in Central America, the U.S. incentive, according to Thomas McCormick, was to pressure nations to abandon economic nationalism, to accept free trade, free capital flows, and currency convertibility. It uses its political power as "ideologue of the world system" to promote the "universal" values associated with the U.S. system; it used its military power to police or protect the system against "external antagonists, internal rebellions, and internecine differences."[27] The United States needed raw materials from throughout the world in the early cold war period and beyond the immediate physical needs, the pursuit of preponderance, according to Melvyn Leffler, required them to create a world environment "hospitable to U.S. interests and values." But just as it sought to assert its preponderant or hegemonic status, many of the peripheral countries wanted to withdraw from the world system, or in the cases of Guatemala and Nicaragua, under the specified periods examined here, there was the desire to renegotiate their position within the system. It is important to note that neither Arbenz nor the Sandinistas cut trade with the United States; Washington took that initiative. McCormick argues that the "tasks . . . envisioned were . . . generic to the periphery: how to defuse neutralism, unseat regimes that were deemed inappropriate role models for the periphery, and build new nations that would showcase the merits of internationalism," centered around modernization and later neoliberal economic theories.[28] But Washington could not appeal to such self-interested motivations in the pursuit of its foreign policy, which was ideologically presented as benevolent, universal, selfless. To a large extent, despite specific U.S. intelligence and understanding, both Guatemala of the early 1950s, and Nicaragua of the 1980s were presented as communist puppets, subservient to either Moscow, later Havana, or manipulated by internal communist forces. This was far from true. Nevertheless, Washington's primary interest was, as specifically stated by the National Security Council (NSC) in 1982, to prevent the "proliferation of Cuba-model states," though in the same document the NSC specifically acknowledged that they had serious difficulties with U.S. public and congressional opinion. Similarly, they acknowledged that international opinion worked against them.[29] As far as U.S. policy for Guatemala was concerned, in the 1950s there was a greater degree of social consensus, especially in the area of foreign policy, and the U.S. media largely accepted and reported the administration's explanations of the events. Abroad, things were not so simple. At the time of the CIA operation against Arbenz, Louis Halle informed Robert Bowie of the Policy Planning Staff, "that the widespread impression abroad is: (a) that the U.S. has become hysterical about the communist menace so that it is losing its head in dealing with it; and (b) that this is leading the U.S. to commit acts of international lawlessness."[30] Still, the simplification of policy was important. It played into reductionist ideological imperatives, or as Noam Chomsky has written about, the "necessary illusions" to maintain order in a society, or to provide the necessary paradigm to motivate action. The utility of U.S. Ambassador John Peurifoy's often cited and ridiculous statement, "I came away definitely convinced that if [Arbenz] . . . is not a Communist he will certainly do until one comes along" is more and more evident. The actuality had to be tailored to fit the ideology.[31]

In 1948 the Department of State concluded in a report to the NSC (no. 16) that "International Communism . . . must be regarded as the tool of the Kremlin, which the latter utilizes to advance Russian imperialistic designs and to supplant democracy throughout the world." Consequently it was regarded as a threat to not only the United States but to the "security of all other American Republics." Nevertheless, this document also concluded that the threat was "potential" rather than "immediately serious." Later policy continued to be made by Dulles and Eisenhower in the name of national security. Stephen Rabe convincingly argues that such policy was derived "more from inference and analogies" than from a detached analysis.[32] A similar process of simplification occurred under the Reagan administration when dealing with Nicaragua. While Gleijeses points out there was a considerable change in official U.S. reporting on Guatemala from the late 1940s to the early 1950s, from "arrogance . . . ethnocentricism, [and] immense ignorance," (many trying to assess whether Arévalo was a communist were "simply bizarre"), bearing no relationship to the reality in Guatemala, inhabiting a "deranged world of nightmares." In the 1950s the reports were still ethnocentric but reflected an understanding of the country.[33] Halle reported to Bowie that the revolution in Guatemala was an "expression of the impulse to achieve equality of status" for both individuals and groups within society and for "the nation-state within the international community." That basically Guatemala's historic conditions provided "fuel to fire the revolution." Similarly, Carter administration reports on the Nicaraguan revolution indicated clearly that it was a "Nicaraguan phenomenon . . . Sandinismo . . . is a Nicaraguan, home grown movement. Sandino predates Castro." The picture dramatically changes as you move up the level of policy makers in both the Eisenhower and Reagan administrations. Obviously a new administration engages in personnel changes, but in Central America several personnel with regional experience were removed or retired because their advice was being ignored. In the 1980s they were replaced by diplomats who had largely gained their experience from service in Vietnam. The policy debate significantly changed from a question of whether poverty or communism caused the instability to a question of the degree of regional communist penetration. The process of simplification served the policy analysis. (Not in a direct parallel. It is still curious to note that Ambassador John Peurifoy too lacked regional experience, but had demonstrated his anticommunist credentials while stationed in Greece in the late 1940s, during the implementation of the Truman Doctrine).[34] In both examples, in terms of policy presentation and the image the various administrations wanted to present of either Guatemala or Nicaragua ranged, as Martha Cottam argues for the former, from "simplified to extremely simplified." Similar contentions hold true for administration presentations of Nicaragua. Reagan's Office of Public Diplomacy largely pursued the task of reshaping public perception of the Nicaraguan situation.[35]

The key part of the official argument on both Guatemala and Nicaragua was that there had been an injection of communism into the western hemisphere. It was specifically alleged that this not only presented a threat to U.S. national security, with the Reagan administration taking it to extremes when in May 1985 the United States declared a state of national emergency because of the "unusual and extraordinary threat to the national security and foreign policy of the United States."[36] In both cases it is silly to argue that these countries posed a physical threat to the United States or to its neighbors, but that they perhaps posed a challenge to U.S. foreign policy is more plausible; they offered an alternative, by way of example, not by force or the "export" of subversion, to other countries in a similar predicament. U.S. hostility occurred in both cases when Washington was seeking greater cohesion in the Western or free world. If this drive toward greater cohesion was threatened in any way the most effective way for the executive to gain a political consensus was to present it as a Soviet threat.

Soviet support for the revolutions in Central America has always been cautious and was extremely limited in the case of Guatemala. The first load of Eastern Bloc arms arrived from Czechoslovakia shortly before the U.S.-backed overthrow of the Arbenz government. Soviet support for the Sandinistas was cautious, providing defensive military equipment, and it was in reaction to stepped up U.S.-backed aggression. The Soviets indicated that they would support the Sandinistas in every political way, but were unwilling to give any military guarantees. Reports conducted by both the CIA and the Department of State reached similar conclusions, but they were largely ignored by the ideologically driven policy makers. On Nicaragua the CIA reported: "in reviewing Soviet policy toward Nicaragua since 1979, one is struck by the general caution with which Moscow has proceeded"; or Carl Jacobsen, writing for the State Department argued that "all too many US claims proved open to question." The historiography on Soviet influence in Central America generally supports these contentions.[37] Regardless, as policy was made at higher levels of government the approach was more ideological. Eagleton's argument that in "the sphere of ideology, concrete particular and universal truth glide ceaselessly in and out of each other, by-passing the mediation of rational analysis" can be used appropriately to describe Washington's mediation of the "apparent Soviet threat."[38]

A further fiction pursued in both cases were the allegations that Arbenz and the Sandinistas "exported their revolution." While Arévalo did initially involve his government in the internal affairs of other countries, and weapons were passed from Nicaragua to El Salvador till 1981, it was a fiction by 1951 that Arbenz continued these practices. In the case of Nicaragua, the International Court of Justice could find no evidence to implicate the Sandinistas in an attempt to export their revolution or militarily aid neighboring revolutionaries.[39]

The 1944 Guatemalan revolution was a middle class movement dominated by university students and army officers. Elections held later in the year, judged to be the freest elections held in the country, gave the presidency to Juan José Arévalo.

When he assumed power in March 1945 the prospects for democracy in Central America seemed reasonable and the dictators of the region were slightly distanced from Washington. Arévalo described himself as a "spiritual socialist" who disliked the extremes of communism, which he considered totalitarian, and the extremes of individualism, which he considered excessive; he believed in the concept of *vitalismo* (the vital minimum), where everyone would be provided with "minimum standards for housing, nutrition, education, health, work, justice, rest." He claimed to model his administration on Franklin Roosevelt's, believing that the reforms he had introduced in Guatemala were less radical than those introduced by Roosevelt in the New Deal. Arévalo's unsystematic approach in either ideology or tactics forced him to rely more and more on left-wing political factions to introduce his reforms. His 1947 Labor Code extended the rights of workers considerably, hurting the interests of the American-owned United Fruit Company (UFCO). From this time, Gleijeses points out, the State Department repeatedly talked about Guatemala's "persecution" of U.S. companies, and further, Arévalo had erred in his "irresponsible attitude toward communism."[40] Walter LaFeber argues that the U.S. "confusion of Arévalo's reforms with communism allowed the Communists to take undeserved credit for correcting centuries of injustice."[41]

There was a distinct change with the presidential transition of Arévalo to Jacobo Arbenz in 1950. For Washington, Arbenz was even worse. His sympathy with the communists was obvious, though he was not a communist yet. But perhaps more importantly in 1952 Arbenz passed an Agrarian Reform Law that tried to break Guatemala's dependency on foreign investors, grow more staple foods for the indigenous population, and to free rural laborers to work their own plots of land that had been confiscated from the UFCO. From Washington's perspective these changes were an "outrage."[42] It is true that Washington had found accommodation with Bolivia's more radical revolution in part because the U.S. interests were adequately compensated. Arbenz, however, was only willing to compensate UFCO to the value they had put on the land in their tax returns.[43] The Arévalo and Arbenz governments had not just challenged the private interests of the UFCO, they had also challenged U.S. hegemony by pursuing a more independent line in both domestic and foreign relations. With the Labor Code and the Agrarian Law Reform, Arévalo and Arbenz had made moves toward dramatically improving the living conditions of most Guatemalans, thus posing a threat to the veracity of modernization theories of development, which were increasingly linked to U.S. national interests and liberal, Western, and capitalist values.[44]

If the Guatemalan revolution challenged the modernization approaches to development, the Sandinista revolution challenged the emerging neoliberal theories. The revolution, which was finally successful in July 1979, was described by Christopher Hitchens as conducted by a broad "coalition of revulsion" against the brutal and corrupt U.S.-backed regime of Anastasio Somoza Debayle. Elizabeth Dore and John Weeks suggest the Sandinista movement primarily evoked the appeal to nationalism because it lacked the class base to articulate a coherent ideology. They argue if a unifying aspect of their ideology can be found it rests around the conviction that Nicaragua would free itself from U.S. domination and that the economy would be reorganized to benefit the poor.[45] The movement, and later the government, was divided, though most of its members made reference to or cited Marxism as a source for their political thought, it was not treated as a doctrinaire or fixed canon, but as an adaptable tool useful to analyze their situation. It needs to be pointed out that this Marxism was blended with the nationalism and anti-imperialism of Augusto Sandino; with aspects of social democracy; with lessons from Castro's experience; and with liberation theology. And while the Sandinistas also made considerable improvements in several social and economic areas—in health, education, agrarian reform, social programs, and human rights, their policies as implemented could not be described as Marxist. Whatever the most apt particular description of the Sandinista ideology, and maybe *Sandinismo* would serve just as well to identify the unique phenomenon, in the anticommunist culture of Washington, and especially through the simplistic prism of the Reagan vision, anything on the left was essentially communist.[46] Again, whatever the particularities of the revolution, by 1983 Reagan had staked the credibility of his administration on removing the Sandinistas from power.[47]

The revolutions in both Guatemala and Nicaragua had dramatically improved the standards of living for the majority of peoples in the respective countries, thus also improving the opportunities for national self-determination. In the former case the revolution was terminated with a CIA-backed operation, and in the latter, a ten-year low intensity conflict ultimately eroded the initial gains of the revolution and pressured the Sandinistas into implementing an austerity package vaguely similar to neoliberal "solutions." In both revolutions, democracy, not understood merely as the formal process of holding elections, but rather an attempt to increase and improve popular participation was extended. While these changes did diverge from the other isthmian countries, with which Washington by and large maintained good relations, the Guatemalan elections of 1944 and 1950, or the Sandinista elections of 1984 and 1990, were comparatively "free and fair."[48]

Washington, however, did not like these revolutions and the regimes associated with them. Because they threatened U.S. hegemony, providing an alternative model to mere compliance with the efforts toward internationalization and subordination to U.S. economic interests, Kolko argues, neither Dulles nor Eisenhower wanted a mere coup that would rid the hemisphere of this kind of challenge. Had they simply wanted to remove Arbenz they could have done so as early as 1953. Instead, "they sought to exploit the occasion to inhibit nationalists in the other nations of the hemisphere, many of whom had supporters and programs comparable to those in Guatemala."[49] Prior to the ousting of Arbenz, at the Tenth Inter-American Conference in March 1954 the United States tried to isolate Guatemala by pushing through a resolution that in effect declared that communism was incompatible with the "concept of American freedom." The resolution was passed 17 to 1, with Guatemala obviously in opposition. At the Conference Guatemalan Foreign Minister, Guillermo Toriello, indicated Guatemala remained a capitalist state that was willing to continue to receive foreign investment, so long as the corporations abided by their national laws. Toriello accused Dulles of internationalizing McCarthyism and of violating the OAS Charter, which guaranteed self-determination. In a post-Conference NSC meeting, Dulles conceded that it was not easy to get Latin American foreign ministers to support the resolution and indicated that he had encountered "much unhappiness and anxiety with respect to the commercial and financial policies which the Administration was following in Latin America." Others indicated that the resolution was nothing more than a pretext for U.S. intervention, but Dulles saw it as "an extension of the Monroe Doctrine to include the concept of outlawing foreign ideologies in the American Republics." Ultimately he argued that communism was "tantamount to external aggression" and therefore any U.S. resistance could not be "described as American intervention." In this way, Hunt points out, U.S. counterrevolution has been reconciled with the concept of maintaining the self-determination of these nations even if the governments were constitutionally elected; if they exhibited "neutralism in foreign affairs . . . economic nationalism . . . labour unrest, or land reform—American leaders turned the economic and political screws and, as a last resort, sent in the troops or unleashed the CIA." In this regard Chomsky cites the National Planning Association who in 1955 argued that the primary threat of communist powers was economic transformation "in ways which reduce their willingness and ability to complement the industrial economies of the West."[50]

Even if Washington had tried to squash the possibility of ideological diversification in 1954 resistance would of course continue. By 1975 the United States had signed the Protocol of Amendment to the Rio Treaty, which accepted the principle of "ideological pluralism," pledged nonintervention, and recognized the right of every state "to choose freely their political, economic, and social organisations." Still, such considerations were of no value to the Reagan administration, which was determined to reassert the Monroe Doctrine, had staked its prestige and credibility on removing the Sandinistas, or making the Sandinistas "say Uncle," and his administration was bent on confining Marxism-Leninism to the "ash heap of history," not in any real sense, but in the world view, cultural assumptions, or ideology of Washington policy makers and their political imperatives.[51]

The basic point is these revolutions were not so much a communist problem, but much more importantly these revolutions provided local solutions that were advanced and implemented to some extent. As Eduardo Galeano suggests they provided a "dangerous and contagious example of a people that lost patience. . . . [People who found] that they'd be better off making history from below and from inside than continuing to suffer history made by others from above and from outside." But these alternative examples, these challenges to U.S. hegemony could not be tolerated. The U.S. hostility to revolution stems from the eighteenth century. If revolutions diverge from the U.S. model, dramatically altering the internal structure of society, the United States usually responded in a hostile manner. Guatemala, Vietnam, Cuba, and Nicaragua were a part of this process. In these twentieth-century cases, Hunt contends, the problem was exacerbated because the typical social revolution did not adhere to the unilinear patterns of development

Washington expected: "development policy was an ethnocentric exercise in trying to fit a diverse world on the Procrustean bed of the American experience." The Guatemalan revolution would have been overthrown even without the UFCO and its close connections to the Eisenhower administration; this relationship obviously affected the quality and speed of the response. But Eisenhower's policy, according to Gleijeses, "was no abberation. . . . It fit within a deeply held tradition, shared by Democrats and Republicans alike and centered on the intransigent assertion of U.S. hegemony over Central America and the Caribbean."[52] A similar contention could be made for the Sandinista revolution. Where governments, whatever their ideology, try to alter the prevailing patterns of development they are usually confronted with U.S. resistance. According to Chomsky the internal record of U.S. diplomacy confirms that U.S. interests are threatened by nationalistic regimes responsive to popular pressure for "immediate improvement in the low living standards of the masses" and diversification of their economies.[53] To suggest it had anything to do with supporting democratic regimes in the isthmus or the hemisphere is ludicrous when considered in the historical context of Washington's friendly relationship with right-wing dictatorships.

CONCLUSIONS AND ELABORATIONS

In the initial section on ideology and U.S. foreign policy I tried to set out general observations on how the United States has constantly approached the world in a dualistic fashion; constantly formulating their identity in opposition to something else: the new world against the old world; the republican democracy against monarchical authority; the Democratic West and the Communist East; and so forth. While U.S. diplomatic language has always contained a messianic tone, this dualism was not confined to the cold war period, though crucially it was globalized in this time. The result was a continued process where the heterogenous and complex world was reduced to an unsophisticated conceptual approach, reflected in the ideology of the Cold War, but premised on the power imperatives of the U.S. way of life. In the second section I tried to demonstrate how the Guatemalan and Nicaraguan revolution were subjected to this approach, which knit together the national interests of the United States with its ideology. The contention is that in the process the United States trammeled the ideals it claimed to stand for centered around conceptions of simultaneously promoting democracy and self-determination and free trade. Part of this is explained through the U.S. attempts to create a national identity, and part of the explanation rests with the requirements of power—economic, strategic, and ideological. For Edward Said the "development and maintenance of every culture requires the existence of another different and competing alter ego." The construction of an identity, he argues in *Orientalism,* is still a construction, open to constant interpretation and reinterpretation according to the age or historical period, but crucially it is bound up with power and powerlessness in any particular relationship.[54] It is no irony that after the deposition of Arbenz, Arévalo urged the rest of Latin America to no longer regard the United States as the leader of the Occidental world.[55]

In the two incisions into the inter-American relationship made above there are a number of coincidences, and they may be no more than coincidences. That is, I am not suggesting that they shaped the quality or timing of the U.S. response, but in various respects they are related to the challenges to the U.S. identity, to its hegemony, to its power, and to the cultural understanding of its ideology. They are: the conscious emergence of new development theories (modernization and neoliberalism); heightened tension in the cold war; and following (though not directly connected to) offers of "Peaceful Coexistence" from Khrushchev and Malenkov, or "Perestroika and New Thinking" from Gorbachev, the U.S. "intellectuals" have engaged with debates on the end of ideology and the end of history. These were attempts to close out the ideological debate, assert U.S. power to reinforce its hegemony, and delegitimize any challenge to the prevailing world system. Geertz commenting on Edward Shils suggests that this kind of thinking is dualistic, opposing the pure "we" to the evil "they," proclaiming that he who is not with me is against me. It is alienative in that it distrusts, attacks, and works to undermine established political institutions. It is doctrinaire in that it claims complete and exclusive possession of political truth and abhors compromise. It is totalistic in that it aims to order the whole of social and cultural life in the image of its ideals, futuristic in that it works toward a utopian culmination of history in which such an ordering will be realized.[56]

Similarly, Isaiah Berlin argues that the pursuit of the universal ideal, systems that subject peoples "to a single ideology, no matter how reasonable and imaginative, robs men of freedom and vitality." It is in a sense the attempt to impose an artificial order on "a reluctant humanity, of trying to fit human beings, like bricks, into a preconceived structure, force them into Procrustean beds, and vivisect living men in the pursuit of some fanatically held schema." Such systems, Berlin argues, usually ends in suffering, disillusionment, and failure.[57]

There is little doubt about the suffering both countries have endured as a result of U.S. intervention, or little doubt about the suffering that preceded the revolutions, or the suffering that returned with the fall of these governments. The revolutions were unprogramatic, not faultless or perfect in any sense, but had made attempts to introduce alternatives that were more democratic, nationalist in a world system that undermines local consent—pluralist, and essentially anti-imperialist.[58] Arévalo, Arbenz, and the Sandinistas, among other revolutions, had challenged U.S. hegemony by introducing prospects for pluralism; undermined U.S. notions of self-determination by pursuing their own through social revolution; and threatened the U.S. sphere of influence through the pursuit of democracy. As Secretary of State George Shultz wrote on Nicaragua, though the comments are also somewhat relevant to the Guatemalan revolution: "We have to safeguard . . . Central American countries against the Nicaraguan virus."[59]

NOTES

1. For more detail on this argument see my article "US Expansionism: From the Monroe Doctrine to the Open Door," in Philip Davies (ed.), *Representing and Imagining America* (Keele: Keele University Press, 1996), pp. 181–90.

2. Michael H. Hunt, "Ideology," in Michael J. Hogan and Thomas G. Paterson (eds.), *Explaining the History of American Foreign Relations* (Cambridge: Cambridge University Press, 1991), p. 196.

3. Edward W. Said, *Culture and Imperialism* (London: Chatto and Windus, 1993), p. 7.

4. Lars Schoultz, *National Security and United States Policy toward Latin America* (Princeton: Princeton University Press, 1987), p. 63; David Ryan, *US-Sandinista Diplomatic Relations: Voice of Intolerance* (London: Macmillan, 1995), pp. 6, 8–10.

5. Michael H. Hunt, *Ideology and U.S. Foreign Policy* (New Haven: Yale University Press, 1987), p. 12.

6. Terry Eagleton, *Ideology: An Introduction* (London: Verso, 1991), pp. 18–19.

7. Peter Novik, *That Noble Dream: The "Objectivity Question" and the American Historical Profession* (Cambridge: Cambridge University Press, 1988), pp. 61–62; Clifford Geertz, *The Interpretation of Cultures* (London: Fontana, 1993 [1973]), pp. 204–5.

8. Hunt, *Ideology,* p. 12.

9. Hunt, "Ideology," pp. 193–94.

10. Richard H. Immerman, "Psychology," in Hogan and Paterson (eds.), *Explaining,* p. 160.

11. Hunt, *Ideology,* p. 178.

12. Novik, *Noble Dream,* pp. 61–63; Hunt, "Ideology," p. 201; David Ryan, "Asserting U.S. Power," in Philip Davies, *An American Quarter Century* (Manchester: Manchester University Press, 1995), pp. 103–26.

13. George Kennan/Policy Planning Staff, PPS/23, "Review of Current Trends U.S. Foreign Policy," 24 February 1948, *Foreign Relations of the United States, 1948*, vol. 1 (Washington, D.C.: U.S. Government Printing Office, 1976), pp. 524–25; Walter LaFeber, *Inevitable Revolutions: The United States in Central America* (New York: W. W. Norton, 1993), p. 109.

14. Hunt, "Ideology," p. 201.

15. David Ryan, "The Monroe Doctrine: The Evolution of U.S. Foreign Relations with Latin America in the Nineteenth Century." Conference on Latin America in the Nineteenth Century, De Montfort University, Leicester, England, 27 May 1995; Walter LaFeber, *The American Search for Opportunity, 1865–1913* (Cambridge: Cambridge University Press, 1993), p. 237.

16. Theodore Roosevelt, "Annual Message," 6 December 1904, reprinted in Henry Steele Commager (ed.), *Documents of American History,* vol. 2 (New York: Appleton-Century-Crofts, 1963), pp. 33–34.

17. Hunt, *Ideology,* p. 129.

18. Ibid., pp. 125, 189; Louis Hartz, *The Liberal Tradition in America: An Interpretation of American Political Thought Since the Revolution* (New York: Harcourt, Brace and Company, 1955), p. 289.

19. Serge Ricard, "The Exceptionalist Syndrome in U.S. Continental and Overseas Expansionism," in David K. Adams and Cornelis A. van Minnen (eds.), *Reflections on American Exceptionalism* (Keele: Keele University Press, 1994), p. 76.

20. Arthur Schlesinger cited in Novik, *Noble Dream,* p. 300.

21. Novik, *Noble Dream,* pp. 298–300, 333; Byron E. Shafer, review of *American Exceptionalism,* by Seymour Martin Lipset, in the *Times Literary Supplement,* no. 4852 (29 March 1996), p. 7; for the wider arguments see Daniel Bell, *The End of Ideology: On the Exhaustion of Political Ideas in the Fifties* (New York: The Free Press, 1962); Francis Fukuyama, *The End of History and the Last Man* (Harmondsworth: Penguin, 1992).

22. Novik, *Noble Dream,* pp. 299, 301; Eagleton, *Ideology,* p. 5.

23. Shafer, *TLS,* 29 March 1996, p. 7; Ricard, "Exceptionalist Syndrome," p. 73.

24. Novik, *Noble Dream,* p. 552; Geertz, *Interpretation of Cultures,* p. 5; Ricard, "Exceptionalist Syndrome," p. 74; Hunt, *Ideology,* pp. 12, 189, 191.

25. I have not attempted to present a chronological narrative of U.S. reaction to the Guatemalan or Nicaraguan revolutions. For specific histories see: Piero Gleijeses, *Shattered Hope: The Guatemalan Revolution and the United States, 1944–1954* (Princeton: Princeton University Press, 1991); Richard Immerman, *The CIA in Guatemala: The Foreign Policy of Intervention* (Austin: University of Texas, 1982); Stephen Schlesinger and Stephen Kinzer, *Bitter Fruit: The Untold Story of the American Coup in Guatemala* (New York: Doubleday, 1982); Blanche Wiesen Cook, *The Declassified Eisenhower: A Divided Legacy* (New York: Doubleday, 1981); Walter LaFeber, *Inevitable Revolutions: The United States in Central America* (New York: W. W. Norton, 1993); James Dunkerley, *Power in the Isthmus: A Political History of Modern Central America* (London: Verso, 1988); Thomas W. Walker (ed.), *Revolution and Counterrevolution in Nicaragua* (Boulder, CO: Westview Press, 1991); Noam Chomsky, *The Culture of Terrorism* (London: Pluto Press, 1987); Ryan, *US-Sandinista Diplomacy.*

26. Hunt, *Ideology,* pp. 152–53; James William Park, *Latin American Underdevelopment: A History of Perspectives in the United States, 1870–1965* (Baton Rouge, LA: Pluto Press, 1995), pp. 167, 171; NSC 144/1, "United States Objectives and Courses of Action With Respect to Latin America," 18 March 1953, in *Foreign Relations of the United States 1952–1954: The American Republics,* vol 4 (Washington, D.C.: U.S. Government Printing Office, 1983), pp. 6–7.

27. Thomas J. McCormick, "World Systems," in Hogan and Patterson (eds.), *Explaining,* p. 94.

28. Melvyn P. Leffler, *A Preponderance of Power: National Security, the Truman Administration, and the Cold War* (Stanford: Stanford University Press, 1992), pp. 18–19; Thomas J. McCormick, *America's Half Century: United States Foreign Policy in the Cold War* (Baltimore: Johns Hopkins University Press, 1989), pp. 118–19.

29. Ryan, *US-Sandinista Diplomacy,* p. 30.

30. Gleijeses, *Shattered Hope,* pp. 369–71; Louis J. Halle to Robert Bowie, 23 June 1954, Records of the Policy Planning Staff 1954, Record Group 59, Lot 65D101, Box 79.

31. Noam Chomsky, *Necessary Illusions: Thought Control in Democratic Societies* (Boston: South End Press, 1989), passim; Ambassador John Peurifoy telegram to the Department of State, 17 December 1953, *FRUS 1952–1954,* vol 4, p. 1093.

32. Department of State, report to the National Security Council, "U.S. Policy Regarding Anti-Communist Measures Which Could be Planned and Carried Out within the Inter-American System," NSC 16, 28 June 1948, document 00045, fiche 8, Presidential Directives on National Security, National Security Archive, Washington, D.C.; Stephen G. Rabe, "Dulles, Latin America, and Cold War Anticommunism," in Richard H. Immerman (ed.), *John Foster Dulles and the Diplomacy of the Cold War* (Princeton: Princeton University Press, 1990), p. 173.

33. Gleijeses, *Shattered Hope,* pp. 362–63.

34. Louis J. Halle to Robert Bowie, 28 May 1954, Policy Planning Staff, Record Group 59, lot 65D101, box 79; U.S. Congress, House, Committee on Foreign Affairs, Subcommittee on Inter-American Affairs, *Central America at the Crossroads,* 96th Cong., 1st sess., 11–12 September 1979, pp. 24–25, 29; Ryan, *US-Sandinista Diplomacy,* pp. 4–9; LaFeber, *Inevitable Revolutions,* p. 122.

35. Martha L. Cottam, "Decision Making in 'Successful' Interventions: The Cases of Guatemala and Chile," in Jonathan R. Adelman (ed.), *Superpowers and Revolution* (New York: Praeger, 1986), p. 89; Robert Parry and Peter Kornbluh, "Iran-Contra's Untold Story," *Foreign Policy,* no. 72 (Fall 1988), p. 3, passim; and see also Eldon Kenworthy, "Selling the Policy," in Thomas W. Walker (ed.), *Reagan versus the Sandinistas: The Undeclared War on Nicaragua* (Boulder, CO: Westview Press, 1987), pp. 159–81.

36. Executive Order 12513 issued by President Reagan, "Economic Sanctions Against Nicaragua," 1 May 1985, document 554, *American Foreign Policy Current Documents 1985* (Washington, D.C.: U.S. Department of State, 1986), p. 999.

37. Carl G. Jacobsen, *Soviet Attitudes Towards, Aid to, and Contacts with Central American Revolutionaries* (Washington, D.C.: U.S. Department of State, 1984), pp. 17, 31; Vladimir I. Stanchenko, "Soviet Views of the Caribbean and Central America 1959–1991," (Cork: Irish Institute of International Relations, 1991); Stephen Kinzer, "Soviet Help to Sandinistas: No Blank Check," *New York Times,* 28 March 1984; Center for Defense Information, "Soviet Geopolitical Momentum: Myth or Menace?" *The Defense Monitor* 15, no. 5 (Washington, D.C.: Center for Defense Information, 1986), p. 31; Ryan, *US-Sandinista Diplomacy,* pp. 45, 61; more generally see: Nicola Miller, *Soviet Relations with Latin America 1959–1987* (Cambridge: Cambridge University Press, 1989), pp. 188–216; Cole Blasier, "The Soviet Union," in Morris J. Blachman and others (eds.), *Confronting Revolution: Security through Diplomacy in Central America* (New York: Pantheon Books, 1986), pp. 256–70; Wayne Smith (ed.), *The Russians Aren't Coming: New Soviet Policy in Latin America* (Boulder, CO: Lynne Rienner, 1992), passim.

38. Eagleton, *Ideology,* p. 20.

39. Gleijeses, *Shattered Hope,* p. 365; Judgement of the International Court of Justice, *Nicaragua v. The United States of America* (The Hague: International Court of Justice, 27 June 1986), p. 63, paragraph 134, and p. 75, paragraph 160.

40. Gleijeses, *Shattered Hope,* pp. 85, 223; LaFeber, *Inevitable Revolutions,* pp. 114–17; Sheldon B. Liss, *Radical Thought in Central America* (Boulder, CO: Westview Press, 1991), pp. 37–38.

41. LaFeber, *Inevitable Revolutions,* p. 115.

42. Gleijeses, *Shattered Hope,* pp. 361–62; LaFeber, *Inevitable Revolutions,* p. 118.

43. Gabriel Kolko, *Confronting the Third World: United States Foreign Policy 1945–1980* (New York: Pantheon, 1988), pp. 100–102; Cole Blasier, *The Hovering Giant: U.S. Responses to Revolutionary Change in Latin America* (Pittsburgh: University of Pittsburgh, 1983), pp. 211–38.

44. Blasier, *Hovering Giant,* p. 211; Peter F. Klaren, "Lost Promise: Explaining Latin American Underdevelopment," in Peter F. Klaren and Thomas J. Bossert (eds.), *Promise of Development: Theories of Change in Latin America* (Boulder, CO: Westview Press, 1986), pp. 8–9; John Brohman, "Universalism, Eurocentrism, and Ideological Bias in Development Studies: from Modernisation to Neoliberalism," *Third World Quarterly* 16, no. 1 (March 1995), p. 133.

45. Christopher Hitchens, "A Dynasty Divided," *The Independent Magazine* (London), no. 76 (17 February 1990), p. 25; Elizabeth Dore and John Weeks, *The Red and the Black:*

The Sandinistas and the Nicaraguan Revolution (London: Institute of Latin American Studies, 1992), pp. 29, 22.

46. Liss, *Radical Thought,* p. 169; Dennis Gilbert, *Sandinistas: The Party and the Revolution* (Cambridge, MA: Blackwell, 1988), p. 23; Dore and Weeks, *Red and Black,* p. 21; For analyses on the gains and losses of the revolutionary period see: Walker (ed.), *Revolution and Counterrevolution*; and Dianna Melrose, *Nicaragua: The Threat of a Good Example* (Oxford: Oxfam, 1985); Noam Chomsky, *The Culture of Terrorism* (London: Pluto Press, 1987); Ryan, *US-Sandinista Diplomacy.*

47. Ryan, *US-Sandinista Diplomacy,* pp. 41–43.

48. Ryan, *US-Sandinista Diplomacy,* pp. 88–106, 170–88, passim; John A. Booth and Mitchell A. Seligson (eds.), *Elections and Democracy in Central America* (Chapel Hill: University of North Carolina Press, 1989); William I. Robinson, *A Faustian Bargain: U.S. Intervention in the Nicaraguan Elections and American Foreign Policy in the Post-Cold War Era* (Boulder, CO: Westview Press, 1992); David Held (ed.), *Prospects for Democracy: North, South, East, West* (Cambridge: Polity Press, 1992).

49. Kolko, *Confronting,* p. 103.

50. Walter LaFeber, *America, Russia, and the Cold War 1945–1990* (New York: McGraw-Hill, 1991), p. 159; Liss, *Radical Thought,* p. 51; Memorandum of Discussion . . . of the National Security Council, 18 March 1954, *FRUS 1952–1954,* vol. 4, pp. 304–5; Kolko, *Confronting,* p. 104; Hunt, *Ideology,* p. 167; Noam Chomsky, *On Power and Ideology: The Managua Lectures* (Boston: South End Press, 1987), p. 10.

51. Walter LaFeber, "The Evolution of the Monroe Doctrine from Monroe to Reagan," in Lloyd C. Gardner (ed.), *Redefining the Past: Essays in Diplomatic History in Honor of William Appleman Williams* (Corvallis: Oregon State University Press, 1986), pp. 138–39; Ryan, *US-Sandinista Diplomacy,* p. 2; Holly Sklar, *Washington's War on Nicaragua* (Boston: South End Press, 1988), p. 260.

52. Eduardo Galeano, *We Say No: Chronicles 1963–1991* (New York: W. W. Norton, 1992), p. 195; Hunt, *Ideology,* 174–75; Gleijeses, *Shattered Hope,* p. 366.

53. Noam Chomsky, "The Third World in the New World Order," paper delivered at CIIR conference, 18–19 January 1991, Regents College London, p. 1.

54. Edward Said, *Orientalism: Western Conceptions of the Orient* (Harmondsworth: Penguin, 1995), p. 332.

55. Arévalo, cited by Liss, *Radical Thought,* p. 42.

56. Geertz, *Interpretation of Cultures,* pp. 197–98.

57. Isaiah Berlin, *The Crooked Timber of Humanity: Chapters in the History of Ideas,* Henry Hardy (ed.) (London: Fontana Press, 1991), pp. 45–48.

58. Guillermo Toriello, cited by Liss, *Radical Thought,* p. 53.

59. George P. Shultz, memorandum for the President, "Managing Our Central American Strategy," 25 May 1983, document 00106, fiche 18, National Security Archive, 1990; Ryan, *US-Sandinista Diplomacy,* p. 48.

chapter 8

Ideology and Opportunism in the Regime of Alfredo Stroessner, 1954–1989

Peter Lambert

INTRODUCTION

When General Alfredo Stroessner came to power via a military coup in May 1954, he had the support of large sections of the ruling Colorado party, the military, and the United States. He also inherited certain structures of political control, such as Colorado hegemony, a nascent Colorado-military alliance, and a corporativist state, constructed under the authoritarian government of General Morínigo (1940–1947). However, he was also the eighth president in seven years, inheriting a political system characterized by factionalism and instability.[1] Indeed there was little to suggest that he would create not only a new regime, but also dominate Paraguayan politics for longer than any other president in the country's history.

Stroessner successfully transformed an unstable political system into a strong personalist dictatorship (the *stronato*) based on a triangular structure of power between the armed forces, the Colorado party, and the government, under his own absolute and undisputed control.[2] Through adroit political skill and the use of certain mechanisms of control that went beyond mere repression, Stroessner was able to impose political order and stability through a regime characterized by "the fascination for state power, the permanent concern to strengthen the decision-making nucleus and an emphasis on peace and internal stability that allowed no room for dissent."[3]

Academic work on ideology in Paraguay is scarce, and the concept of ideology has often been loosely applied. Guido Rodríguez Alcalá argues that an authoritarian ideology, running intermittently but noticeably through Paraguayan post-independence history, resurfaced under Stroessner,[4] yet he does not analyze satisfactorily what that ideology entails. Carlos Miranda goes further by arguing that *stronismo* was a new political ideology in itself, that it was a coherent structure of images, ideas, and values that sought to apply theory to practice with the aim of remodeling society.[5] Yet he neglects to define ideology, and uses it as an all-embracing term to describe nonideological elements of the Stroessner regime.

This chapter argues that the exploitation and development of existing ideologies and mentalities were important factors in explaining the longevity of the regime. Not only did they enable Stroessner to harness a high degree of elite, mass, and international support, but they also served as an important mechanism of civil control. However, the contradictions between Stroessner's rhetoric, indicating firm adhesion to prevailing ideologies and mentalities, and his political actions suggest that Stroessner was more guided by opportunism than by ideology. Ideology was merely a tool, albeit a powerful one, to strengthen Stroessner's hold on power.

THE REBIRTH OF NATIONALISM

The emergence of Colorado nationalism can be traced back to the removal of the Colorado party from power by the Liberal party in 1904. Although a strong sense of national identity remained from the nationalist period (1814–1870), neither the Colorado party in power nor the Liberal party had tapped it as a source of popular support. Instead, nationalism had been devalued, state assets sold off, and the leaders of the nationalist period officially vilified.[6] However, in opposition, the Colorado party began to turn toward nationalism and against the laissez-faire capitalism that they had previously espoused. With the Liberal party firmly in government, nationalism, supported by the emergence of a revisionist interpretation of history, was resurrected as a pillar of Colorado ideology.

The intellectual catalyst of Colorado nationalism was Juan O'Leary, who sought in his writings to rediscover the essence of *paraguayidad*. Central to this was the creation of a cult of national heroism and the conversion of the disgraced leaders of the nationalist period into national heroes.[7] The nationalist period was turned from one characterized by brutal personalist dictatorship ending in mass genocide, into a glorious and heroic past of national strength, unity, and sovereignty, overseen by heroic leaders.[8]

Rodríguez de Francia (1814–1840), seen by many as a ruthless dictator, became the "creator of Paraguay" the father of the nation, who defied foreign advances to create an independent and powerful sovereign state. In particular, the image of Francisco Solano López (1862–1870), known as *El Mariscal* (the Marshall) was resurrected from one of an egoistical megalomaniac who led Paraguay into a pointless and disastrous military defeat against its neighbors, to become one of a president who gave his life to the highest cause, the defense of the "patria"; "a man and a people. A judge and a cause. In one word he is the personification of Paraguay at the most glorious moment of its history . . . López was and is Paraguay."[9]

The Colorado party thus portrayed itself as the party of Paraguayan nationalism, "the guardians of the spirit of the Marshall."[10] This was in contrast to the ruling Liberal party, who it portrayed as bearing the interests of foreign capitalism. This ideological shift was exemplified not only by party rhetoric but also by the launch of the Colorado party newspaper, *Patria*, in 1917, and the increasing use of the indigenous language, Guaraní, at the time shunned by urban elites.

Natalicio González, the most famous propagandist of the Colorado party, expanded on O'Leary's definition of *paraguayidad*. González emphasized the images of land, race, and history, exalting the *autóctono*, which was Paraguayan and therefore to be valued, and attacking the prevalence of the *exótico* (in this case Liberal ideology), which was imported, anti-Paraguayan, and therefore intrinsically opposed to the national interest. He also argued in favor of a strong, unified, nationalist, and interventionist state that would protect the Paraguayan peasant (the embodiment of *paraguayidad*), and recreate the alleged strength, prosperity, and independence of the nationalist period.[11]

The nationalist cause adopted by the Colorado party was immeasurably helped by the outbreak of the Chaco War (1932–1935) with Bolivia, for which the ruling Liberal party was inadequately prepared. Paraguayan victory served to reinforce the concept of innate Paraguayan superiority, while emergent nationalism and the poor preparation and conduct of the war by the Liberal party were successfully exploited by González among the peasant majority.[12] The resurgence of nationalism at a government level began in the postwar period under the *Febreristas* and continued under the corporativist dictatorship of General Higinio Morínigo (1940–1947).[13] Growing nationalism was exploited by the radical nationalist wing of the Colorado party, the *guión rojo* (red banner), associated with Natalicio González.

The civil war of 1947 led to the victory of the Colorado party over the rebel forces, comprising of Liberal, Communist, and *Febrerista* parties. Despite some significant rebel advantages,[14] the Colorado party successfully exploited the nationalist cause among the Paraguayan peasantry, claiming for itself the mantle of nationalism and portraying the rebels as foreign-inspired and anti-Paraguayan. The brutal repression of the rebels and the destruction of the rebel military structure allowed the Colorado party to reform the military, realign it with the party, and consolidate its political hegemony.

NATIONALISM UNDER STROESSNER

Stroessner fitted the nationalist mold perfectly. As an artillery officer, he was a hero not only of the Chaco War but also of the civil war, in which he was acclaimed for his defense of the Colorado cause. From the outset, he sought to identify himself with Colorado nationalism to strengthen his own position. Under his rule, history was modified and manipulated to create the myth of a glorious and heroic past, enhancing the standing of the party, the military, and most importantly, Stroessner himself.

Stroessner succeeded in taking up the banner of nationalism as his own, adapting it to his own ends and using it as a powerful pillar of the regime. However, although the works of González and O'Leary were regularly reedited and quoted, what emerged was a distortion of Colorado nationalism and the promotion of an ambiguous and undefined nationalist ideology that was molded and redefined by Stroessner to strengthen his own base of support.

There is little to suggest that Stroessner's exploitation of nationalism was anything more than a highly effective mechanism of control both within the Colorado party and of civil society. As in the civil war, nationalism was used to cement popular support for the regime, not just against external threats but, more importantly, against internal opposition. If the regime were nationalist, *autóctono*, in the words of González, the assumption was then that all opposition to the regime could only be, by default, *exótico*; in other words, antinationalist, anti-Paraguayan, and foreign-inspired. In brief, all opposition to the regime was thus portrayed as being supported by traitors to the *patria*. Such powerful imagery was not only used in periods of armed conflict (1959–1963) but as a constant official accompaniment to the repression of opposition throughout the *regime*.

Despite its nationalist rhetoric, the *stronato* undermined Paraguayan sovereignty and the very nationalist values it claimed to represent. It used the images of nationalism, but never attempted to implement the values expressed by nationalist ideologues, such as independence, economic power, the empowerment of the peasant class, and government honesty. Instead, institutionalized corruption permeated society, contraband undermined local Paraguayan industry, and the indigenous peoples, the essence of the exalted "raza guaraní," remained the most marginalized sector of the population.[15] Far from achieving greater independence, Paraguay became increasingly dependent on foreign support, especially from Brazil and the United States. By 1970 it is estimated that foreign capital controlled 80 percent of major private enterprises, 90 percent of the private banking system, and 80 percent of merchandise exports.[16]

Rather than a government in favor of the peasantry, the *stronato* oversaw a period characterized by continued concentration of land. By 1991, 1 percent of landholders owned 77 percent of the land.[17] Efforts by peasants to improve their condition were met with brutal state repression, the most notorious case being that of the *Ligas Agrarias* in the mid 1970s.[18] The 1970s also witnessed a dramatic increase in Brazilian immigration and the operations of foreign agribusiness in the agriculturally fertile Eastern Border Region, as a result of the construction of the Itaipú dam.[19] Indeed, while Paraguayan peasants faced eviction and a constant struggle for land, Stroessner increasingly came to represent the interests of foreign agro-export transnationals and large landholders grouped in the *Asociación Rural del Paraguay* (ARP).[20]

EL ÚNICO LÍDER

Unlike the case of neighboring military regimes, power was exerted not directly by the military, but personalized in Stroessner himself. Domination was guaranteed through a system of reward and punishment that guaranteed loyalty to the regime.[21] With loyalty to Stroessner taking precedence over loyalty toward any particular ideology, Stroessner became the architect of his own political system, molding an authoritarian tradition to suit his own ends.

Stroessner continued the historical tendency in Paraguayan political culture of personalization and centralization of power characteristic of the nationalist period. Despite his own lack of charisma, Stroessner encouraged a cult of personality to develop around himself, succeeding in becoming an integral part of the national identity, a symbol of Paraguay.[22] Portraits of a youthful Stroessner adorned all public offices, schools, libraries, and many private shops and bars. The national airport bore his name as did the major city on the Brazilian border (today Ciudad del Este). Barrios, streets, and plazas, even a polka were named after him, while stamps and electoral posters made his features a daily presence. Stroessner became a father figure, whose ever-present image pervaded daily life.

The cult of personality was fortified by the regular accolades he received in newspapers, on the radio, in political rallies, and at all public occasions, as ministers, party members, businessmen, and the public sought to outdo each other in their praise. Stroessner encouraged this constant stream of praise that eulogized him as *el Gran Líder* (the Great Leader), *el benefactor*, *el Único Líder* (the Sole Leader) and *el abanderado de la Paz y el Progreso* (the Flag Bearer of Peace and Progress).[23]

Stroessner sought not to create a cult of personality based solely around himself, but also on his role as heir to the great leaders of the nationalist period. He encouraged the images of himself as *el continuador* (the continuer), *el segundo reconstructor del país* (the second rebuilder of the country—following in the footsteps of the founder of the Colorado party, Bernardino Caballero) and *el heredero inmarcecible de los Próceres de la Patria* (the Unyielding Heir of the Founding Fathers).[24] By encouraging such parallels between himself and the exalted (authoritarian) leaders of the nationalist period,[25] by portraying these leaders (and thus by implication himself) as the embodiment of *paraguayidad,* Stroessner ensured himself a central role in national cultural identity.[26] To criticize the past leaders (or indeed Stroessner), or to offer a different version of history became anti-Paraguayan, a betrayal of nationalist values and of the *patria*.

Stroessner also placed great emphasis on his ceremonial role throughout the country, opening schools, roads, and hospitals, meeting local people, giving the impression at least of response to local demands. His omnipresence at state and public events and his manipulation of traditional Paraguayan symbolism and ceremony, gave legitimacy to his role,[27] reinforcing the impression that Stroessner was a symbol of national unity, the embodiment of the nation itself.

LA UNIDAD GRANÍTICA

The role of the Colorado party was not merely to give a civilian facade to the regime but represented the regime's principal instrument to control and (de)mobilize civil society.[28] Through its patronage networks, based on an extensive network of local *seccionales* (party branches), Stroessner ensured that the party pervaded all sectors of society. Such local organization was not designed to encourage local democracy but instead strengthen social control on the local level.[29] This in turn, created a politically passive civil population, dominated more by fear than by repression.[30]

Party membership was compulsory for all civil servants from civil administrators to teachers and members of the armed forces.[31] Patronage made party membership an essential prerequisite of social or economic advancement, as reflected in the fact that by 1986, according to government figures, it had reached 1,300,000 members out of an electoral population of 1,442,607.[32] Unlike other Southern Cone dictatorships, it was the party and the police, rather than the armed forces, that played the major role in internal national security.[33]

Despite attempts to portray Stroessner's struggle for control of the party in the 1950s and 1960s as guided by ideological conflict between Colorado factions,[34] his purging of various sectors was based on pragmatism and the desire to retain power.[35] It is striking that Stroessner's control of the party was not based on ideology. Indeed, there was an absence of any overriding political ideology to guide the party, besides a vague concept of nationalism. Instead, its direction was defined by Stroessner.

Stroessner inherited a Colorado party beset by factionalism and instability. By the end of the 1960s, Stroessner had successfully created an organized, verticalist, and disciplined political machine, a party dominated by himself that "unifies all the political forces of the party, so that there is only one force, without internal dissidence and without any other ideal than the patriotic zeal to create a stable, firm, and authoritative government with a wide base of political support."[36]

Through coercion, purges, and promotions, Stroessner had created, or according to nationalist rhetoric, "recreated," *la unidad granítica* (the granitic unity) of the party. The Colorado party, at least to all appearances, had become a *stronista* Colorado party.[37] Loyalty to the party became synonymous with loyalty to the patria and to the president. To be Paraguayan was to be Colorado and to be Colorado was to support Stroessner.

DEMOCRACIA SIN COMUNISMO

Unlike neighboring authoritarian regimes, the *stronato* did not inherit a democratic system, did not have to suppress the electoral arena, or dismantle democratic institutions in order to consolidate his power. On the contrary he inherited an authoritarian constitution, a political system based on the exclusive power of the Colorado party, and a nascent Colorado-military alliance. However, Stroessner carefully constructed and strictly adhered to the formalities of a legal and democratic facade to the regime, based on regular multiparty elections and strict adherence to the Constitution, enabling him to claim to rule a democracy.

The cornerstone of the democratic facade was the electoral arena, with elections held regularly, every five years, as stipulated by the Constitution. After an initial period of single party democracy, Stroessner allowed limited political activity to selected opposition parties from 1962.[38] The opposition role was essentially decorative,[39] serving to mask the authoritarian nature of the regime. Political power was monopolized by the Colorado party, and the opposition was exiled or confined to the sidelines of political legality. Although, under Paraguayan electoral law, the opposition automatically gained 33 percent of the seats in Congress, Stroessner won elections with immense majorities. In the eight elections held between 1958 and 1988, Stroessner gained over 90 percent of the vote on five occasions.[40] This limited democracy also succeeded in fueling factionalism within opposition parties (between abstentionists and participants) and between opposition parties (recognized and nonrecognized).[41]

Multiparty elections did not contribute to the democratization of the country. As the existence of a permanent state of emergency reflects, the intention was not to encourage political activism or participation. Under Stroessner, civil society could not organize, participate, or even deliberate on politics. Politics thus became a ritual with the aim of creating a politically apathetic and demobilized civilian population.[42]

Limited multiparty democracy may have been an obvious facade for the excluded and persecuted opposition to Stroessner, but democracy played a central ideological role in public discourse. Stroessner made constant reference to his role as a democrat and to the regime's adherence to its own unique brand of *democracia sin comunismo* (democracy without communism), a reference that was constantly echoed by his supporters:

This is *Stronista* Paraguayan democracy. With liberty, without hatred . . . but also with the strength to defend liberty and our national values that international marxism seeks to crush . . . when we speak of *Stronista* Paraguayan democracy, we are expressing the loyalty of our people towards an era of national greatness, whose interpreter is President Stroessner.[43]

Democracy also played a vital role on an international level. Not only did the *stronato* escape the international condemnation directed toward neighboring Southern Cone dictatorships, but it facilitated much-needed foreign support. Until the Carter administration in 1977, the United States recognized successive fraudulent reelections while quietly ignoring the systematic violation of human rights.

Stroessner strictly adhered to constitutional legality, allowing him to equate legality with democracy. In legal terms the regime was based on the markedly authoritarian Constitution of 1940 (replaced in 1967 and amended in 1977), which gave it wide powers.[44] For example, although under the 1940 Constitution the state was formally divided into distinct powers, the legislature and judiciary were in practice dependent on the executive.[45] Stroessner further fused the roles of the executive, legislative, and judiciary under his own rule. The executive appointed the members of the Supreme Court, and thus all judges and magistrates (1967.Art.195),[46] while, in practice, all judges had to belong to the Colorado party. The executive could also dissolve congress (which could not convene itself), while neither the legislature nor the judiciary could sanction the executive.[47] Through a constitutional amendment of 1977, Stroessner could be indefinitely reelected.[48]

The Constitution also justified the detention of opposition leaders and the prohibition of opposition meetings and demonstrations (Article 79). When constitutional articles could not be used to justify certain acts, they could be circumvented through the state of emergency, regularly renewed every 90 days, which became "the principal legal device employed to justify repression against political dissidents,"[49] or through the penal laws, especially law 294 (1955) and 209 (1970).[50] The ambiguity of such laws allowed them to be widely used to repress civil and political opposition, giving the regime almost unlimited powers of ostensibly legal repression.

ANTICOMMUNISM/THE NATIONAL SECURITY DOCTRINE

The *stronato* was clearly more anticommunist than democratic. Central to its virulent anticommunism was the National Security Doctrine (NSD), created by the United States in the context of the cold war, in defense of hemispheric security.[51] In Paraguay, this export came to represent an important element of ideological cohesion for the regime.

The NSD viewed internal political change as a potential threat to national security. It demanded that all political, economic, and social activities within a nation be subordinated to national security, which it equated with national survival. There was no room for dissent within this ideology. Protests or opposition were seen as not due to structural inequality, but to subversion and communist infiltration. The enemy became not merely external but internal, active within movements, organizations, and parties that opposed the status quo. The defense of national security, order and stability became paramount, justifying repression.[52]

The *stronato* adopted anticommunism as a crusade. Official newspapers, magazines, and radio and television broadcasts put great effort into combating and denouncing "subversive ideas." Repression meted out against peasants, unions, students, human rights groups, and opposition politicians was justified in the name of anticommunism. Anticommunism became an official ideology, written into the Constitution.[53]

The NSD was used and adapted to extend regime control over civil society. In what was portrayed as a permanent struggle between Paraguay (state and society) and international communist subversion, it served to legitimize repression under the banner of internal security.[54] It was adopted precisely because it was in harmony with the efforts of the regime to impose order and repress dissent.

However, throughout the *stronato*, the Communist party was exiled, factionalized, and lacking support within Paraguay. Nor did any legal left-wing party emerge to threaten the status quo. This suggests an evident contradiction between the vociferous and constant anticommunist campaign waged by the dictatorship and the absence of any real communist threat within Paraguay. Strikingly, in an interview given in 1990, Stroessner admitted that he considered the communist threat as of little importance in Paraguay.[55]

However, anticommunism was not merely a mechanism of internal security, nor based on ideological commitment. Rather the potential economic, and diplomatic advantages of the cold war, made anticommunism an essential official ideology for Paraguay and other struggling dictatorships.[56] Anticommunism, together with the democratic facade, was decisive in gaining Stroessner diplomatic support, above all from the United States.[57] Indeed, from the coup in 1954 until 1977,[58] the United States viewed Stroessner as one of their most trustworthy allies in Latin America.[59] With Stroessner as the most faithful supporter of the United States in the United Nations and the Organization of American States, Paraguay remained a bulwark of U.S. cold war hemispheric policy.[60]

Above all, as Domingo Laíno (1979) has argued, anticommunism was a sound economic strategy and a lucrative business. Materially, in the period 1954–1989, Paraguay received over $31 million in military aid and $240 million in technical and economic assistance.[61] Although this figure may seem small, U.S. aid as a percentage of GDP reached 2.73 percent (1953-61), rising to 4.9 percent between 1962 and 1965. The regime also benefited indirectly from U.S. support in terms of World Bank loans, totaling $504 million. The largest lender to Paraguay, however, was the Inter-American Development Bank (IDB), which lent $619 million during the Stroessner years.[62] In 1979, the president of the IDB, Antonio Ortiz Mena, stated that the bank supported Paraguay "because we know that Paraguay lives and prospers with democracy and liberty."[63]

PEACE, ORDER, AND PROGRESS WITH STROESSNER

Stroessner repeatedly evoked the instability and violence of Paraguay's twentieth-century history to emphasize the benefits of peace and stability his regime had brought. For those who remembered the political instability of the years prior to Stroessner, the concepts of peace, order, and stability were powerful images. This message, emblazoned on electoral posters and billboards in the capital, contrasted sharply with the brutality of the regime. Official propaganda created the myth of "peace under Stroessner," harmony, unity and progress, amidst a reality of injustice, corruption, and repression.

By expropriating and manipulating these concepts, Stroessner turned opposition to the regime into the antithesis of peace, order, and tranquillity, a threat to national accord. If the regime brought peace, prosperity, stability, and progress, then the opposition, by definition, would bring instability, conflict, and social chaos. Repression of opposition thus became synonymous with the defense of peace and stability.

The mechanism to ensure peace was not merely repression but material reward. The price of peace, stability, and order, was corruption at all levels of society. In the pyramid of power, the higher the position of the individual the more opportunity for illicit gain.[64] Corruption became a base of loyalty to the regime and the majority of high-ranking party and military officials involved themselves in some branch of corruption, from illicit business, to land appropriation through the *Instituto de*

Bienestar Rural (Rural Welfare Institute), to construction work.[65] Contraband became rife throughout society, ranging from household appliances, to foodstuffs, to clothes, and to cars. The pervasiveness of corruption created a passive compliance, from the powerful general to the poorest urban dweller.[66]

Given the lack of ideological motive, loyalty to Stroessner (and civil acquiescence) was strengthened by personal, political, and economic patronage that tied people to the regime on all social levels in a convergence of economic and political interests. In the 1960s and 1970s, the modernization of the national infrastructure, new opportunities for financial gain, and the expansion of the public sector allowed a rapid expansion of the patronage system. The path to economic wealth and political power increasingly lay in an allegiance to the Colorado party and thus to Stroessner.

Material progress was not only exploited through patronage, but also served as a powerful image for propaganda purposes. As absolute ruler, Stroessner took the credit for all material signs of development, from each new health center to each new kilometer of roadway or power line. By constantly emphasizing developmental improvements under his government, Stroessner successfully sought to equate himself with Paraguayan modernization and development. According to the new mythology, not only had Stroessner brought peace, but peace and progress *(paz y progreso)*.

CONCLUSION

Ideology has been defined as a "systematic and all-embracing political doctrine, which claims to . . . derive therefrom a programme of political action."[67] Ideology may guide political action, or, as in the case of Stroessner, it may also be reactive, used to legitimate political action or arrangements and defend the interests of a certain class or group.[68] Because ideology is based on a basic, all-embracing and coherent world view, it represents a form of social control, both impeding reflective self-awareness by society and justifying repressive action against opposition.[69]

Linz distinguishes between ideology and mentalities.[70] Ideology is based on intellectual or academic theory and suggests a comprehensive political doctrine that may include a projected transformation of society. In the case of the *stronato*, ideology would refer to nationalism, anticommunism, and democracy.[71]

Mentalities, on the other hand, describe emotional elements used to unite society. As myths, symbols, values, and images they are commonly exploited in reaction to certain situations as an instrument of legitimization, to promote and defend the regime. In the case of Paraguay, the powerful array of mentalities used by Stroessner would include heroism, unity, legality, strength, leadership, peace, order, and progress.

As this chapter has sought to show, the *stronato* lacked a cohesive or coherent ideology. Stroessner had no messianistic quality, no visions of a greater Paraguay with which to unite the people. He may have sought to rewrite Paraguayan history to equate his regime with those of the nationalist period, but he did not attempt to project a new social order. Instead his political vision was limited to the personal maintenance of power and the perpetuation of his regime. Stroessner sought not to transform social reality, but to defend and perpetuate his own position.[72]

Yet, despite Stroessner's lack of coherent ideology, it would be a mistake to state that ideology played no role in the *stronato*. Stroessner was a highly skilled opportunist who expropriated and redefined existing ideologies, myths, and mentalities in order to gain and consolidate support at a national and international level. Stroessner was far from being a democrat, but promoted democracy without communism throughout his regime. Communism was not a significant threat to the regime, yet anticommunism represented an ideological pillar of the regime. Stroessner's policies arguably undermined Paraguayan sovereignty yet Stroessner expounded the values of extreme nationalism. The *stronato* was a repressive dictatorship, yet Stroessner manipulated the concepts of peace, progress, and tranquillity.[73]

In the absence of any ideological fervor to transform society, the longevity of the *stronato* owed much to this skillful manipulation of ideology displayed by Stroessner in his overriding quest to retain power. The *stronato* was not guided or defined by ideology. Instead, as with all else in the regime, ideology was defined and manipulated by Stroessner.

NOTES

1. P. Lewis, *Paraguay under Stroessner* (Chapel Hill: University of North Carolina Press, 1980).

2. See B. Arditi *Adiós a Stroessner. La reconstrucción de la política en el Paraguay* (Asunción: Centro de Documentación y Estudios, 1992).

3. Ibid., p. 18.

4. G. Rodríguez Alcalá, *Ideología Autoritaria* (Asunción: RP Ediciones, 1987), p. 5.

5. C. R. Miranda, *Paraguay y la Era de Stroessner* (Asunción: RP Ediciones, 1990).

6. An example of the antinationalist sentiment of successive Liberal governments was the systematic relegation of the indigenous language, Guaraní.

7. Rodríguez Alcalá, *Ideología*, p. 92.

8. This image still dominates official interpretation of Paraguayan history today, and reference to this period is still referred to as a golden age in much political discourse.

9. J. O'Leary, *Prosa Polémica* (Asunción: Napa, 1982) , p. 152.

10. R. Roett, "Paraguay after Stroessner," *Foreign Affairs* 68:2 (1989), p. 126.

11. See P. Lewis, *Paraguay under Stroessner*.

12. See R. A. Nickson, "The Overthrow of the Stroessner Regime: Reestablishing the Status Quo," *Bulletin of Latin American Research* 8:2 (1989).

13. The importance of nationalism was reflected in the title of Morínigo's *Gobierno Nacionalista Revolucionario* (Nationalist Revolutionary Government).

14. For example, the rebels had the support of approximately 90 percent of the officers of the armed forces.

15. See M. Chase-Sardi, "The Present Situation of the Indians in Paraguay," in W. Dostal (ed.), *The Situation of the Indian in South America* (Geneva: World Council of Churches, 1972).

16. Figures are from R. A. Nickson, *Historical Dictionary of Paraguay* (London: Scarecrow Press, 1993), p. 233.

17. Figures are from the 1991 National Census: *El Censo Nacional de 1991* (Asunción: Dirección General de Estadística y Censos/Secretaria Técnica de Planificación, La Presidencia de la República, 1991).

18. The *Ligas Agrarias* were grass-roots peasant communities that sought to create a new model of peasant organization, cooperation, and education. Their growth and the nature of their demands for agrarian reform had led them into direct conflict with vested interests. This, in turn, led to their brutal repression by the state in 1976.

19. See R. A. Nickson, "Brazilian Colonization of the Eastern Border Region of Paraguay," *Journal of Latin American Studies* 13:1 (1981), pp. 111–31.

20. The *Asociación Rural del Paraguay* became an extremely powerful organization, lobbying on behalf of large-landholders and against the demands of peasant organizations. It remains an extremely powerful group in Paraguay today.

21. Arditi, *Adíos.*

22. Lewis, *Paraguay under Stroessner.*

23. Ibid.

24. R. A. Meza, *El Triángulo de la Opresión* (Asunción: Imprenta Salesiana, 1990).

25. During the *stronato*, the heroism of the nationalist leaders became rooted in the Paraguayan education system. From an early age, children learned of Rodríguez de Francia and López as the embodiment of Paraguay, whose example had to be honored and followed (thus reinforcing the ideas of discipline, obedience, and authority).

26. In this context, it is ironic that rather than a descendant of a long line of Paraguayans, Stroessner was the son of a German immigrant.

27. P. C. Sondrol, "Totalitarian and Authoritarian Dictators: A Comparison of Fidel Castro and Alfredo Stroessner," Journal of Latin American Studies 23:3 (1991) pp. 599–620.

28. Arditi, *Adíos.*

29. F. Masi, *Stroessner: La Extincción de un Modelo Político en Paraguay* (Asunción: Nandutí Vive/Intercontinental Editora, 1989).

30. Miranda, *Paraguay y la Era.*

31. Affiliation to the Colorado party began to become a necessary requirement for political, economic, or military advancement in the period between 1947 and 1954, and not as is commonly believed during the *stronato*.

32. Figures are from Nickson, "The Overthrow of the Stroessner Regime," p .191. As Nickson points out, this figure is undoubtedly exaggerated.

33. M. A. Riquelme, *Stronismo, Golpe Militar y Apertura Tutelada* (Asunción: CDE/RP Ediciones, 1992).

34. Miranda, *Paraguay y la Era.*

35. Stroessner inherited a Colorado party divided into three main factions: the *democráticos*, the *Guionistas*, and the *Epifanistas*. Ideology played a minimal role in the struggle for power between these factions. Stroessner's success in gaining control of the party was in great part due to his success in exploiting these divisions, using and then purging contending factions to strengthen his own power (for an in-depth explanation of the contending factions under Stroessner, see Lewis, *Paraguay under Stroessner.*

36. Complete text in Luis Vittone *Dos Siglos de Política Nacional* (Asunción: Imprenta Militar, 1976) pp. 122–23. Also quoted in V. J. Flecha, C. Martini, and J. Silvero Salgueiro, *Autoritarismo, Transición y Constitución en el Paraguay* (Asunción: BASE ECTA, 1993) p. 32.

37. Lewis, *Paraguay under Stroessner*.

38. Following a political opening in 1963 allowing for limited multiparty elections, the political sphere was divided into four groups. The dominant party (ANR); recognized parties (PL, PLR, and PRF); tolerated parties but nonrecognized (Christian Democrats); and prohibited parties (Communist party and MOPOCO). After the Constituent Assembly of 1977, these parties divided into participating parties (ANR, PL, PLR) and abstentionist parties (PLRA, PDC and PRF). See Arditi, *Adíos*.

39. Riquelme, *Stronismo*.

40. The percentage votes for Stroessner in presidential elections between 1954 and 1988 were as follows: 98.4 percent (1954), 97.3 percent (1958), 90.6 percent (1963), 70.9 percent (1968), 83.6 percent (1973), 90 percent (1978), 90.1 percent (1983), and 88.6 percent (1988).

41. The cleavages brought about by the constant participation/nonparticipation debate within the Liberal party from 1962 onward led to the emergence of five factions all claiming to be the "authentic" liberal opposition.

42. Arditi, *Adíos*.

43. Luis María Argaña, "Historia de las ideas políticas en el Paraguay" (1983), quoted in Meza, *Triángulo*, p. 137.

44. Miranda, *Paraguay y la Era*.

45. Riquelme, *Stronismo*.

46. Under Article 195 of the Constitution, the executive appointed members of the Supreme Court. These in turn appointed all judges and magistrates (Art. 180).

47. For a more in-depth discussion of the balance of powers of the Executive, judiciary and legislature, see Arditi, *Adíos*.

48. The 1967 Constitution, which originally limited presidential office to two terms, was amended in 1977, allowing for the indefinite reelection of Stroessner.

49. R. A. Nickson, *Historical Dictionary of Paraguay* (London: Scarecrow Press, 1993), p. 550.

50. Law 294, "The Defense of Democracy," made "ostensible or secret" membership of the Communist party a crime. Law 209 "Defense of Public Peace and Personal freedom," reinforced law 294 and made "the fostering of hatred among Paraguayans" a criminal offense.

51. Meza, *Triángulo*, p. 187, describes the National Security Doctrine as "the notorious creation of the United States that with its egoistic and machiavellian mentality, crushed the unalienable rights of peoples south of the Rio Bravo."

52. Riquelme, *Stronismo*.

53. Article 71 of the 1967 Constitution states that "The promotion of hatred among Paraguayans or class struggle are not permitted."

54. Riquelme, *Stronismo*.

55. In a fascinating interview with Isabel Hilton, Stroessner consistently denied the presence of revolution or communism in Paraguay. Despite Hilton's efforts to extract information about the communist threat, Stroessner "simply refused to worry about communism." See I. Hilton, "The General," *Granta* 31 (London: Penguin, 1990).

56. B. Arditi, *Cálculo y contingencia en las transiciones a la democracia* (Asunción: CDE, 1994).

57. Although the United States provided the bulk of economic aid to Paraguay, Stroessner benefited from military and economic links to other anticommunist countries. These included Brazil, South Africa, and later Taiwan (Riquelme, *Stronismo*, p. 60).

58. U.S.-Paraguayan relations foundered in 1977, due to pressures on the Stroessner regime resulting from the Carter Human Rights Doctrine. Relations temporarily improved with the Reagan administration until they foundered in the mid-1980s, as the United States sought to promote hemispheric "democratization" in order to justify its policies in Central America.

59. A. Seiferheld, *La caída de Federico Chávez: Una visión documental norteamericana* (Asunción: Ediciones Históricas, 1987).

60. Roett, "Paraguay after Stroessner." The U.S. embassy in Asunción is the largest in the Southern Cone, a tribute to U.S.-Paraguayan relations under Stroessner. In turn, Stroessner was quoted in March 1968 as saying that he considered the U.S. Ambassador to be a member of his cabinet (Nickson, *Historical Dictionary*, p. 607).

61. Figures are from Roett,"Paraguay after Stroessner," p. 132.

62. Figures are from Nickson, *Historical Dictionary*, p. 608.

63. Quoted in D. Laíno, *Paraguay: Represión, Estafa y Anticomuni$mo* (Asunción: Ediciones Cerro Corá, 1979), p. 77.

64. Arditi, *Adiós*.

65. Riquelme, *Stronismo*.

66. For an in-depth analysis of the extent and forms of corruption, see Arditi, *Adiós*.

67. R. A. Scruton, *Dictionary of Political Thought* (Basingstoke: Macmillan, 1982), p. 213.

68. M. A. Riff, *A Dictionary of Modern Ideologies* (Manchester: Manchester University Press, 1987).

69. G. Roberts and A. Edwards, *A Dictionary of Political Analysis* (New York: Routledge/Chapman and Hall, 1991).

70. J. J. Linz, "An Authoritarian Regime: Spain," in E. Allardt and S. Rokkan (eds.), *Mass Politics: Studies in Political Sociology* (New York: Free Press, 1970), p. 257.

71. This classification concurs with the ideologies discussed in Riff, *Modern Ideologies*.

72. See Sondrol, *Totalitarian*. Although Sondrol is perhaps guilty of loosely applying the term "ideology," his article on the authoritarian and totalitarian features of the Stroessner regime is a thought-provoking and insightful analysis of the theme.

73. This imbalance between rhetoric and political practice has was not unique to Stroessner, nor is it unique to Paraguayan politics (as suggested by Rodríguez Alcalá, *Ideología*). However, Paraguayan politics since 1870 has been characterized by an absence of strong ideological positioning by political parties. Far more common, even in modern-day "democratic politics," is the manipulation of existing ideologies and mentalities in order to retain or gain access to power.

chapter 9

Feminism, Ideology, and Low-Income Women's Groups in Latin America

Anny Brooksbank Jones

This chapter looks at the changing relations between feminist and low-income women's groups in Latin America.[1] In particular it focuses on the impact among low-income women of certain feminist assumptions and proposes a non-binary framework for the evaluation of different forms of women's activism. There are three principal difficulties associated with such a task. First is the fact that any discussion can only begin to engage with the exceptional diversity of women's activism in a Latin American framework, and with the quality and quantity of insights key researchers have offered into it in recent years.[2] The second problem is that any attempt to ground larger analyses and claims on these detailed studies risks charges of willful homogenization. Despite having argued for many years in a feminist frame against such homogenization, however, I remain convinced that some temporary reduction of specificity is unavoidable if (as here) larger strategic questions are to be raised. The final problem relates to the difficulty of defining "ideology" and "feminism" as they operate in a Latin American framework. For the purposes of this discussion the use of the word ideology is restricted to the three senses that emerge most frequently from my sources. Two can be traced back to Marx and Engels: the first evokes "the set of ideas which arise from a given set of material interests or, more broadly, from a definite class or group"; the second evokes "illusion, false consciousness, unreality, upside-down reality."[3] The other use of the term (which can be traced back to Napoleon Bonaparte) implies an "abstract, impractical or fanatical theory."[4] Defining feminism is even more tricky. Particularly in an Anglo-American context, feminism's broadly egalitarian and emancipatory impulse has led to its association with the post-Enlightenment modernizing project.[5] But researchers in Anglophone and European countries are increasingly recognizing the feminist claims of thinkers and activists influenced by postcolonial, poststructuralist, difference and postmodern theories that question that project,[6] and the effects of this questioning are being felt (to differing extents) within some metropolitan feminist groups in Latin America. For the purposes of this discussion, what matters is not the competing claims of antihumanist and socialist, radical or broad equality feminisms, but rather what makes each of these different ideological perspectives recognizably feminist. And I would argue that their chief (and in some cases only) common characteristic is the systematic privilege of gender as an analytic category. In the discussion that follows, groups and individuals will thus be referred to as feminist, whatever their particular ideological orientation, only if they share this characteristic.[7]

In 1985 Maxine Molyneux described the gender-based analysis and macrosocial orientation of most Latin American feminism as "strategic."[8] This she contrasted with the "practical gender interests," which (in her view) arise from women's positions in the division of labor, are articulated in more locally based activism, and tend not to address the wider social relations that circumscribe them. Though ground-breaking at the time, Molyneux's distinction has since been hotly contested.[9] I do not propose to dwell on it here, except to question (with Radcliffe and Westwood) what now seems an artificial and potentially hierarchizing opposition, and one that tends to promote the no less artificial separation of public and private spheres. However, my necessarily schematic overview of the development of feminist and other women's groups will initially collude to some extent with Molyneux's binary by emphasizing differences rather than common ground.

Feminism in Latin America can be traced back to the 1970s, and almost invariably to small numbers of middle-class, educated, mostly professional women and students. They were particularly influenced by U.S. radical feminists. Like them, they privileged gender above class and other factors, and focused on women's subordination as a structural necessity of patriarchy. There were few other women's groups in Latin America at this time and those there were tended to be conservative in orientation: official women's organizations in Chile, for example, promoted self-abnegation and the maternal virtues, while women active with *El Poder Femenino* (Feminine Power) actively contributed to the overthrow of Salvador Allende. Independent feminists allied with the left were obliged to organize clandestinely, in order to avoid having their struggles subsumed by male-dominated left groups.[10] Meanwhile "las políticas" (the women who fought within opposition parties or groups—in Chile, Peru, and Argentina, for example) were broadly suspicious of the single sex organizing of "las feministas," and disinclined to support feminist demands around such issues as abortion rights or violence against women. As Villavicencio notes with reference to Peru, despite some joint action in the large-scale popular and trade union mobilizations of the 1970s, their different priorities and approaches meant that party women's sections, early women's organizations, and the first feminist groups tended to develop independently.[11] Over time, however, organization within opposition groups around gender-linked issues became more common and more open, to the point where some activists began to characterize themselves as "doble militantes" (double militants). These women were an important stimulus to joint "feminista/política" mobilizations in Peru in the late 1970s, for example, and in Chile in the late 1980s. In some cases the success of double militants' demands led to the establishment within opposition parties of women's commissions and secretariats. These enabled gender-based claims to be pursued in a more focused way and with some success. More generally, however, they institutionalized the sidelining of women activists' demands. Within unions, too, women activists tended to find demands for equal employment rights blocked or sidelined. And as the Mexican case indicates, even when a measure of politico-juridical equality was achieved it did (and still does) not always materialize in practice. These setbacks led some disillusioned women to abandon gender-based activism altogether and others to defect to independent feminist groups.[12]

Throughout the 1970s and early 1980s, the number of women's groups with a gender dimension to their demands continued to grow. The year 1983 saw the establishment of Chile's MEMCH-83, an umbrella organization with twenty-four member groups, all oriented toward some notion of women's emancipation. Since by means all members systematically prioritized gender in their demands, however, this does not imply the growth of mass support for feminism. Instead, I would argue, in Chile, Peru, and Argentina, for example, the ability of a relatively small number of feminists to influence the left's political agenda helped raise their profile disproportionately. Even in Chile, however, this influence has not been great and to date feminists have rarely seen their efforts rewarded with significantly increased representation in government.[13] Not all independent feminists would wish to participate in what they see as profoundly patriarchally structured political systems. Much more widespread, however, is the concern that feminist demands would not necessarily be met overnight even if democratic parity were achieved. As Jelin observes, even the exceptional 25 percent representation for women in the current Argentinian Congress—more than twice that of Britain or the United States, for example—does not in and of itself mean an equality agenda.[14] This remains true even where women enjoy the highest political status. It is evident in Violeta Chamorro's pronouncements on abortion, for example, and even more unambiguously in a statement by Martha Chávez, leader of the Peruvian congress, to mark last year's International Women's Day: "el lugar de la mujer debe ser el hogar con su familia" (women's place should be at home with their family).[15] Conversely, although Chile's Congress is currently made up of only 7 percent women, the establishment in 1990 of SERNAM (the government-created National Women's Service) does appear to be advancing the cause of institutional feminism in that country, despite some reservations on the part of independent feminists.[16]

All of this underlines the (albeit unstable) ideological differences that separate not only feminists from non- or antifeminists, but also independent or institutional or double-militant feminists from each other. Throughout the 1970s, however, most feminist groups continued to focus on the macropolitical rather than more local, social, issues that concerned the majority of women's groups. By the mid-1980s, however, encouraged partly by their raised profile and by contacts with left-allied exile groups, some were beginning to think of themselves as the vanguard that would lead the broader women's movement out of false consciousness.[17] Particularly in Chile, Brazil, and Peru, middle-class feminists began to develop contacts with women's survival and other groups on the urban periphery. As Álvarez puts it in the context of Brazil, "feminists embraced the struggle of poor and working class women."[18] The great majority of women who were able or inclined to attend metropolitan feminist-led women's workshops nevertheless rejected much of what they heard. In particular, most work with Latin American women's groups confirms Fisher's findings that, with the possible exception of Chile, "the label 'feminist' . . . was almost unanimously rejected by working-class women."[19] Although, as her own work demonstrates, to oppose the label is not necessarily to oppose all feminist demands, many women clearly do dismiss feminism (as they understand it) as ideological in one of the senses I have outlined. One of the mothers of Argentina's Plaza de Mayo rejects it as abstract theorizing, for example: "we don't defend ideologies: we defend life."[20] In a Brazilian context, Vieira Machado traces similar objections back to the early 1970s, when feminism tended to be "rather undefined, and largely restricted to 'established; Marxist categories and analysis . . . and in general women's 'specific' needs were seen as secondary to the need for 'general social transformation.' "[21] More common, however (and a reminder that members of women's groups do not all mobilize exclusively *as women*), is a rejection of feminism on the grounds that it attempts to impose the priorities of one particular class or group on another. As Corcoran-Nantes notes, the majority of low-income women still find that "feminism . . . has very little to do with the reality of their lives."[22] But as feminists in the late 1970s and 1980s began to question left analyses—and in particular the view that women's demands could wait until after the struggle—they elaborated gender-based alternatives, which, in some cases, would serve to alienate them even further from other women's groups.[23] For example, within broad sociopolitical contexts that privileged solidarity—and in particular mixed activism—feminist separatism was (and continues to be) regarded with suspicion. Independent feminists were accused by left groups of being *petit bourgeois* and of diverting attention from the main struggle; the Catholic church charged them with being antifamily and egotistical; the more polemical sections of the conservative press represented them as man-haters and lesbians.[24] Women organizing around survival or human rights issues were especially unsympathetic toward their early early focus on identity, sexuality, and pleasure; the feminist promotion of contraception and abortion in particular tended to be seen as a direct attack on the family which, for all its ambiguities, was (and remains) many low-income women's principal base and support.[25]

So far the differences between feminism and other forms of women's activism have been emphasized at the expense of common ground. There are clear theoretical and political advantages to insisting on common ground in certain circumstances, and if I have so far resisted them it is from an uneasy sense that some feminists—in and outside of Latin America—have assumed them rather too hastily. What is at issue here is not an attempt to police the borders of "real" feminism by excluding insufficiently ideological or other supposedly inferior forms; rather it is a recognition of the different motives and imperatives that condition low income women's activism and of their widely expressed desire to evaluate that activism in their own terms, whether or not this is linked explicitly to a wider struggle for interpretive power.[26] The voluntaristic elision of feminism with the broader women's movement—or with any women's activism with a general focus on increasing women's power, or that has a gender dimension or is in some other way undertaken by women *as women*—makes it more difficult than it need be to register differences, to think through changes in women's feminist and nonfeminist activism over time (for example, to plot their changing relations), and to trace how those relations are inflected by ethnicity, class, and other factors.

If feminism is understood as the more or less systematic privileging of gender above other analytic categories, Küppers is probably right to suggest that it has been until quite recently the domain of a provocative middle-class minority made up of "academics, scholars, women in the media and artists."[27] This predominantly middle-class urban perspective arguably made early feminists less sensitive not only to differences of class and location, but also to the racial component of some women's discrimination.[28] Since then, serious attempts have been made to broaden contacts with marginalized groups. However, as activists with Peru's Bartolina Sisa and FENAMAD peasant federations have underscored, there is still some way to go where indigenous women's groups in particular are concerned.[29] Critics often link their charges of insensitivity to claims that feminism is an alien ideology. The spread of feminism in Latin America from the late 1970s was indeed stimulated largely by activists and delegates exposed to the views of Anglo-European and other feminists at international conventions—at first directly and later via other Latin American feminists.[30] This process intensified as exiles began to return from Paris, London, and elsewhere, bringing with them radical perspectives elaborated by exile collectives and their feminist contacts in the host country.[31] During the early 1980s, however, metropolitan feminism in the United States and Europe turned increasingly from the early emphasis on sisterhood toward attempts to theorize women's heterogeneity. Partly as a result, so-called Third World women's activism came under closer scrutiny at a time when economic restructuring and other factors were already helping to make women more prominent as social actors not only in Latin America but also in North America and Europe. By the early 1990s, as talk of postfeminism began to take hold in metropolitan centers, Sheila Rowbotham (a key figure in British second-wave feminism) was not alone in looking to Latin America for new feminist models.[32]

Most of the women's groups that came under scrutiny were locally based survival or human rights groups oriented toward specific, usually small-scale and short-term goals, and there was a tendency to disband when the goal was achieved.[33] Women's mobilization had begun to increase dramatically from the mid-1970s and by the mid-1980s they formed the clear majority across almost all the social movements.[34] By this time the economic crisis of the 1980s, IMF-imposed austerity programs, and (in particular) cuts in national welfare resourcing was throwing many working-class men into unemployment and weakening the unions that had supported them. The importance of women's groups in palliating the worst effects of these processes grew, and their work outside of the family to reduce poverty and hunger and to secure basic services was increasingly—if ambiguously—foregrounded. As the crisis deepened, campaigns around immediate needs like a clean water supply or a health center displaced more open-ended activism, particularly where the absence of the basic state welfare "cushioning" (such as that afforded by PRONOSOL in Mexico) made self-reliance essential. Following Caldeira, Foweraker has underlined material and ideological shifts arising from women's activism during this period: their increased levels of autonomy, for example, and signs of negotiated changes in their domestic sphere.[35] But as Chant and others underline, while women's increased participation in the so-called public sphere has led to some democratization of household decision-making, this should not be overstated; even when menfolk are unemployed, for example, domestic responsibilities continue to fall largely if not exclusively to women family members.[36] At the same time, the tendency of men demoralized by chronic unemployment to feel trapped in the home, suspicious of women's activities outside of it, and resentful of their partner's increased self-confidence and economic power, has also contributed to increased levels of alcoholism and domestic violence.[37] In such tense situations, many low-income women place the need to support their partners' self-esteem before their own personal needs and those of the family as a whole.

This may be a case of ideological changes being overridden at times by short-term necessity,[38] or it may reflect the fact that significant ideological change has not, or has not yet, taken place. In neither case, however, can low-income women's activism be said simply to reinforce their traditional roles. The stresses and conflict produced by unfamiliar and rapidly changing circumstances and the negotiations required to accommodate them have helped to precipitate "the emergence into visibility and contestability of problems and possibilities that cannot be solved or realized within the established framework of gendered roles and institutions."[39] Feminists frustrated by the unwillingness of most low-income women to embrace a feminist analysis of these new situations have in some cases interpreted it as a sign of ideological weakness or complicity. In the words of Nicaraguan publisher Sofía Montenegro, a woman who denies feminism in these circumstances "is either talking nonsense or simply revealing her alienation."[40]

Overviews, as noted, tend to highlight differences between feminist and women's groups at the expense of the differences within them. Montenegro's charge of false consciousness and the blank incomprehension with which feminist ideologues like Julieta Kirkwood have been greeted by low-income women mark extreme points in the relations of feminists and low-income women.[41] In practice, as their exposure to external—continental but also Anglo-American and European—bodies grew through the 1980s, some members of low-income women's groups became more familiar with core aspects of feminist ideology and with key demands arising from them.[42] While certain issues raised in feminist-led meetings were (and continue to be) rejected by most members, either for pragmatic reasons or (as in the case of abortion) on principle, some members have been less resistant. These more responsive women have included a relatively high proportion of group leaders, partly as a result of special targeting by certain feminist groups. But feminist assumptions may also influence women's organizations more indirectly. While women campaigning together *as women* on particular issues may not derive their gendered standpoint directly from feminists, even mediated and/or resisting contact with elements of feminist ideology can help more generally to condition the development of such a standpoint. Once again, there is no suggestion that a gendered standpoint is necessarily a feminist one. On the other hand, if organizations like Chile's SERNAM are able to secure the incorporation in national and local social policy of key feminist assumptions and demands, gendered standpoints may (in time and in favorable conditions) be encouraged to develop into a broad acceptance of some of these assumptions.[43]

The influence of feminist and other external groups on women's activism should not be overstated, however. And not least because the field that confers significance on sociocultural relations and practices is complex and unstable, making the impact of outside influences—which in any event are rarely entirely "outside"—vary in often unpredictable ways.[44] The development of forms of feminism in Chile or Peru, for example, does not reflect a process of direct acculturation, nor a simple dialectical negotiation with Anglo-American and European feminisms—which are themselves less homogeneous and more contested than some Latin American critics tend to assume.[45] After the mutual incomprehension of the early years and the well-intentioned but invariably fractured dialogues of the 1980s, feminism today enjoys a generally less asymmetrically powered relationship with other forms of women's activism in Latin America. The blurring of lines between mobile, locally based tactics and metropolitan, ethically grounded strategies is manifest in the demands of this Argentinian union activist, for example: "[f]eminism may help to explain reality but it has to be adapted to the conditions of the people. In some senses we are feminists but we want it to have its proper meaning—an Argentine feminism for the mass of Argentine women."[46] It is also evident in the words of feminist Virginia Vargas who, as coordinator of Latin American and Caribbean NGOs at the 1995 Beijing World Conference on Women, placed women's need for "la ciudadanía plena" (full citizenship) alongside a focus on "la multiculturalidad y pluricidad de nuestra región" (the multicultural and plural nature of our region), and acknowledged that "[l]os intereses de las mujeres son múltiples, no solamente se reducen a los intereses exclusivamente de género" (women's interests are manifold, and are not reducible to gender alone).[47] This underscores the extent to which, like other women's organizations, Latin American feminists of different persuasions increasingly have the self-confidence and awareness to reject what they do not need from other sources, to appropriate what they do, and to shape it to local conditions. In such cases the term "femenism" might be used, not to describe the end results (which may vary significantly between and within Latin American countries and according to the particular feminist ideology subscribed to), but to mark the "will to critical appropriation" that animates them. Giving due weight to this process in femenist but also other women's groups helps to explain why not only a gendered perspective but also, in some cases, certain femenist assumptions are now shared by women in nonfeminist organizations. In this case, the term "womenist"[48] could serve to designate nonexclusive, solidary activism among women (and supportive men) who include gender as one factor among others in their assessment of specific situations of discrimination, exploitation, and injustice. Their analysis may include some recognizably femenist claims and demands, but is characterized particularly by a supple mix of "negotiations, appropriations and negations."[49]

Partly because of the powerfully appropriative and recuperative tendencies of hegemonic neoliberalism, suppleness has had an increasingly important place in oppositional activism since the 1980s. At the same time, however, the lack of a clear ideological framework for action has lead at times to an overemphasis on pragmatism and made successes difficult to sustain. Particularly significant in this context is the crystallization from among womenist negotiations and appropriations of forms of self-styled "grassroots feminism"—or femenism—which combine inflected elements of womenist and femenist tendencies in variable proportions. Chile's MOMUPO, for example, does not share the overall theoretical focus of any particular version of metropolitan feminism, but it does prioritize gender over other factors in low-income women's lives and rejects the subordination of women's demands and priorities to those of the left.[50] It differs from metropolitan feminism, however, in its clear class base and commitment to bottom-up activism, while acknowledging the difficulties of sustaining this impulse over time in practice. MOMUPO's activists are also disinclined to confront questions of women's sexuality, and particularly abortion, despite the fact that metropolitan femenists have gone some way to breaking down womenist resistance to these questions by raising them under the heading of reproductive rights.[51]

Despite MOMUPO's relatively modest claims to the title, its feminist label has been enough to place the organization's relations with other women's groups on a different and more contradictory footing. As noted above, such contradictions can (in the right conditions) promote changes in practices and in consciousness.[52] But particularly at times of rapid change individuals are often able to accommodate relatively high levels of contradiction before feeling obliged to try to resolve it—or to displace or decathect it in myth or ritual, for example. In MOMUPO's case, its sustained community links and insight into their individual situations have encouraged many local women to continue attending meetings even when they reject out of hand certain explicitly feminist aspects of its activism. It may be that if MOMUPO and other grassroots feminist organizations can avoid alienating womenist activists—for example, by becoming too remote from their concerns—this ongoing contact may, over time, enable aspects of grassroots femenism to spread. This does not necessarily mean that even the most open of womenists will think of themselves as femenists, although some might. More likely in the short term is that even avowed antifeminists will find it easier to adopt femenist positions or analyses unselfconsciously, in certain circumstances.

However, neither this prospect nor the spread of grassroots femenism is likely to represent the next stage in an evolution toward generalized femenism in Latin America. This is chiefly because the ideological crisis of feminism goes well beyond talk of backlash and postfeminism in the United States and elsewhere. It involves the questioning of rationality, coherence, systematicity, evolution, justice, and other post-Enlightenment values fundamental to virtually all forms of feminism.[53] And the context for this questioning is a range of sociocultural and politicoeconomic phenomena—grouped under such headings as postmodernity, globalization, the communications revolution[54]—that presuppose the fragmentation of the (feminist or other) subject itself. These phenomena are making their presence felt (albeit unevenly) across Latin America in a neoliberal, modernizing frame that privileges pluralism and pragmatism at the expense of solidarity and ideological commitment. The pragmatism of womenist groups is complicitous with that of the neoliberal state to the extent that they tend to supplement shortfalls in government services. In the absence of feminist alternatives, however, some intellectuals will continue to seek to ground their social critique in womenist and grassroots femenist mobilizations.[55] Whatever its impact on activists (some of whom will continue to exploit the femenist/nonfemenist binary for their own purposes[56]) this strategy marks a timely reinforcing of feminism's, and feminism's, macropolitcal edge.

NOTES

1. I am particularly grateful to Sarah A. Radcliffe for her thought-provoking comments on an earlier draft, while absolving her of any responsibility whatsoever for my conclusions.

2. I am thinking here of work as diverse as: Sarah A. Radcliffe and Sallie Westwood, *Viva: Women and Popular Protest in Latin America* (London: Routledge, 1993); Sylvia Chant, "Women, work and household survival strategies in Mexico, 1982–1992: Past trends, current tendencies and future research," *Bulletin of Latin American Research* 13:2 (May, 1994), pp. 203–33; Jo Fisher, *Out of the Shadows: Women, Resistance and Politics in South America* (London: Latin American Bureau, 1993); Jo Fisher, "Women and democracy: For home and country," *NACLA: Report on the Americas* 27:1 (1993) pp. 30–36; Debra A. Castillo, *Talking Back: Toward a Latin American Feminist Criticism* (Ithaca: Cornell University Press, 1992); Jean Franco, "Going public: Reinhabiting the private," in George Yúdice, Jean Franco, and Juan Flores (eds.), *On Edge: The Crisis of Contemporary Latin American Culture* (Minneapolis: University of Minnesota Press, 1992), pp. 65–83; Jane S. Jacquette, *The Women's Movement in Latin America: Feminism and the Transition to Democracy* (Boston: Unwin Hyam, 1989); Elizabeth Jelin, "Citizenship and identity: Final reflections," Elizabeth Jelin (ed.), *Women and Social Change in Latin America* (London: Zed Books, 1990), pp. 184–207; Janet H. Momsen and Vivian Kinnaird (eds.), *Different Places, Different Voices: Gender and Development in Africa, Asia and Latin America* (London: Routledge, 1993); Gaby Küppers, *Compañeras: Voices from the Latin American Women's Movement* (London: Latin America Bureau, 1994). Although these have particularly influenced my discussion, many other studies are referred to during the course of the chapter.

3. Raymond Williams, *Keywords: A Vocabulary of Culture and Society* (London: Flamingo, 1981; orig. 1976), p. 156. Unless indicated otherwise, my own use of the term ideology will be restricted to the first definition.

4. Ibid., p. 154.

5. On this see, for example, Linda Nicholson (ed.), *Feminism/Postmodernism* (London: Routledge, 1990) and Michele Barrett and Anne Phillips (eds.), *Destabilizing Theory: Contemporary Feminist Debates* (Cambridge: Polity, 1992).

6. See, in particular, Barrett and Phillips, *Destabilizing Theory*; Chandra Talpade Mohanty, "Under Western eyes: Feminist scholarship and colonial discourses," Chandra Talpade Mohanty, Ann Russo, and Lourdes Torres (eds.), *Third World Women and the Politics of Feminism* (Bloomington: Indiana University Press, 1991), pp. 51–80; Gayatri Chakravorty Spivak, *The Post-colonial Critic: Interviews, Strategies, Dialogues*, Sarah Harasym (ed.) (London: Routledge, 1990); Gayatri Chakravorty Spivak, *Outside in the Teaching Machine* (London: Routledge, 1993); Judith Butler, *Gender Trouble: Feminism and the Subversion of Identity* (London: Routledge, 1990); Judith Butler, *Bodies that Matter: On the Discursive Limits of "Sex,"* (London: Routledge, 1993); Luce Irigaray, *Je, Tu, Nous: Toward a Culture of Difference*, Alison Martin (trans.) (London: Routledge, 1993); Elizabeth Grosz, *Volatile Bodies: Toward a Corporeal Feminism* (New York: Columbia University Press, 1994); Chantal Mouffe, "Feminism, citizenship, and radical democratic politics," Linda Nicholson and Steven Seidman (eds.), *Social Postmodernism: Beyond Identity Politics* (Cambridge: Cambridge University Press, 1995), pp. 315–31.

7. As emerges below, this definition is not designed to promote one particular version of feminism at the expense of others, but precisely to question the tendency to assimilate all women's activism to feminist models.

8. Maxine Molyneux, "Mobilization without emancipation? Women's interests, the state and the revolution in Nicaragua," *Feminist Studies* 11:2 (1985), pp. 227–54.

9. For accounts of this debate see Jennifer Schirmer's "The seeking of truth and the gendering of consciousness: the Comadres of El Salvador and the Conavigua widows of Guatemala," in Radcliffe and Westwood, *Viva*, pp. 30–64, and Sarah Radcliffe's " 'People have to rise up—like the great women fighters': The state and peasant women in Peru," in the same volume, pp. 197–218. For a sophisticated critique of the public/private division in a Latin American framework see Franco, "Going public."

10. On this see Joe Foweraker, *Theorizing Social Movements* (London: Pluto, 1995).

11. Maritza Villavicencio, "The feminist movement and the social movement: Willing partners?," in Küppers, *Compañeras*, pp. 59–70.

12. See Nancy Saporta Sternbach, Marysa Navarro-Aranguren, Patricia Chuchryk, and Sonia Alvarez, "Feminisms in Latin America: From Bogotá to San Bernardo," *Signs: Journal of Women in Culture and Society* 17:2 (1992), pp. 393– 434.

13. On this see Jo Fisher, "Women and democracy: For home and country," *NACLA: Report on the Americas* 27:1 (1993) pp. 30–36.

14. Cited in Lucien Chauvin, "Ser y hacer política," *Noticias Aliadas* 32:23 (22 June, 1995), p. 4.

15. Elizabeth Jelin is cited in Dafne Sabanes, "Argentina: Menem provoca debate sobre aborto," *Noticias Aliadas* 31:28 (28 July, 1994), p. 1, and Marta Chávez in Chauvin, "Ser y hacer."

16. Institutional feminism of whatever ideological persuasion tends to be viewed with suspicion by independent groups, since it is invariably designed to obviate, or more cynically to mask, the need for independent feminist activism. If SERNAM is (arguably) an example

of the first of these, El Salvador's Departamento de la Mujer (Woman's Department) is an example of the second. On SERNAM, see Fisher, *Out of the Shadows*, and on the Departmento de la Mujer, see Yance Urbina, "Building a feminist organization inside the social movement," in Küppers, *Compañeras*, pp. 23–29.

17. Two influential studies from this period are Latin American and Caribbean Women's Collective, *Slaves of Slaves: the Challenge of Latin American Women*, (London: Zed Books, 1980; orig. 1977) and Miranda Davies (ed.), *Third World, Second Sex: Women's Struggles and National Liberation: Third World Women Speak Out* (London: Zed Books, 1983), which includes a section on Latin America.

18. Sonia E. Alvarez, "Women's movements and gender politics in the Brazilian transition" Jacquette, *The Women's Movement*, p. 265.

19. Cited in Fisher, *Out of the Shadows*, p. 205.

20. Cited in Jelin, "Citizenship and identity," p. 204.

21. Leda Maria Vieira Machado, " 'We learned to think politically': The influence of the Catholic church and the feminist movement on the emergence of the health movement of the Jardim Nordeste area in São Paulo, Brazil," Radcliffe and Westwood, *Viva*, pp. 88–111.

22. Yvonne Corcoran-Nantes, "Female consciousness or feminist consciousness?; women's consciousness raising in community-based struggles in Brazil," in Radcliffe and Westwood, *Viva*, pp. 136–55.

23. On this see Villavicencio, "The feminist movement."

24. On mixed activism and the overrepresentaion of men at higher levels see María Teresa Blandón, "The impact of the Sandinista deafeat on Nicaraguan feminism," Küppers, *Compañeras*, pp. 97–101, and Sofía Montenegro, "The future from a female point of view," in the same volume, pp. 173–77.

25. On this see Radcliffe, " 'People have to rise up,' " pp. 216–17, and Fisher, *Out of the Shadows*, p. 93.

26. For more on this struggle see George Yúdice, "Postmodernity and transnational capitalism," in Yúdice, Franco, and Flores, *On Edge*, pp. 1–28.

27. Küppers, *Compañeras*, p. 4.

28. Chabela Vicenta Camusso "Black women in a white world: The search for a new identity," Küppers, *Compañeras*, pp. 120–25.

29. See Radcliffe, " 'People have to rise up,' " and more recently María Esther Mogollón, "El derecho a ser diferente," *Noticias Aliadas* 32:23 (22 June, 1995), p. 16.

30. See, for example, Blandón, "The impact" (especially p. 98), and Villavicencio, "The feminist movement."

31. See Davies, *Third World*; Fisher, *Out of the Shadows*, pp. 13, 15, 185; Lady Elizabeth Repetto, "Women against violence against women," Küppers, *Compañeras*, pp. 126–37.

32. In a lecture at Nottingham Trent University in the U.K. in 1993, Rowbotham referred explicitly to her search for inspiration in Latin America, although it seemed to focus more on leading feminists like Virginia Vargas and Julieta Kirkwood than on leaders of women's groups themselves. For a U.S. example of this tendency, see the closing pages of Sternbach et al., *Feminism*.

33. See Tessa Cubitt, *Latin American Society* (Harlow: Longman Scientific, 1995), p. 198.

34. Foweraker, *Theorizing Social Movements*.

35. Ibid.

36. See Chant, "Women, work," and Fisher, *Out of the Shadows*, p. 93.

37. Ibid., p. 29; Repetto, "Women against violence."

38. On the overriding of ideological see Molyneux, "Mobilization."

39. Nancy Fraser, cited in Franco, "Going public," p. 65.

40. Montenegro, "The future," p. 173.

41. On Kirkwood's reception by Chilean low-income women see Fisher, *Out of the Shadows*, p. 186.

42. Chile's MOMUPO (Movement of Women from the *Pueblos*), for example, has received advice and funding from Oxfam, as well as visits from foreign researchers and visitors (Fisher, *Out of the Shadows*, pp. 183–88). At the same time, increased coordination between groups has meant that even where there have been no direct external contacts of this kind, advice and information found useful by one group is more likely to be passed on to others.

43. I base this observation on studies of SERNAM's model, Spain's Instituto de la Mujer. See, for example, my "Spain's Institute for Women," *European Journal of Women's Studies* 2 (June, 1995), pp. 261–69.

44. On this, see the opening and closing sections of Néstor García Canclini's *Hybrid Cultures: Strategies for Entering and Leaving Modernity*, Christopher L. Chiappari and Silvia L. López (trans.) (Minneapolis: University of Minnesota Press, 1995).

45. See, in particular, Villavicencio, "The feminist movement."

46. Cited in Fisher, *Out of the Shadows,* p. 173.

47. Virginia Vargas "Construyendo la ciudadanía femenina," *Noticias Aliadas* 32:10 (23 March, 1995), p. 15.

48. This is based on the term "mujerista," with its echoes of Alice Walker's "womanist," which has gained some academic recognition, particularly in Mexico and the United States. However, its implication that women are somehow better than men simply by virtue of their femaleness has led to its rejection by others on the grounds that it tends to promote separatism—hence my suggested alternative. On this see Marta Lamas, *"Debate feminista*: A bridge between academia and activism," Küppers, *Compañeras*, pp. 160–62.

49. Radcliffe, " 'People have to rise up,' " p. 217.

50. See Fisher, *Out of the Shadows*, pp. 177–200.

51. On this see Virginia Vargas, "Construyendo la ciudadanía femenina," *Noticias Aliadas* 32:10 (23 March, 1995), p. 15.

52. For key contributions to this debate see, for example, Joan W. Scott, "The evidence of experience," *Critical Enquiry* 17 (1991), pp. 773–97; Schirmer, "The seeking of the truth"; and Radcliffe, " 'People have to rise up.' "

53. See Mridula Udayagiri, "Challenging modernization: Gender and development, postmodern feminism and activism," Marianne H. Marchand and Jane L. Parpart (eds.), *Feminism/Postmodernism/Development* (London: Routledge, 1995), pp. 159–77.

54. For a broad-ranging discussion of these phenomena in a nonfeminist Latin American framework, see García Canclini, *Hybrid Cultures.*

55. See Franco, "Going public."

56. For more on this see also Marianne H. Marchand, "Latin American women speak on development: Are we listening yet?" in Marchand and Parpart, *Feminism/Postmodernism/Development*, pp. 56–72, especially pp. 63–64.

chapter 10

Jaime Guzmán and the *Gremialistas*: From Catholic Corporatist Movement to Free Market Party

Marcelo Pollack

The military coup that overthrew the democratically elected socialist government of President Salvador Allende in September 1973 gave previously peripheral elements of the Chilean right the opportunity to exercise almost unlimited power within the new regime. The *gremialista* movement, which first emerged as an organized grouping in the 1960s, was one of the most significant of these ideological tendencies. By the late 1980s, the organization had transformed itself from an obscure movement based on a primarily archaic ideology into one of the country's leading and most influential right-wing parties with significant representation in both houses of Congress. The central preoccupation of this study will therefore center on the question of how the *gremialistas* and the right in general, politically dominant in a time of authoritarianism, have adapted both to functioning within a democratic framework and as a "loyal" opposition. This is an important question given that the right, and the *gremialistas* in particular, was the dominant civilian force in policy implementation within an authoritarian political system (1973–1990). This work will thus not only analyze the origins, development, and achievements of the *gremialista* movement, but examine the role of the right as a whole during the democratic transition and consolidation process.

THE IDEOLOGICAL AND POLITICAL ORIGINS OF THE *GREMIALISTA* MOVEMENT

The ideological origins of the *gremialistas* lie with the most integrationist versions of social Catholic thought, in particular the French and Spanish traditionalists of the nineteenth century, whose main exponents were Vasquez de Mella and

Donoso Cortez in Spain and De Maistre and De Bonald in France. Its principal *criollo* source of ideological inspiration came from the Chilean philosopher and historian Jaime Eyzaguirre, one of the foremost intellectual representatives of mid-twentieth century conservative thought in Chile. Eyzaguirre embraced a traditionalist interpretation of Catholic social doctrine as expressed by the papal encyclicals of Leo XIII and Pius XI, and promoted a corporatist political schema similar to the fascist organizational project of regimes such as Salazar's Portugal and Franco's Spain.

The *gremialistas* emerged as an organized movement among law students at the prestigious Catholic University in Santiago in the mid-1960s, under the tutelage of Jaime Guzmán, a law lecturer at the university, who became the movement's spiritual, ideological, and political leader. The *gremialista* movement was born out of a desire to promote and encourage a wide-ranging process of university reform and to channel such reforms through nonpolitical student federations, in accordance with the corporatist thesis of depoliticized intermediary organizations. In particular, the *gremialistas* sought to challenge the university reform program proposed by the Christian Democrat administration of President Eduardo Frei, which sought to "popularize" Chile's elitist system of higher education.

The *Movimiento Gremial de la Cátolica* became an official entity in March 1967 following the publication of its Declaration of Principles. The document stressed that the "nature" of universities was alien to any ideological or political conceptions of society and that universities possessed their own specific objectives that were both universal and permanent. In this way, the movement sought to depoliticize higher education.[1] While professing to be a university movement inspired simply by a student-focused ideology, the *gremialista* doctrine went far beyond these purely parochial concerns.

Guzmán developed a modern interpretation of archaic corporatist dogma. His principal premise stemmed from the belief of man as a dignified and transcendental entity whose nature was superior to that of society's. According to Guzmán, man is ontologically superior to society given that, while temporal societies disappear through time, man not only exists within it, but transcends it. Therefore, society is at the service of man and not vice versa. The recognition of man as the axis of all societal action led Guzmán to conclude that the multiple societies that man creates between the family and the state (to secure his full spiritual and material development) should be respected as a sign of the "sociable" nature of man and his right to create various associations with the objectives as outlined above. Although the family is the basic cell of society, it does not satisfy all the requirement's of man's sociability. The groupings that tie individuals, for reasons of proximity and work, emerge due to their functions in terms of complementarity and variety. Because they are larger than the family and smaller than the state they are referred to as "intermediary organizations," and include social groupings such as trade unions, student federations, professional associations, and business guilds (*gremios*).

Guzmán promoted the notion that social autonomy was the basic principle of a free society. Each intermediary organization has the ability to achieve its own specific objectives and so should be given the autonomy to do so. As the concept of governance entails the attempt by a community to achieve its specific goals, this autonomy extends only to a group's precise aims and objectives. This concept of social autonomy is today better known as subsidiarity. Guzmán argued that if all intermediary organizations were to benefit from this autonomy, it was improper for another society, superior to it, such as the state, to assume what an organization lower down the scale could do for itself. The state exists to administer those areas that individuals cannot adequately perform for themselves, such as foreign affairs and defense. Moreover, Guzmán rejected the politicization of these nonpolitical intermediary organizations on the grounds that it "denaturalized" their objectives; politicization limits a group's autonomy, thereby weakening one of the fundamental pillars of a free society.[2]

The August 1967 student occupation of the Catholic University marked the single most important turning point for the *gremialista* movement during this period. The Christian Democrat-dominated *Federación Estudiantil de la Universidad Cátolica* (FEUC) organized the occupation in protest at the university's reactionary position vis-à-vis Frei's educational reform program. The *gremialistas* thus made their mark as the most vociferous opponents of the FEUC position. Their campaign against the occupation, together with their populist antiparty line, enabled the *gremialistas* to win the FEUC presidency for the first time in October 1968. This enabled the movement to garner campus-wide support, extending its web of influence far beyond the myopic and privileged ivory towers of the law faculty. The *gremialistas* soon took control of a significant number of student unions around the country.

Their oppositional activities during the Allende Popular Unity government ensured that their realm of influence far exceeded their origins as a student-based movement.[3] The FEUC, headed in 1973 by the *gremialista* Javier Leturia, transformed the Catholic University into the symbol and bastion of right-wing opposition to the Allende government. In an attempt to qualify their overtly political opposition to the administration, the *gremialistas* strove to situate it within a specific student context. Yet their support for striking miners, providing them with safe houses within the university campus, and their mobilization of the first national demonstration against the government, revealed the extent to which they were prepared to go in securing its defeat. Revealingly, in June 1973, Leturia published an open letter in the right-wing establishment newspaper, *El Mercurio*, demanding Allende's resignation. By the time of the 1972 insurrectional strike, the *gremialistas* had become the principal mass organizer, mobilizing the middle and various popular sectors in opposition to the government.

THE *GREMIALISTAS* AND THE 1973 MILITARY COUP

Following the coup, *gremialismo* began to organize through linked yet autonomous groups. Many of its followers occupied various legislative and politically related government posts. Moreover, the *gremialista* concept of subsidiarity played an increasingly important part within the regime's ideological base, with "liberty" defined in opposition to the concentration of power in the hands of the state. Subsidiarity was thus used to justify the dismantling of the state apparatus. As a counterweight to this liberal interpretation of subsidiarity, the *gremialistas* developed the concept of *poder social*. Consisting of the intermediary organizations, the *poder social* would protect the freedom of the citizen, thereby safeguarding the autonomy of civil society and acting as an instrument of support for the state. In this way, the military government sought to substitute the Western liberal ideals of participation and representation with those of *gremialismo*.

Why did the military choose to adopt this archaic strain of thought? First, because the Catholic component within it conferred Christian legitimacy, an ethical basis capable of justifying the economic and social transformations imposed by force. Second, the closeness of the movement's members to the increasingly influential neoliberal Chicago Boys economists. Third, it facilitated the attempt to keep together the regime's heterogeneous support coalition. Given its leadership of the anti-Allende coalition, *gremialismo*, more than any other ideology, had succeeded in solidifying this counterrevolutionary group. The increasingly harsh social consequences of the 1975 economic "shock," and the political discontent that invariably ensued as a result, led the military to call on the *gremialistas* to create a movement that would help bring together the regime's civilian supporters. This was an explicit attempt to keep morale high and prevent the erosion of this heterogeneous and fragile coalition. Guzmán was keenly aware of the potential benefits, especially for the *gremialista* movement, of developing a morale-boosting, cadre-building organization. To this end, he devised and organized the *Frente Juvenil de Unidad Nacional* in 1976 along *gremialista*-structured lines.

Although the *Frente* failed as a mass movement, it succeeded in grooming and molding young *gremialista* leaders in readiness to occupy the many, and increasingly powerful, posts in the municipalities.[4] The *gremialistas* built their power base within the realm of local government, through their stranglehold on key public administration posts. This was a new generation, lacking the necessary pre-1973 political experience. They were young ideologues, socialized within the authoritarian regime, who were, in essence, the right's new and dynamic political generation. As the municipalities were given ever increasing responsibilities, the political power of these barely postadolescent *gremialista* administrators became wide-ranging, covering areas such as health, education, and welfare. Appointed by *Junta* leader General Augusto Pinochet himself, they provided the regime with an invaluable source of ideological coherence and control.

IDEOLOGICAL FUSION: THE CHICAGO BOYS AND THE NEOLIBERALIZATION OF THE *GREMIALISTAS*

The ties of personal solidarity that developed between the neoliberal Chicago Boy economists, who became the dominant economic expression of the military regime, and the *gremialistas*, and the influence of *gremialismo* over a predominantly conservative and antipolitical economics faculty, created the foundations that facilitated a process of reciprocal influence. As an elitist movement, the Chicago Boys developed their cadre base at the economics faculty of the Catholic University. This was accomplished through the successful screening and control of both the economists and students involved within the faculty. Through the unreserved and systematic use of terror and intimidation, the state apparatus, with the tacit consent of the Chicago Boys, marginalized and barred from academia many of those who opposed the ideas and practical consequences of the economic model. In the same way that the *gremialistas* began to increase their control of public and political life through the manipulation of the municipalities, so the monetarist technocrats guaranteed future docile public administrators and economists for the regime through their control of the universities and their relevant faculties.

The first signs of this process of mutual ideological insemination became more apparent during the government of Popular Unity, during which the *gremialistas'* defense of the *poder social* and the autonomy of the intermediary organizations were picked up by the neoliberals. The Chicago Boys believed it would infuse an ideologically maligned entrepreneurial movement with the necessary global discourse. The Chicago Boys soon absorbed the nonliberal notion of the "subsidiary state," as denunciations of statism and the market as the basis of a free society were picked up by the *gremialistas,* who had few qualms about adopting "the invisible hand of the market" to execute the "common good." The most important aspect of this association was the bond that the liberal technocrats forged with an ideological group that rejected liberal democracy on doctrinarian grounds.[5] In the face of the democratic advances and statist leanings of Allende's socialism, the emphasis that the *gremialistas* placed on the alternative organizations of civil society over the base of nonpoliticized intermediary organizations found an echo in the apoliticism and antistatism of neoliberalism and its strong critique of democratic constructivism.

The Chicago Boy's thesis that the state's redistributive pretenses must be removed, otherwise it would create an artificial social order that would dominate and suffocate the spontaneous order that individual action generates, enabled the *gremialistas* to converge with neoliberalism. Both groups endorsed the notion of a naturally spontaneous order while the neoliberals readily recognized the concept of subsidiarity. This entailed the silencing of fundamental corporatist ideals, such as the more detailed proposals of a corporatist regime, including the economic role assumed by the state, the moral regime of the economy and social justice, and its critique of liberalism. Yet their shared anticonstructivism had different origins. The *gremialistas* held communitarian ideals in which man was perceived as a social being. Neoliberalism, on the other hand, is individualist, in which man is perceived as an independent and free individual. The market, and not the family or the natural intermediary organization, is the social paradigm par excellence.

The economists needed an all-encompassing ideology with which to justify a rather uninspiring technical and economic revolution. The *gremialistas'* corporatist rhetoric and "florid" ideology provided just the right combination of mysticism and authoritarianism to an economic plan that had no apparent moral attraction nor justification. The *gremialistas* lacked the economic sophistication with which to launch their own specific revolution. Abandoning the impractical elements inherent in economic corporatism in favor of neoliberalism was a necessary compromise. By attaching themselves to the liberal technocrats, the *gremialistas* discerned a monumental opportunity to carry out the political and social elements of their ideology.

Given the success of the neoliberal economic model, the *gremialistas* were thus forced to abandon the remaining vestiges of their corporatist habits. As these became increasingly incompatible with the growingly radical liberalism of the political economy, the *gremialistas* were left without a coherent political vision with which to justify the *revolución capitalista* to which they now adhered. Neoliberalism was able to fill the *gremialista* ideological void. It provided the movement with a global vision of society that satisfied both the anti-interventionism and the depoliticizing elements of the initial *gremialista* project. There was now a reinterpretation of subsidiarity and the once sacrosanct intermediary bodies. These were now scornfully accused of monopolistic and oligarchic tendencies. It was now up to individuals to defend freedom and not the *gremio*, the neighborhood group, or the trade union. This spectacular volte face was justified by the assertion that these groups had, in the face of an omnipotent state, been necessary. As this type of state was no longer a reality, the intermediary organizations had become an irrelevant anachronism. Although the general rhetoric used by the regime still breathed the air of traditional *gremialismo*, the actual substance did not. Guzmán was keenly aware of the unfeasibility of corporatism within a world order that abhorred both the state and any form of collective organization.

After 1977, the demands for political reform became increasingly strong and technical justifications were no longer sufficient. There was an urgent need to develop an ideology that could globalize the problems of both the political and the economic spheres of national life. This became the raison d'être of the neoliberalized *gremialista* movement, which now espoused the mercantile-individualism of Hayek and Friedman rather than the Catholic-inspired integrationist concepts of thinkers such as Eyzaguirre, although at a rhetorical level it remained unchanged, thus enabling it to continue as a force to legitimize and justify the regime and its program.

With the introduction of so-called Seven Modernizations in the late 1970s, covering labor, pensions, education, health, agriculture, justice, and regionalization, the revolutionary dimensions of the neoliberal project began to permeate into all aspects of Chilean society. The modernization's had, as a common objective, the infusion of market forces into the country's social relations network. It involved the extension of subsidiarity into noneconomic spheres with the official aim of ensuring efficiency and rationality in decision-making, expanding equality of opportunity, and increasing the limits of individual freedom to cover all aspects of everyday life. The reforms involved the decentralization of public institutions so as to place much of their responsibility in the hands of the private sector. This would allow market decision-making to operate, thereby guaranteeing freedom of choice in the provision and access to basic social services. This was vindicated as necessary to free the individual from the monopolistic *gremio* and trade union, stimulate efficiency and progress by submitting individuals' decisions to the logic of the market, and by transferring responsibility for social services from an inefficient state to a dynamic private sector.

The 1980 Constitution, which reflected *gremialista* thinking almost in its entirety, served to provide the political and legal assurances needed to ensure the permanence of the neoliberal model.[6] While no longer advocating corporatist forms of representation, the *gremialistas* continued to distrust universal suffrage, but were forced to accept it as an option of *mal menor*. In recognizing this, they proposed to set up a protected democracy to prevent the rise of totalitarianism, statism and demagogy. Universal suffrage would become the predominant, but not the exclusive, method of generating political authority. Moreover, universal suffrage would have to recognize and respect the essential values of *chilenidad* defined as dignity of the human person, the family as the basic nucleus of society, social integration in opposition to the class struggle, the state as objective and impersonal and—maintaining *gremialista* rhetoric—the autonomy of intermediary groups. The constitution thus limited universal suffrage to the election of the president, the deputies, and two-thirds of the Senate. The remaining one-third would be nominated by the military and a number of nonelected institutions.

The *gremialistas* also wished to create an institutional framework for what they called the "responsible and constructive exercising of universal suffrage."[7] The concentration of political power is therefore an underlying feature of the Constitution. In placing very little power in the hands of the legislature, the regime chose to concentrate this faculty in the hands of the president. Parliaments were deemed the source of all that had gone wrong with pre-1973 Chile. Moreover, the *gremialistas* wished to establish a number designated institutional bodies that would safeguard the contents of a future constitution against the possible demagogic and populist tendencies of elected government. The military would play a crucial role acting as guardians of the *institucionalidad* with majority representation in the proposed quangos as well as extra powers that would place it in a virtually autonomous position vis-à-vis the government. The constitution, therefore, removed the source of power from elected representatives placing it in the hands of unelected and unaccountable military-dominated bodies.

FROM MOVEMENT TO PARTY: THE INDEPENDENT DEMOCRATIC UNION

The failure of the neoliberal model to resolve the problems of growth, investment, employment, and an increasingly unjust distribution of national income had been obscured until 1981 by apparent success according to certain indicators publicized by the government and, above all, by an international economic situation that allowed an excessive flow of foreign capital into Chile. The collapse of this financial system, combined with the dogmatism and incompetence of the economic team, laid bare the profound weaknesses hidden beneath the triumphant official discourse. What had been called the "Chilean miracle" showed its true face: increasing economic concentration in the hands of a few groups engaged in irresponsible plundering and speculative manipulation, one of the highest external debts in the world, destruction of national means of production, acute economic stagnation, 30 percent unemployment, and the lack of an economic project with solid investment bases for the future.[8]

The first signs of mass popular discontent were expressed in May 1983. The government made no political response to this crisis until August 1983, when it named the moderate nationalist leader, Sergio Onofre Jarpa, as interior minister. Jarpa's plan consisted of opening up a dialogue with the democratic opposition and replacing the neoliberal economic team with a more pragmatic and flexible group. His aim was to decompress political tensions rather than carry out more wholesale liberalization. Although Jarpa's strategy failed, it did have one significant effect: the de facto creation of a series of political parties that were still illegal but were now tolerated. The economic crisis, the protests, and the government's response had shown that an accommodation with opponents of the regime was not a viable option. The right now realized that the system could not be fine-tuned, and so sought to adapt and mobilize, via political parties, to ensure the survival of the regime's principal accomplishments.

Despite their self-professed distaste for political parties, the *gremialistas* and other representatives of the bureaucratic technocracy of the military regime set up the Independent Democratic Union (UDI) in August 1983. Although politically and socially conservative, the party represents the most extreme form of neoliberalism. It is classified as an urban right, economically modern but at the same time paternalistic and authoritarian, representing those most loyal to the military re-gime's economic and political model. Despite its claims to be an independent movement, UDI was, and still is, the party most closely associated with the military government; an attempt by Guzmán and his followers to secure the prolongation of the regime's "achievements" in a postmilitary Chile.

Several features characterize UDI and its leadership, which, rather than ideology itself, have largely differentiated the party from other right-wing forces. First, the leadership is drawn almost exclusively from former Catholic University law student activists. Second, the party is generational in its composition with UDI's hard-core activists drawn almost exclusively from the 35–45 age bracket, corresponding to Guzmán's tutelage of the Catholic University's law faculty during the military period. Third, most of the leadership gained valuable political experience in the municipalities or other government departments during the military government. This intrinsic relationship between UDI and the previous regime has played an important part in its continued adherence to the military government in general, and to Pinochet specifically. Fourth, UDI is highly religious, with Catholicism playing a fundamental part in the party's development. However, unlike the now-defunct Conservative party, its Catholicism is integrationist rather than confessional, and the party, unlike the Conservatives, does not have the backing of the Chilean

Catholic church, given its implicit responsibility in human rights abuses. UDI does however have close links to the conservative Catholic *Opus Dei* movement, founded in Spain in 1928 by the Spanish Bishop Jose María Escrivá de Balaguer. Fifth, the party has been marked by its extreme homogeneity reflecting in part its evolutionary process as a movement and party. The fact that virtually the totality of its leadership emanates from a very tightly knit sector grouped around Guzmán's "mystical" leadership has infused UDI with a high degree of discipline that is difficult to find outside Leninist-structured organizations.[9]

UDI is an elite-based, cadre organization and it has systematically failed to develop a national and regional organizational structure necessary for the successful development of a modern, Western-style political party.[10] It recognizes itself to be an organically organized, *Falangist*-style movement that seeks to "cut across society" and represent all social sectors.[11] The party has therefore sought to represent society "vertically" rather than "horizontally": to represent the views of the whole of society rather than promote the aspirations of one particular class or determined economic interests. Consequently, UDI claims to be a popular party, seeking to displace the left as the traditional standard bearers of the urban working class.[12] It is most active in those areas where, through the manipulation of municipal structures, it succeeded in building a clientelistic network of supporters. As such, UDI has been most successful at the local level, with most of its activity concentrated in the urban working-class areas and the *poblaciones*, centers traditionally associated with the left, and particularly the Communist party. UDI has sought to create as many neighborhood groups as possible, in many instances setting up rival organizations to compete with those that it has been unable to infiltrate successfully. The party has also stressed the role of Mothers' Centers, whose role is to set up support schemes and training in issues such as welfare, with youth clubs and sporting centers also targeted. This *blitzkrieg* on working-class local organizations is intended to deliver *una llegada rápida a las personas*, and the party admits that it has cloned this strategy from both the Christian Democrats and the Communists, UDI's main electoral competitors in the *poblaciones*.

UDI is also a hierarchical party with strong central control and internal unity based on the authority of its leaders. It has therefore sought to develop popular roots different from those associated with mass-based parties, where there exists a feedback between the leadership and the mass. UDI has instead sought to ferment its ideology on the mass. As such, it has a longer-term perspective than other political parties. Like the Communist party, UDI is seeking to convert prospective sympathizers rather than engage in a game of interaction between the leadership and the mass, in which there is only partial commitment to the party. UDI is therefore seeking *un lazo de compromiso más fuerte* exactly because it wishes to convert these individuals; to become members of UDI's ideology and to articulate it within a very coherent organization.[13] It lacks what can be regarded as a modern party machine and has as yet to developed a nationwide presence. It is this amateurish approach to party politics that marks it out from other mainstream parties. The formalization of party activity is anathema to it. With Guzmán as supreme leader there was no need to develop a complex and modern party machine. He created a made-to-measure party of former colleagues and students that organized themselves around him. Guzmán created the doctrine, the strategic changes, the tactical shifts, and the designation of key posts. He thus created a homogeneous machine, capable of standing up to the many radical twists of the transition process.

Guzmán's assassination by left-wing terrorists in April 1991 led to several important developments within the party. UDI experienced a mass increase in its membership, owing to a wave of public sympathy. Moreover, several important independent right-wing personalities, not previously associated either with UDI or the *gremialista* movement, joined the party in solidarity, including the former Pinochet minister, José Piñera, and the former presidential candidate, Hernán Büchi. This allowed the party to claim that it now included the principal architects of the military regime's revolutionary program. Although some welcomed this expansion in membership, and especially the incorporation of prominent liberal figures, most felt uneasy given that most of the new recruits were not from the *gremialista* tradition. Indeed, this could in the long term undermine the party's strategy to become a popular, mass-based Christian party, in the same tradition as the Christian Democrats. The new recruits threaten the homogeneous nature of UDI, especially its generational element, which has so far acted as an ideological adhesive. However, Guzmán's legacy so far remains intact. The party's leaders have remained in those posts that Guzmán created for them during the movement's inception. As such, the new neoliberal members of the party have been unable to take up key positions and many have left as a result.

ELECTORAL EFFECTIVENESS

Traditionally, the right in Chile has never felt at ease with electoral politics. The lack of party institutionalization and the informal power networks it had nurtured and developed over decades, as well as its fear of fermenting mass mobilization, has left it unable, and often unwilling, to participate fully in the democratic process. This suspicion of Western liberal democracy became evident in the immediate post-coup period, when it readily abandoned even its formal adherence to Chile's party political system and to any semblance of democratic forms of representation. The economic crisis of 1981–1983 and the subsequent political difficulties that engulfed the military regime demonstrated that the institutional status quo would not endure. Consequently, the right arrived at the conclusion that electoral politics would once again become a reality in Chilean politics. A central preoccupation has therefore centered around the question of the degree to which the right has been able and willing to insert itself into this nascent democratic framework.

The role of the nonparty right, most notably, the economic conglomerates, entrepreneurs, the media, and the military in right-wing party politics has been a vexing issue for decades. The right's institutional weakness has forced it, rather willingly, to rely on forces outside the party structures. This has severely weakened the sector's attempts to strengthen the role of political parties. UDI has persistently supported the right of nonparty sectors within the right to "interfere" in party activity, not only because of ideological considerations, but more importantly because the party enjoys the overwhelming support of these individuals and groups. The lack of a party political culture within the right becomes all too evident during electoral campaigning. The involvement of nonparty activists, almost exclusively hostile to, and ignorant of, the rules of the democratic game, have resulted in UDI adopting a relatively amateurish approach to politics. The nod-and-a-wink approach has been adopted to the detriment of modern and professional techniques. The institutionalization of the party right has been hampered as a result. Moreover, the absence of a historical democratic party trajectory has resulted in a right that is both politically immature and lacking in confidence.

Although the right has failed to elect a president from the sector in both the 1989 and 1993 polls, and remains in opposition at the parliamentary level, its electoral performance has far outweighed the expectations of not only its many critics, but of the right itself.[14] In the 1989 presidential elections, the candidate of the then center-left opposition coalition, Patricio Aylwin, won in the first round with 55.17 percent of the vote. The candidate of the right, the independent technocrat Hernán Büchi, supported ostensibly by UDI and the moderate National Renewal (RN), now the largest right-wing party, trailed on 29.40 percent, while the independent center-right populist candidate, Francisco Javier Errázuriz, obtained 15.43 percent of the popular vote.[15] The results in 1993 followed a similar trend with the candidate of what was now the center-left government coalition (the *Concertación*), Eduardo Frei, obtaining an even clearer majority with 58.1 percent. The right's candidate, again an independent, Arturo Alessandri, obtained only 24.39 percent, while the maverick right-wing former minister and former UDI activist, José Piñera, trailed on 6.18 percent.[16]

The right's parliamentary performance proved more successful both in 1989 and 1993. In the 1989 congressional elections, the right-wing pact *Democracia y Progreso*, made up of UDI and RN, obtained 34.18 percent of the vote in the lower house elections, while the center-left *Concertación* won 51.48 percent of the vote. RN emerged as the larger of the two principal right-wing parties with 18 percent of the vote to UDI's 10 percent.[17] In terms of seat distribution, the Christian Democrats (PDC) emerged by far as the largest party in the Chamber of Deputies with 38 representatives. RN became the second largest with 29, followed by the center-left party for Democracy (PPD) on 17, UDI (11) and the Socialist party (4).[18] In the senate, the PDC obtained 13 seats, RN 6, the PPD 4, and UDI 2.[19] The 1993 congressional results were very similar to those in the previous election. The *Unión Progreso de Chile* pact, again bringing together the principal parties of the right, obtained 33.7 percent of the vote (the right as a whole, including competing lists and other independents, won nearly 37 percent) to the *Concertación's* 55.42 percent. Within the pact itself, RN obtained 16.23 percent and UDI 12.11 percent (right-wing independents won 4.8 percent while Errázuriz's populist vehicle, the Center Center Union (UCC) obtained 3.19 percent). There were only slight changes in terms of parliamentary seat distribution with the PDC again emerging as the largest party in the Chamber of Deputies with 37 seats. RN maintained its position as the second largest political force with 29 seats, while UDI and the PPD both increased their number of deputies to 15, while the Socialist party dropped its level of representation to 15 deputies. In the Senate, where only a proportion (9) of the seats were being contested, the PDC ended up with 13 seats, RN with 11, the Socialist party with 5, UDI with 3, and the PPD with 2.[20]

UDI's limited organizational capacity has prevented it from penetrating both the north and south of the country, with its northernmost deputy representing Valparaiso/Isla de Pascua and its southernmost Los Angeles/Mulchen, both within a relatively short driving distance from the capital. Moreover, in the 4 northern contests in which both parties competed against each other, RN won 3 and UDI 1. The party did not present even one candidate in the 2 most southern regions. UDI did elect 5 deputies in the central-south region, but these have generally surfaced in districts where its candidates are locally known figures or in urban centers, such as Los Angeles and San Fernando. Its strength clearly lies in the industrialized central core region. It has performed spectacularly well in both the wealthiest and poorest urban districts, especially in the capital. It polled more than any other party in Santiago's wealthiest suburb, Las Condes/Vitacura (35 percent) and in very poor urban areas, with high concentrations of *poblaciones*, where it relegated RN's vote to single percentage figures, including the Santiago districts of San Bernardo/Paine (32 percent to RN's 8) and Melipilla/Peñaflor (33 percent to RN's 6). UDI also elected deputies to the Greater Santiago working-class districts of Colina/Pudahuel (29 percent), Recoleta/Independencia (25 percent), Macul/La Granja (27 percent), El Bosque/La Cisterna (28 percent), and San Miguel/Lo Espejo (23 percent). UDI has performed well in the upper-class suburbs of Santiago because its political rhetoric and style, its total commitment to the free market model and the reputation of its candidates as faithful and capable civil servants under the Pinochet administration echoes well with the most privileged sectors of Chilean society.

Although the *poblaciones* continue to represent fertile ground for the PDC and the left, UDI's electoral penetration in these areas has been remarkable. While its general level of support continues to be lower than that achieved by its ideological opponents, the party has succeeded in obtaining parliamentary representation in areas previously thought of as anathema to the right. This demonstrates the existence of a popular right, unafraid and knowledgeable about utilizing political techniques more commonly associated with the radical left, primarily the Communist party. It reflects the ideologically inspired work carried out by *gremialista* administrators in these working-class areas during the military regime. It also marks the successful development of clientelistic networks and relationships that have delivered to UDI a significant portion of the urban working class.

Although the bulk of right-wing support has come from urban areas with relatively high standards of living, and the right is rooted in the financial, industrial, and agricultural elites of the country, the sector has actively sought, and to some extent succeeded, in attracting sectors not normally associated with the right. The problematic for RN and UDI, however, is that it has had to hand-tailor its political rhetoric and style to suit its respective and more often than not mutually exclusive, non-core constituencies. This has invariably led to the development of two very different right-wing parties that are both responsive to very different audiences. This may inevitably make coexistence very difficult, but because of the political and electoral legacy of the military regime, of which they were to varying degrees a part of, coexistence, if not often peaceful, may prove the only viable and realistic electoral option for the right. Despite these problems, the right's electoral performance has been both relatively strong and stable, especially given the difficulties inherent in competing with such a solid political grouping as the *Concertación*. Moreover, the fact that the sector is divided into two, very different parties may have even helped boost its electoral representation. Each represents very distinct social and political sectors and ideological positions that may have been lost to other political groupings if the right were to be represented by a single monolithic movement.

Why was RN and even UDI's performance so impressive considering the circumstances? Part of this, of course, can be explained by the Pinochet-inspired electoral system that exaggerated the right's electoral support while underestimating that of the center-left coalition. With a fairer system it seems unlikely that UDI would have obtained any seats in the Senate and much fewer in the Chamber of Deputies. The right's clientelistic approach is also an important factor, especially among UDI politicans. While an important proportion of the population has traditionally supported right-wing candidates it cannot account for the scale of their 1989 and 1993 vote. It is therefore reasonable to suppose that the regime's process of decentralization, at the municipal level, of public services such as education, health, housing, and subsidies for the poorest, combined with a structure of limited participation, would have provided the right with a powerful clientelistic network among the country's popular and lower-middle classes. It is no coincidence that many of the regime's young, former mayors, notably *gremialistas*, obtained good electoral results in popular urban areas. Finally, in the 1989 election at least many still feared the consequences of an opposition government. The military regime's electoral campaign attempted to maximize these fears and in some respects it seems to have been successful. Pinochet's strategy was made all the easier by the economic boom that Chile had experienced since 1985, which appeared all the more spectacular when set against the 1981–1983 recession. The subsequent economic growth after 1990 does not seem to have had much effect on the electoral core of the right, at least at the congressional and municipal level. This suggests that there is in Chile a solid block of the electorate loyal to the right: a political subculture of the right, historically rooted, and not susceptible to the attractions of the other political parties.

PARTY POLICY: IS UDI A DEMOCRATIC PARTY?

UDI's position vis-à-vis a number of defining domestic political issues enable us adequately to assess to what degree it feels an inherent bond with Western-style liberal democratic system. Since the initiation of the transition process, political debate in Chile has focused on three principal issues: civil-military relations, the violation of human rights, and constitutional reform. Moreover, the successful resolution of these three key areas will determine the real success of the democratic transition and consolidation process.

Civil-Military Relations

The 1980 Constitution set up a "protected democracy" under the tutelage of the armed forces. As such, considerable political power lies in the hands of the military, whose high degree of autonomy would be deemed unacceptable in any Western liberal democracy. The commanders-in-chief have tenure during their term of office and responsibility for selecting, promoting, and retiring military officers. They are also voting members of the all-powerful National Security Council and each names one of the nine designated Senators. It is not surprising that UDI's stance toward the military is both uncompromising and unambiguous and the party does not disguise its ambition to become a civilian alternative to the military regime. UDI has intrinsic links with the military and through Guzmán, liaised, although unofficially, with the institution.

The party's close relationship with the military is played out symbolically every September 11, the anniversary of the 1973 coup, when party activists organize visits to army units and its leaders pay public homage to the *Junta* members. Moreover, crowds of UDI supporters, bussed in from the *poblaciones*, gather outside Pinochet's house to proclaim their loyalty, while wealthy, and principally young, sympathizers organize motorized calvacades around the streets of uptown Santiago and the UDI hierarchy attends the various celebrations organized by the military high command. This annual civic-military operation has sought to regroup the *fuerzas leales* that were dispersed by the electoral defeats of 1989 and 1993, as well as by the 1988 plebiscite that opened the way for contested democratic elections. The ultimate aim of this *cabal* is to bring together Pinochet, his civilian supporters, and those military officers who make up the general's praetorian guard. The military component revolves around the figure of Pinochet, while the civilian element is orchestrated by UDI in its capacity as the *derecha cuartelera*. The unambiguous link with the military helps to reinforce UDI's antiparty posture, one of its defining characteristics. However, political parties, within a democratic framework, should not act as the civilian representatives of the armed forces. This lack of political independence has hindered UDI in terms of developing a modern and efficient party structure. Moreover, it has led UDI to act as spokesperson and unquestioning defender of the military. This explains the party's dogmatic reluctance to consider the possibility of negotiating reform of even the most uncontroversial and undemocratic elements of the constitution's military articles and the Organic Law of the Armed Forces.

Human Rights

The 1978 Amnesty Law, passed by the armed forces, granted an amnesty to all military personnel who had committed acts of violence between 1973 and 1978, the period in which most human rights violations were perpetrated.[21] In an attempt to redress the balance in favor of the victims of these violations, the government of President Patricio Aylwin set up the Commission of Truth and Reconciliation (the Rettig Commission), which aimed to investigate all human rights abuses that had resulted in death between September 11, 1973 and March 11, 1990, dates when the military transferred power to the civilian authorities.

UDI has adopted a particularly hard-line and uncompromising stance toward the issue of human rights violations. This does not only stem from its unquestioning support for the military regime but is the result of its particular interpretation of human rights. It recognizes that certain personal rights can be restricted by the political authorities during what it calls *régimenes de excepción*, ostensibly during disturbances that threaten the stability of a particular nation. Moreover, the party supports the notion that there exists a hierarchy of rights. It is therefore justifiable to violate certain "lesser" rights in the defense of other more important rights. Although UDI has reiterated its support for the investigation of abuses committed after 1978, it has stated that officers bear individual responsibility and that the armed forces should not be involved as an institution. Moreover, the party has been consistently luke warm in its support for investigating post-amnesty violations as well as those that occurred prior to 1978, but are not covered by the amnesty law.

Constitutional Reform

UDI perceives the 1980 Constitution as the legislative embodiment of the military regime and as the principal mechanism for defending Pinochet's political, economic, and social legacy. It is the fundamental sacred cow, the ultimate and defining benchmark by which loyalty to the *ancien régime* is gauged. Its loyalty to the constitution is compounded by the fact that Guzmán played an instrumental ideological and political role in its creation. The constitution was a *gremialista* creation and as such it symbolizes the movement's fundamental principles and values. UDI's position vis-à-vis the constitution is therefore both highly emotional and uncompromising. The party has categorically rejected the possibility of further reform and has dogmatically refused to discuss the prospect of any future modifications.

CONCLUSIONS: PROSPECTS FOR THE RIGHT

Although the right as a whole has been relatively successful electorally, many factors continue to work against it. Until these issues are addressed, the right may be unable to expand its current levels of support. The sector, especially UDI, still lacks a well-established and fully democratic party political culture. This has led it to adopt various positions that have contributed to its ineffectiveness as a political and electoral force. At the most fundamental level, the sector has still not shed its traditional strategy of *mal menor*. This not only resulted in its support for the PDC presidential candidacy of Eduardo Frei in 1964, rather than its own option, but in its unconditional support for Pinochet. This fear of being *desplazada* by competing electoral forces may continue to force it to rely on seemingly attractive, quick-fix, independent personalities to rescue it from possible electoral oblivion. This lack of a party political tradition has prevented the right from uncovering a natural party leader capable of representing the sector at a national level and to unite it around a single programatic banner.[22] Since the return to democracy in 1990, the right, as in the past, has sought out "providential" leaders who can wave a magic wand but who invariably fail to deliver. The right, notably UDI, has thus for too long relied on figures whose importance lie outside the political parties. The entrepreneurial sector, the large economic and financial conglomerates (the economic groups), and the right-wing media have been unwilling to respect the political autonomy of the parties to which they adhere.

The absence of a well-defined and stable democratic political culture has had serious organizational and strategic repercussions for the right, not only in terms of its parliamentary oppositional activities, but within the parties themselves and in relations with each other. RN and UDI have not overcome their long-standing differences, which in many respects have proven significantly more fundamental than those that affected the "unrenovated" left until the mid-1980s. The post–cold war socialist parties at least share a common political agenda. They are also not divided in terms of the past (the legacy of the military regime). The parties on the right are ideologically similar. However, their political and strategic differences are enormous. They do not possess a common history nor do they share a common perception about the fundamental nature of democratic institutions, most notably what role the parties should play in the new democratic order. Moreover, their animosity is rooted at the most personal level: they simply do not like each other. They are also divided by their vision of the past, most importantly by disagreements over the level of loyalty that both should express toward the political and economic legacy of the military regime.[23] This has severely weakened its capacity to become an effective oppositional force. The right has thus been unable to create a consistent oppositional model. In Congress, it has failed to develop an efficient and solid scheme while the Aylwin and Frei governments have been successful in weakening the parliamentary right through a strategy of divide and rule. The performance of its parliamentarians, especially those from RN, has been divisive and ineffective. RN and UDI parliamentarians are all too ready to hammer out deals with the center-left coalition in an attempt to undermine their sectoral opponents. This has not only facilitated the government's divide-and-rule strategy but has highlighted the immature nature of right-wing parliamentary politics.

The right has also failed to establish a cultural dialogue since the collapse of the Berlin wall. The right has always acted reactively when threatened. This is how its various tendencies kept together and dynamic. With the collapse of the Eastern European communist model, the right has no overriding ideological preoccupation, and its components are left squabbling with each other over the minutia of party politics. This has resulted in a failure in its strategy. Both RN and UDI have adopted, as main themes, support for the economic model, personal liberty, security, and efficiency. However, the governing *Concertación* has also taken up these issues and made them their own. The right does not have an alternative project and is relying on being portrayed as the most efficient political sector to carry out these generally accepted ideals.

Pinochet's legacy has therefore been contradictory for the liberal-conservative bloc. On the one hand, the military regime initiated a radical political and socio-economic modernizing project, while on the other it opted to lead by itself in the political arena, thus making the parties redundant. Moreover, Pinochet abandoned power at the precise moment when Chilean and world socialism ceased to be the dangerous bogeyman of the past. However, he left the civilian supporters of the regime without an all-encompassing project and a coherent set of ideals that could propel it toward the future. This has left the right with a sterilizing contradiction that it has been unable to resolve. This is why two competing models now coexist uneasily within the right: a conservative, nationalist, traditional, and moralist right, represented by UDI; and one that perceives itself as liberal, democratic, and modern, exemplified by RN. Moreover, neither project is dominant enough to prevail over the other. This dichotomy, exacerbated by the present need to present large electoral pacts, will continue to act as a double-edged sword for the sector. On the one hand, its electoral representation may well be boosted by the existence of two competing right-wing parties, each able to attract support that the other would find difficult to capture; but on the other, the ensuing debilitating struggles that both have experienced will weaken its prospects of expanding into previously marginal electoral constituencies.

Most on the right privately conceded that the sector would not win either in 1989 or in 1993. Its underlying strategy has therefore been to prevent the possibility of any kind of substantial constitutional reform. The present institutional formula has prevented the full adoption of a democratic system. It includes a series of power instruments that the right needs to maintain: the Supreme Court, the greater autonomy of the armed forces, and several institutions that do not emanate from popular sovereignty that can veto the actions of the legislature and the executive—the designated senators, the Constitutional Tribunal, and the National Security Council. These institutions have given the opposition a level of power far superior to that delegated to it by the electorate. For the right, it is fundamental to maintain these institutional controls. But it has to defend them without weakening its already fragile democratic credentials. This has been the implicit function of the nonparty right. Both RN and UDI have ensured that the most hard-line elements of their political and electoral strategy come from the sectors of civil society that the right controls so as to leave its purely political agents to stress their democratic credentials.

This process of mutual collaboration has compensated for the right's continued inability to function effectively within the party political system and is a further example of the weakness of its party structures. Until this is corrected both UDI and RN will continue to be dominated and undermined by forces outside the parties' structures. This neither help the right expand its current level of electoral support nor help Chile's process of democratic consolidation. Nevertheless, elements within it have made a concerted effort to reinsert the sector into the country's democratic processes fully. Even UDI has until now chosen to function within the fundamental confines of the democratic game. This is a relatively pragmatic new right, which bears little resemblance to the insurrectionist right that existed prior to 1973. It recognizes that authoritarian systems of government are no longer a viable option and that its interests will best be served under a democratic political system, although residual sectors may still be inclined to prefer authoritarian solutions.

NOTES

1. See UDI's Declaration of Principles, 1983.

2. See Jaime Guzmán, *Escritos Personales* (Santiago: Zig-Zag, 1992), pp. 46–53.

3. See *Qué Pasa*, no. 652, 6 October 1983.

4. The movement failed principally because Pinochet was an authoritarian, not a totalitarian, leader and as such was instinctively opposed to any form of political mobilization. Moreover, there was general hostility from the traditional party right, which, although it had voluntarily dissolved its structures, resented any attempt to usurp their influence via nonparty means.

5. See Juan Gabriel Valdés, *La Escuela de Chicago: Operación Chile* (Buenos Aires: Editorial Zeta, 1989), pp. 303–4.

6. Guzmán was head of the military regime's constitutional commission, which since the early 1970s had responsiblity for drawing up an eventual constitution.

7. For an examination of Guzmán's interpretation of universal suffrage see Guzmán "El Sufragio Universal y la Institucionalidad Politica," *Realidad*, no.1 (June, 1979).

8. See Manuel Antonio Garretón, "Mobilization and the Military Regime in Chile: The Complexities of the Invisible Transition," Susan Eckstein (ed.), *Power and Popular Protest: Latin American Social Movements* (Berkeley: University of California Press, 1989), p. 151.

9. A universally common sight in the parliamentary offices of UDI deputies and senators are three photographs, representing the three heroes of the party: Guzmán, Pinochet, and the Pope.

10. Interview with the Santiago-based Guardian journalist Malcolm Coad (14 July 1992).

11. Interview with UDI Senator Eugenio Cantuarias (20 August 1992).

12. Interview with UDI Deputy Carlos Recondo (20 August 1992).

13. Interview with the Chilean political scientist Oscar Godoy (22 July 1992).

14. Its electoral effectiveness has generally been underestimated for three principal reasons. First, the political right represents the civilian legacy of a military regime rejected, although not overwhelmingly, by the civilian population. Although its association with the Pinochet administration has acted as a break to any potential growth, this intrinsic link has not relegated the sector to the fringes of the political system. Second, the lack of strong and well-established party political organizations has, in the past, hindered the right's prospects for electoral growth, most notably at the parliamentary level. In both 1989 and 1993, this deficiency did not prevent it from obtaining levels of parliamentary support far higher than one would have expected. Third, opinion poll data had persistently underestimated the right's

level of support, especially at election time. This helped boost the impression that the sector had performed better than anticipated. This phenomenon can be explained by the general reticence of right-wing supporters, especially in the Chilean context with its laden symbolism: the military regime, publicly to admit their political preferences.

15. *Apsi*, no. 335, 18 December 1989.

16. *La Nación*, 13 December 1993.

17. The apparent shortfall in the overall right-wing figures and those of RN and UDI can be explained by the fact that independents stood both for the parties themselves and within the coalition.

18. Following a series of defections from independent candidates, RN increased its number of deputies to 32 and UDI to 14, while in the Senate RN increased its representation to 13.

19. *Ercilla*, no. 2838, 20 December 1989.

20. For a detailed examination of the 1993 elections, see Alan Angell and Benny Pollack, "The Chilean Elections of 1993: From Polarisation to Consensus," *Bulletin of Latin American Research* 14:2 (May, 1995), pp. 105–25.

21. Around 60 percent of the most serious violations were committed during this period.

22. A majority center-right faction within RN, led by the party president Andrés Allamand, has sought to insert the party into the democratic fold, including the adoption of a presidential candidate from within the party ranks. This modernizing agenda has been vociferously opposed not only by hard-line elements in RN but by UDI.

23. RN has adopted a more independent line vis-à-vis the military, especially its political dimensions. It has, since its inception, sought to distance itself from the military regime, unlike UDI.

chapter 11

El Mercurio's Editorial Page ("La Semana Económica") and Neoliberal Policy Making in Today's Chile

David E. Hojman

INTRODUCTION

El Mercurio is Chile's oldest daily newspaper. It is also well known for its views: conservative in social matters, right-wing in politics, and free-market in economics. The purpose of this chapter is to examine the contents of the economic section of *El Mercurio*'s editorial page, "La Semana Económica" (SE), which is published on Saturdays. One of the aims of the chapter is to assess the extent to which SE has affected the economic policies of the center-left government coalition in the mid 1990s. These policies are largely free-market, open economy ones (neoliberal). The SE contents were examined for a period of slightly over two years, between January 1994 and March 1996. Several questions will be addressed. First, what are the messages that SE is trying to put forward? Second, do the messages change over time? What are the patterns of this change? How are they related to the acquisition of new information? Third, why does SE identify some individuals? The answers to these questions should also help to understand several related issues, such as who are the messages addressed to, what are the messages' objectives, and are the messages successful in achieving their objectives?

HISTORICAL BACKGROUND

El Mercurio was founded in Valparaiso in 1827. Its principal daily edition is now published in Santiago. *El Mercurio* has played a fundamental role in Chile's history for most of this country's independent life. It also occupies a special place in the demonology of the Chilean left: it is the media organ that left-wing militants love to hate. For example, a bitter struggle for university reforms was being fought in the late

1960s. University students who were in favor of reform coined the slogan *"El Mercurio* miente" (*El Mercurio* lies). Perhaps unfairly, given the positive contributions that *El Mercurio* has made to Chile's civic life over many years, this slogan was so powerful that it stuck, and it has now become part of many Chileans' everyday language. *El Mercurio* opposed the socialist program of the Allende government in 1970–1973, and during the rest of the 1970s and 1980s it supported the neoliberal stabilization and liberalization policies of the Pinochet military regime (1973–1990).

What is the role played by *El Mercurio* today? How significant is *El Mercurio* in shaping Chile's contemporary public life? Costly mistakes in interpreting *El Mercurio*'s role have been committed in the past. For instance, many observers, including academics in North America and Europe, failed to predict during the 1980s, first, that the neoliberal economic policies of the Pinochet regime would eventually succeed and, second, that these policies would be adopted by the center-left opposition to the military government, once in office during the 1990s. These academics wrongly believed that the Pinochet economic policies would fail, and that in any case they would be replaced immediately after the restoration of democracy in 1990. As explained below, it is possible that this widespread academic mistake was caused, at least partly, by the fact that many scholars overestimated the role played by *El Mercurio* in the 1970s and 1980s, but they underestimated this role in the 1940s, 1950s, and 1960s.

In order to explain the adoption of neoliberal policies after 1973, a lot of emphasis has been put by academic observers on the influence of Chicago-inspired views that were consistently defended during the 1970s by *El Mercurio*. Possibly because of this excessive emphasis by academic observers, these observers tended to ignore the fact that similar policies had been advocated by substantial sectors of Chile's public opinion for many years before 1973. Had these scholars examined old editions of *El Mercurio* more carefully, going back to the 1940s, 1950s, and 1960s, they would have discovered that many serious objections to the import-sub-stituting model of industrialization had been repeatedly raised by sectors of economic activity with an export vocation, both in traditional and nontraditional areas. This export vocation could not be realized, because excessive protection to many branches of manufacturing was punishing potential exporters with negative effective protection rates.[1] At least part of the reason why the Pinochet neoliberal policies succeeded in the second half of the 1980s, and were then adopted by center-left, democratically elected governments after 1990, is that these policies are a lot less alien to the national character, and their roots in Chile are much deeper, than many observers (especially abroad) believe, or used to believe. *El Mercurio*, representing some significant sectors of Chilean public opinion, had been supporting these policies for at least thirty years before the Pinochet military coup in 1973.

THE THEORETICAL MODEL

In recent decades mathematical economists and game theoreticians have developed a body of results that are quite helpful for purposes of the present discussion.[2]

This material can be generically described as repeated cooperative games, informational lobbying, asymmetric information games, signaling games, and strategic information transmission. In general, these analyses examine the different forms and possibilities of interaction between the sender and the receiver of a strategic message. The sender may be an interest group (for instance, the conglomerate that owns *El Mercurio*), and the receiver may be a policymaker (for example, the experts and economic technocrats who were advising Chile's center-left government coalition in the mid 1990s). The sender and the receiver have their own individual agendas that do not fully coincide. However, there is some overlap between these agendas. Otherwise, no communication would exist. Some important variables to consider in these studies are how much the sender's and the receiver's agendas have in common, the cost of sending the message, how much is at stake for the sender, and what are the receiver's prior beliefs, both about the message subject matter and about the sender.

The sender and the receiver may opt for ignoring each other, or confronting each other, or alternatively they may choose to cooperate, explicitly or more often implicitly. A typical result of these theoretical models is that the joint payoff of cooperation between the sender and the receiver is likely to be greater than the sum of individual payoffs in the absence of cooperation. This is because the sender is interested in preserving her reputation or credibility (and therefore she cannot abuse the receiver's confidence, or at least she cannot abuse it systematically), and the receiver stands to benefit from the message by acquiring some new knowledge about the state of the world. Another interesting result is that under certain conditions, the contents of the message may not be as important as the fact that the message is sent at all, or not. A message may not be transmitting any new information to the receiver, but, if the message is not sent, then the receiver may interpret the sender's silence wrongly.

In the remainder of this chapter, "La Semana Económica" will be the sender, and the policymakers in the center-left government coalition will be the receiver. The expressions "*El Mercurio*," "the editorialist," "La Semana Económica," "SE," and "the sender" will be used interchangeably.

SOME KEY MESSAGES FROM "LA SEMANA ECONÓMICA"

This section is devoted to answering the first question asked in the introduction: what are the messages that SE is trying to put forward? If the central message from SE to the government's policymakers was to be captured in one phrase, it would be: "You are doing well, but you could be doing even better." Within this general good-but-could-be-better framework, or attitude, there are six messages that seem to be of crucial importance to *El Mercurio*'s economic editorialist.

In the rest of this section, the SE views will be in italics.

The Labor Market Must Be Flexible

One of the messages that tends to appear more or less frequently in *El Mercurio* is the importance of flexibility in the labor market. The editorialist opposes increases in the legal minimum wage, she opposes expansion of the Chilean version of the welfare state, and she also opposes a larger role for the Confederation of Trade Unions (*Confederacion Unitaria de Trabajadores*, CUT). In this connection, there is also some emphasis in SE on opposing "excessive" levels of compensation for unemployment or dismissal, and some highlighting of the fact that strikes are now only observed in the public sector. *El Mercurio* also argues that the CUT is not really representative of most workers, but a rather artificial entity supported and inflated by certain government politicians to further their own aims. Another argument that is also often put forward by SE is that in an open economy, the enemy of the employees of any particular firm is no longer their own employer, but rather the firms (both employers and employees) in competing countries.

There is no fundamental disagreement between *El Mercurio* and the government on the question of labor market flexibility. Some politicians in the center-left government coalition are in favor of a much higher profile for organized labor, but they are possibly a small minority.

Taxes Should Be Low

A second message from SE is in favor of lower taxes. This includes *El Mercurio*'s argument that the temporary tax increase of 1990, which became permanent in 1993, was unnecessary, because economic expansion alone would have generated as much in tax revenues as the government was able to spend effectively. Moreover, the editorialist believes that, without the 1990 tax increase, economic growth would have been even faster and tax receipts even larger. *This 1990 tax increase, together with the municipal tax increases in 1994, were both negative because they contributed to discourage productive efforts by the private sector and because they may have increased the danger of corruption.*

According to SE, corruption tends to increase with the scale of state ownership and with the amount of resources administered by the government. *Special, and especially punitive, taxes against particularly successful activities, such as fruit, forestry, or the pension funds, are ill conceived and unacceptable. Taxes should come down. A possible starting point could be to reduce import tariffs* (this is related to the third message from SE, that of increasing the economy's degree of openness toward the rest of the world).

The government is in favor of lower import tariffs. However, the size of the government share in national output is possibly the most fundamental area of disagreement between *El Mercurio* and the government (and between the opposition and the government). The difference has little to do with economic theory. The government simply cannot afford to reduce public expenditure because of political economy reasons: a large number of its natural constituencies depend on government jobs or government support.[3]

The Chilean Economy Should Be More Open to International Trade

SE is emphatic about the fact that openness to international trade is good for Chile. *It does not make any sense to attempt to negotiate bilateral tariff reductions with other countries. Unilateral tariff reductions from the current rate of 11 percent are desirable and urgent. Lower tariffs would reduce the costs of exporters, make it easier to control inflation, and help the poor. Lower tariffs would also contribute to prevent further appreciation of the Chilean currency, the peso.*[4] *In particular, the special tariff surcharges on imports of textiles and clothing and of some agricultural products should disappear.* There is no disagreement between *El Mercurio* and the government on this issue. However, the government is interested in minimizing the political costs of reducing import tariffs.

There Should Be More Privatizations

The fourth message from SE is in support of further privatizations, including those of copper, petroleum, the ports, the construction of transport infrastructure, and the water and sewage works. *El Mercurio* argues that neighboring countries such as Argentina are privatizing at a very fast rate, and therefore Chile runs the risk of being left behind.

However, the editorialist chooses to ignore the fact that Chile has already privatized most of the state enterprises that were of a significant size, with the exception of copper. Because of political reasons, copper cannot be privatized openly, but it is in fact being "privatized by the back door."[5] There are substantial incentives for private investment in the development of new copper mines, the state has opted for associating itself with the private sector in the development of other new mines (such as El Abra), and the state copper holding, CODELCO, is being divided into several individual firms in order to prevent cross-subsidization. In 1995, the amount of copper produced and exported by the private sector was larger than CODELCO's output, for the first time since CODELCO was formed in the early 1970s. This trend will become more noticeable as new private mines start production in 1997 and 1998. By the middle of the first decade of the twenty-first century (about 2005), the share of state-produced copper will be less than 20 percent, and maybe as little as 10 percent, of Chile's total output.

The privatization of non-copper state enterprises is going ahead, although at a pace slightly more leisurely than SE would prefer. The government is aware of the economic advantages of privatization but it fears the political consequences, which may be negative, at least in the short run. Thus, *El Mercurio*'s emphasis on further privatizations is unlikely to change policy in the short term, but it may be playing a long-term educational role. Alternatively, or additionally, this may be one of those theoretical cases that were identified before, as "the fact that a message is being sent at all may be more important than the message contents."

Some of the Current Government Measures against Poverty and Inequality May Be Counterproductive

The fifth message from SE is how to deal with the problems of poverty and inequality. *The poor are best helped by economic expansion, which creates new jobs and increases real wages, especially if the labor market is reasonably flexible. All the special tariff surcharges on imports of textiles and clothing and of agricultural produce should be eliminated. These forms of tariff protection to domestic activities damage the poor more than anyone else, because food and clothing represent a larger share in the consumption of the poor, as compared with the nonpoor.*

SE argues that no attempt at poverty alleviation can be successful if it involves increasing taxes. *Higher taxes discourage economic activity and the new tax revenues are often spent on the nonpoor, even if the initial intention was to devote them to the poor.* The government has been made painfully aware of the acute limitations of its antipoverty programs by a self-critical report produced by the Planning Ministry early in 1996. Again, there is little disagreement here between *El Mercurio* and the government. However, redesigning these programs is bound to hurt the interests of some of the center-left coalition's natural constituencies, such as the antipoverty "industry."[6]

Financial Modernization and the Liberalization of the Capital Account Are Urgent Tasks

The sixth message from SE is the need for further modernization of the financial sector and for liberalization of the capital account of the balance of payments. It is argued by the editorialist that the Central Bank's attempts at preventing "excessive" and wildly fluctuating short-term capital movements are unnecessary, and that full liberalization is required in order to make Santiago the most important financial center in the South American region. It is also argued by *El Mercurio* that the controls on the private banks by the Superintendency of Banks and by the Central Bank should be relaxed. SE is also concerned about the high interest rates, which the Central Bank uses in order to keep domestic credit expansion under control, but which, according to *El Mercurio*, help to discourage productive activities and to further appreciate the domestic currency. It is also argued by SE that the Central Bank should abandon any pretensions to control both the real exchange rate and the interest rate at the same time, and instead it should concentrate on controlling inflation.

It is unlikely that the Central Bank will relax its tough stance against the danger of wild fluctuations in short-term capital movements, at least during the 1990s. The Mexican financial collapse of December 1994, which severely damaged not only Mexico but also Argentina and to a lesser extent Brazil, suggests that the policies adopted by Chile's Central Bank were possibly the correct ones. However, it is possible that international capital flows may be gradually liberalized over a period of a few years, possibly starting shortly after the year 2000. If the policies being implemented are both sound and stable, and after the Chilean financial sector has acquired a larger volume and depth, any day-to-day speculative capital movements, no matter how wild, are extremely unlikely to do much harm.

This may be another example of a message from SE that will be unable to change policies in the short term, but that may have a long-term educational value, or which may be sent because "the fact that a message is sent at all may be more important than the message contents."

SEASONS AND LONGER CYCLES IN "LA SEMANA ECONÓMICA"

This section is devoted to explaining the presence of seasonality (one-year-long cycles) in some of the editorialist's messages, and the presence of another cycle that may be much longer than one year. An example of the latter may be offered by the eventual introduction of insights from the public choice school of economic analysis in some of the SE messages.

The annual fiscal budget needs to be sent to Congress and approved before the end of the previous year. This introduces an element of seasonality in the messages from *El Mercurio*. In August and September of each year, messages about the desirability of lower taxes and of less government expenditure become more frequent. Then, after the budget has been sent and approved, in October or November, the columns of SE tend to reflect the editorialist's disappointment. There is also some seasonality following the annual official announcements of GDP (gross domestic product) growth and balance-of-payments results.

There is also another cyclical pattern that is longer than one year, and may be as long as the full length of a presidential period (currently six years). At the beginning of the Frei administration (Frei was elected in December 1993 and took office in March 1994), some of the weekly messages from *El Mercurio* suggested that possibly the editorialist hoped that she would be able to affect government economic policy to a larger extent than she actually managed to do. Again, some disappointment was expressed in this connection after about eighteen months, that is, during the second half of 1995.

Expressions of *El Mercurio*'s disappointment, however, need to be cautious. The tone of the SE message needs to be inviting rather than insulting. The editorialist cannot afford to lose the most sensitive part of her readership. She cannot afford to preach only to the converted. After a hardening of her position in August 1995, SE softened her position again in January 1996. Hardening was expressed, for example, in the fact that the question of public choice was introduced for the first time in August 1995, and a full SE editorial was devoted to public choice in September–October 1995. Presenting an argument in terms of public choice represents a qualitative break with the past. The conventional approach to public finance assumes that the politician who holds office is benevolent: all she wishes is the best for ordinary people. In contrast, the public choice approach assumes that the politician in government maximizes her own objective function, which may not coincide with, or may even contradict the social objective function.[7]

NONCYCLICAL CHANGE IN THE MESSAGE CONTENTS: LEARNING ABOUT THE RECEIVER, THE SENDER, AND THE ECONOMY

A particularly interesting aspect of the dynamic interaction between the sender and the receiver of a strategic message is that the amount of information available (to all the participants in the game) is increasing all the time. This is an essential feature of the process of informational lobbying. In Chile during the mid 1990s, the dynamics of the process of interaction between SE and the government policymakers is such that each one of the players is constantly learning about the other. Furthermore, possibly each one of the players is also learning about herself, and ordinary members of the public (and voters) are learning about both players.

In terms of how much information is available to each player, and to any independent observers, at a particular time, the picture is far from static. Between January 1994 and March 1996 it was possible to learn some important facts about the receiver. For instance, the sender learned that: (1) the GDP growth forecast for the next year, that is produced by the Finance Ministry at the same time as the budget, has always been an underestimate; (2) the fact that next year's growth rate is being officially forecast as relatively low makes it easier for the Finance Ministry to resist pressures to spend more, from other ministries and from government politicians; and (3) the fact that growth will eventually be higher than forecast will give greater freedom to the Finance Ministry in the allocation of these "unanticipated" extra revenues. There is no suggestion here of any impropriety. Simply, a conservative growth forecast has several advantages for the policymaker, including greater flexibility.

This type of learning is qualitatively different from that behind the cyclical messages of the previous section. The present section's learning by the sender about the receiver does not have a cyclical nature. In the present section, any rational government policymaker who is subjected to the same economic, political, and political economy constraints will do the same. This is a question of economic epistemology. Once economic knowledge has progressed so much that it becomes known that, under certain conditions, the optimal behavior for a rational policymaker is action "x," then economists assume that, under similar conditions, all rational policymakers will do "x."

Another example of noncyclical learning about the receiver is offered by her refusal to lower tariffs on food imports, despite repeated invitations by the sender. The receiver also refused to listen to advice from the sender on unilateral tariff reductions instead of bilateral negotiations. However, eventually the government agreed to reduce the protection to agriculture, in the context of the negotiations with MERCOSUR, the trade pact between Argentina, Brazil, Paraguay, and Uruguay. The receiver is possibly as aware of the economic advantages of low import tariffs as the sender, but she is prevented from reducing the protection to domestic agriculture because of political economy reasons.[8] Possibly the receiver thought that the only way she would be allowed to introduce lower tariffs on food imports was if they were presented to the Chilean public opinion as unavoidable, because they were a precondition of success in the negotiations with MERCOSUR. Any posturings by Chilean government officials in relation to MERCOSUR, before the MERCOSUR agreement in March 1996, were not addressed to the MERCOSUR negotiators, but to vested interests at home.

Learning by the sender may also be combined with changes in her ideological and cultural attitudes (her own personal attitudes as well as those of the social group she represents). This is possibly the case of the editorialist's view on the drugs traffic. This is a complex issue because initially (in early 1994) the editorialist favored ethical solutions with emphasis on education, traditional family values, personal responsibility, and rehabilitation. She was against strong controls of money laundering because she feared that they might have led to the complete elimination of bank secrecy (the sender may also have some right-wing libertarian, or even anarchist leanings). However, eventually (in early 1996) she is forced to consider the possibility of legalizing drugs. In principle, she is in favor of legalization, on the grounds that good economics is not about interfering with the operation of markets. On the other hand, she thinks that legalization will not work, and it will create immense problems, unless the individual national legalization experiences are supported by an international coordinating framework.

Another aspect of the process of noncyclical learning by the sender is under the form of changes in the sender's economic model. For example, at the beginning of 1994 SE thought that the peso appreciation might be inevitable. Since 1989, the Chilean peso has been appreciating by about 5 percent per year with respect to the U.S. dollar.[9] Two years later, the editorialist was convinced, not only that the peso appreciation was unavoidable, but also that appreciation helped to control inflation, even if the Central Bank did not intend, explicitly or implicitly, to achieve this result. She was also convinced that appreciation during the 1990s, even if it were similar to the Dutch Disease in some respects, was not really a disease at all, because the supply response of nontradables to higher relative prices was extremely healthy.

It may be interesting to note that learning about the receiver is possibly against the receiver's interest. An incumbent politician may be maximizing her chances of being reelected if she deliberately cultivates an atmosphere of ambiguity about her preferences and objectives.[10] The center-left government coalition in Chile in the mid 1990s may be in a privileged position to project an image of ambiguity, even if it does not intend deliberately to do so, because of the highly heterogeneous composition of the political parties that form this coalition. It may not be an exaggeration to say that for the center-left government coalition, ambiguity (or, at the very least, ideological diversity) is a way of life. For example, in late 1994 the Christian Democratic managing director of the state television channel (*Televisión Nacional*), Jorge Navarrete, was dismissed from his post by the right-wing and the Christian Democratic members of the channel governing board, against the wishes of its Socialist and PPD members. SE saw this incident as proof of the advantages of privatizing the channel. But the incident also highlights the large degree of ambiguity in the government coalition.

Summarizing, in a relatively short period of time some interesting facts have been learned by the sender about the receiver. Possibly the receiver has also learned about the sender, and (the present chapter proves it) voters and independent observers have learned about both players, and everyone has learnt about the economy.

IDENTIFYING AND CONGRATULATING INDIVIDUALS

The SE message is addressed to a rather large number of people, including leading politicians and ordinary members of the public; voters who usually support the center-right opposition, and voters who tend to support the center-left government coalition; those readers who have some formal economics training, or some general awareness of economics, and those who are completely ignorant of economics. However, the editorialist is interested in particular in reaching government policymakers. The present section directs its focus toward a subset of this group, namely, those individuals who are specifically named by SE.

SE is not concerned only with impersonal policies. The editorialist is not afraid of naming names, at least approvingly. In particular, individual politicians, ministers and policymakers are singled out when a policy measure has been proposed or adopted by them, of which the editorialist approves. These individuals are being congratulated on their choice of policy. Support is offered to them, which should make it easier for them to deal with those who oppose their policies. (In contrast, if the editorialist disapproves of a particular policy, this is hardly ever personalized.)

Among politicians who were singled out in this way by *El Mercurio* between January 1994 and March 1996, possibly the most important is President Eduardo Frei. Several times the point was made that Frei is more friendly to free-market, open economy policies than his predecessor Patricio Aylwin ever was. Other names SE mentioned include Education Minister Sergio Molina, Health Minister Carlos Massad, Economics Minister Alvaro García, and the chairman of the Party for Democracy (PPD) Jorge Schaulsohn, who is also a member of the lower house of Congress. *El Mercurio* offered congratulations to Aylwin's former Finance Minister Alejandro Foxley on his election as chairman of the Christian Democratic Party (CDP). The editorialist emphasized that Foxley was an economist, and that an increased participation by economists in active politics was a positive development. Other economists whose work has been mentioned approvingly by SE are Cristian Larroulet, who is head of a free-market think-tank close to the opposition party National Renewal (*Renovación Nacional*, RN), and Felipe Larrain, an academic who teaches at the Catholic University in Santiago.

Individuals are never selected for praise in isolation from particular policy measures. In each of the cases mentioned in the previous paragraph, support was being given by *El Mercurio* to a particular policy measure, and, strictly related to that, to the particular individual or individuals behind, or associated with the measure. For example, Sergio Molina was finance minister in the government of

Eduardo Frei, Sr., in the late 1960s, from which he resigned on a point of principle after his proposal of a forced savings scheme had been rejected. He is a highly competent economist with a distinguished past. However, *El Mercurio*'s support for Molina in the mid 1990s has little to do with his past, and everything to do with Molina's current attempts at modernizing and liberalizing the educational sector. These attempts are being resisted by, among others, the militant teachers' union, which is dominated by members of the Communist party. *El Mercurio*'s support for Carlos Massad is also related to current policymaking. Massad, despite being a Christian Democrat, was one of the first three Chilean economists to receive postgraduate training at the University of Chicago in the 1950s, and he became chairman of the Central Bank in the second half of the 1960s. Massad is now facing an uphill task in his efforts at modernizing the health sector against opposition from the respective unions. The public trajectories of Molina and Massad over several decades suggest to *El Mercurio* that they can be reliable allies, but the key issue in both cases is policies today.

Sometimes a whole political party is congratulated by SE. Examples between January 1994 and March 1996 include the CDP, PPD, and RN. In either case, regardless of whether praise goes to an individual or to a whole political party, the point worth stressing here is that what is really important to the editorialist is the policy, rather than who is behind it. The same policy can be designed or implemented by different individuals, in some cases from different political parties. Policies are more important than political party affiliations. By congratulating individuals from different political parties, *El Mercurio* is showing them, and everyone else, that they are not alone, no matter how unpopular their policies may be, even within their own parties.

Moreover, by congratulating on policy intentions or achievements, SE is making the point that agreement on a particular economic policy is possible among individuals from different parties. This agreement is even more likely if these individuals have a solid training in economic theory. Ever since the 1980s, agreements on economic policies have often been reached among economists, experts or economic technocrats of different political parties, long before the respective political leaders had agreed. Most of these agreements were in favor of free-market, open economy policies.[11] By identifying individuals to be congratulated, *El Mercurio* is contributing to strengthen the so-called *partido vertical*, in other words, that loose association of economic technocrats, over and above their respective political parties, who are in favor of the neoliberal model. Should the current center-left government coalition eventually break down (which is possible in the run-up to the next presidential election in 1999), SE will have made a powerful contribution toward the possible formation of a potential new political coalition, to include moderate (i.e., right-wing) Christian Democrats and PPDs, moderate (i.e., left-wing) members of RN, and even some Socialists. Professional economists would play a fundamental role in this new coalition.

SUMMARY AND CONCLUSIONS

The central message of *El Mercurio*'s SE (the sender) to government policymakers (the receiver) in the mid 1990s is: "You are doing fine, but you could be doing even better." The key themes in *El Mercurio*'s message are labor market flexibility, lower taxes, openness to international trade, further privatizations, the correct ways to approach the problems of poverty and inequality, and financial modernization and the liberalization of the capital account of the balance of payments. The SE message is not addressed only to government policymakers, but to a much wider range of educated readers, including supporters of the main opposition party, RN.

El Mercurio's message has several objectives: to transmit information, to affect and change economic policy in the short term, to educate and form opinion in a longer-term perspective, to congratulate those who have designed or implemented any particular policies that meet with the editorialist's approval, and to contribute to the creation of strategic and tactical alliances in support of particular policies, over and above narrow political party affiliations.

Success has been more substantial in relation to some of these objectives, than in relation to the rest of them. The only case of unqualified success (during the period under study, January 1994 to March 1996) refers to an October 1994 call in SE for more checks and controls on government expenditure, possibly by Congress. Almost exactly a year later, in September 1995, SE was able to report on the results of a study carried out by two business lobbies, the Industrialists' Association (*Sociedad de Fomento Fabril*, SFF) and the National Mining Society (SNM), on the use of the tax receipts generated by the post-1990 tax increases. This is a very important success for *El Mercurio*, because the question of the size of the government share in national output, and with it the rates of tax and the amount of public expenditure, are possibly the most fundamental area of disagreement between government and opposition. The SFF-SNM study revealed some astonishing instances of waste. It was not difficult to associate this evidence of misallocation of resources with the rather disappointing outcome of the government's efforts against poverty and inequality, which were candidly reported in a sharply self-critical study by the Ministry of Planning early in 1996.

There are several cases of policies that were defended by SE and subsequently adopted by the government. However, in all of these cases it can be argued that possibly these policies would have been adopted anyway, as a result of the widespread presence of neoliberal views among policymakers in the government coalition. Because of the internal dynamics of policymaking in the coalition, these neoliberal policies may not be adopted immediately, but they are inevitably adopted with a time lag. A good example may be the liberalization of agricultural trade in the context of the MERCOSUR negotiations in March 1996, which was adopted despite intense opposition by the farming lobbies.

The Chilean evidence seems to provide striking confirmation of the theoretical results offered by the game theory models. It would be tempting to describe the attitude of the receiver toward the sender as "letting them do our dirty work." This may be impolite but it is possibly highly accurate. There is substantial opposition to the free-market, open economy model, among ordinary members of the public and politicians, not least among some of the government's own constituencies. So, by arguing in favor of neoliberal policies, SE is performing a valuable service to the government policymakers. Most—if not all—of these policymakers are convinced of the economic advantages of the neoliberal policies, but they would rather not publicly defend these policies because this may represent a high political cost for them.

El Mercurio, by identifying, supporting, and congratulating some carefully chosen individuals among the government policymakers, is improving the chances of success of certain policies. It is also helping these individuals with their political careers, provided that they are prepared to become increasingly identified as being close to *El Mercurio*'s editorial line. For SE this process is to a large extent one of creating self-fulfilling prophecies.

Perhaps even more could have been learned about the interaction between sender and receiver in this particular case, by looking at those specific problems or incidents in relation to which SE chose to remain silent. This is possibly the subject of another study, but a couple of examples may be mentioned here. First, no SE message was sent in connection with several government decisions to restrict competition in international air travel in favor of the two Chilean national airlines, and against the interests of their foreign competitors and possibly consumers. However, a view was expressed by the editorialist supporting the merger of the two Chilean airlines.[12] The second example refers to the fact that no message has been sent by SE regarding sex discrimination in the Chilean labor market, despite substantive evidence of the presence of this discrimination—strong theoretical arguments in the sense that discrimination is economically inefficient, and in light of *El Mercurio*'s efforts to support labor market flexibility.[13]

When examining the possible determinants of decisions in favor of neoliberal economic policies in Chile in the mid-1990s, it may be a mistake to take *El Mercurio* too seriously. There is a danger of overestimating the role played by *El Mercurio*, at the cost of hiding free-market tendencies in the center-left government coalition. This would be conceptually wrong. It would be similar to the intellectual process by which the Chilean free-market, open economy model implemented in the 1970s and 1980s was blamed by many academic observers on the influence of the University of Chicago, and therefore wrongly perceived as alien to the Chilean national character, history, interests, and institutions.

Neoliberal views among economists in the center-left government coalition are overwhelmingly widespread. Should SE cease to be published, nothing would change in terms of economic policy in the short term. However, *El Mercurio* has played, it plays today, and possibly it will continue to play a fundamental role in educating and forming opinion in a longer-term perspective, and supporting, explicitly and implicitly, formal and informal alliances in favor of particular policies, above or even against the positions of all the political parties.

NOTES

1. See E. N. Baklanoff, "Model for economic stagnation: The Chilean experience with multiple exchange rates," *Inter-American Economic Affairs* 13:1 (Summer 1959), pp. 58–82; L. J. Johnson, "Problems of import substitution: the Chilean automobile industry," *Economic Development and Cultural Change* 15 (1967), pp. 202–16; K. B. Griffin and J. L. Enos, "Policies for industrialization," in H. Bernstein (ed.), *Underdevelopment and Development* (Harmondsworth: Penguin, 1976), pp. 216–31; G. Carey, *Chile sin UF: Vivencias* (Santiago: Zig-Zag, 1989); and D. E. Hojman, *Chile: the Political Economy of Development and Democracy in the 1990s* (London and Pittsburgh: Macmillan and Pittsburgh University Press, 1993).

2. See V. P. Crawford and J. Sobel, "Strategic information transmission," *Econometrica* 50:6 (November, 1982), pp. 1431–51; J. Potters, "Fixed cost messages," *Economics Letters* 38 (1992), pp. 43–47; and J. Potters and F. van Winden, "Lobbying and asymmetric information." *Public Choice* 74 (1992), pp. 269–92.

3. See D. E. Hojman, "Poverty and inequality in Chile: Are democratic politics and neo-liberal economics good for you?," *Journal of Inter-American Studies and World Affairs* 38 (1996), forthcoming; D.E. Hojman, "Rent-seeking and corruption in a successful Latin American economy: Chile in the 1990s," in R. Espindola (ed.), *Problems of Democracy in Latin America* (Stockholm: Institute for Latin American Studies, University of Stockholm, 1996), pp. 35–51; and D. E. Hojman, "Rent-seeking in Chile: Growth, distribution and poverty in a successful third world economy." Paper presented to the 1996 Meetings of the European Public Choice Society (Bar-Ilan and Tiberias, Israel, 10–13 March 1996).

4. For further discussion of the peso appreciation, see D. E. Hojman, "Too much of a good thing? Macro and microeconomics of the Chilean peso appreciation," in D. E. Hojman (ed.), *Neo-liberalism with a Human Face? The Politics and Economics of the Chilean Model* (Liverpool: Institute of Latin American Studies, University of Liverpool, 1995), pp. 225–48.

5. Hojman, *Chile: The Political Economy.*

6. Hojman, "Poverty and inequality in Chile"; Hojman, "Rent-seeking and corruption"; Hojman, "Rent-seeking in Chile."

7. See J. M. Buchanan and R. D. Tollison (eds.), *The Theory of Public Choice II* (Ann Arbor: University of Michigan Press, 1984); D. C. Mueller, *Public Choice II* (Cambridge: Cambridge University Press, 1989); and J. Cullis and P. Jones, *Public Finance And Public Choice: Analytical Perspectives* (London: McGraw-Hill, 1992).

8. See Hojman, "Rent-seeking and corruption"; Hojman, "Rent-seeking in Chile." See also D. E. Hojman, "Chile under Frei (again): The first Latin American tiger—or just another cat?," *Bulletin of Latin American Research* 14:2 (May, 1995), pp. 127–42.

9. Hojman, "Too much of a good thing?"

10. See A. Alesina and A. Cukierman, "The politics of ambiguity," *Quarterly Journal of Economics* 105:4 (November, 1990), pp. 829–50.

11. See Hojman, *Chile*; D. E. Hojman, "The political economy of recent conversions to market economics in Latin America," *Journal of Latin American Studies* 26:1 (February, 1994), pp. 191–219; V. Montecinos, "Economic policy elites and democratization," *Studies in Comparative International Development* 28:1 (Spring 1993), pp. 25–53; and J. M. Puryear, *Thinking Politics: Intellectuals and Democracy in Chile, 1973–1988* (Baltimore: Johns Hopkins University Press, 1994).

12. See M. Zellner, "Cielito lindo," *AmericaEconomia* 97 (July 1995); Hojman, "Rent-seeking and corruption"; and Hojman, "Rent-seeking in Chile."

13. See G. Becker, *The Economics of Discrimination* (Chicago: University of Chicago Press, 1957); and I. S. Gill, "Is there sex discrimination in Chile? Evidence from the CASEN survey," in G. Psacharopoulos and Z. Tzannatos (eds.), *Case studies on Women's Employment and Pay in Latin America* (Washington, DC: The World Bank, 1992), pp. 119–47.

Selected Bibliography

Abel, C. and Torrents, N., eds. *José Martí, Revolutionary Democrat*. London: The Athlone Press, 1988.

Abente, D. "Stronismo, Post-stronismo and the Prospects for Democratization in Paraguay," *Kellog Institute of Notre Dame, Working Paper 119* (1989).

Adams, D. K. and van Minnen, C. A., eds. *Reflections on American Exceptionalism*. Keele: Keele University Press, 1994.

Adelman, J., ed. *Essays in Argentine Labour History, 1870–1930*. Basingstoke: Macmillan, 1992.

Adelman, J. "State and Labour in Argentina: The Portworkers of Buenos Aires, 1910–21," *Journal of Latin American Studies* 25:1 (1993).

Adelman, J. R., ed. *Superpowers and Revolution*. New York: Praeger, 1986.

Aguilar, L. E. *Cuba 1933: Prologue to Revolution*. Ithaca: Cornell University Press, 1972.

Albendea, G. *España a la deriva*. Madrid: Huerga y Fierro Editores, 1995.

Albert, B. *South America and the First World War. The Impact of the War on Brazil, Argentina, Peru and Chile*. Cambridge: Cambridge University Press, 1988.

Albornoz, O. *Education and Society in Latin America*. Basingstoke: Macmillan and St. Antony's, 1993.

Alesina, A. and Cukierman, A. "The politics of ambiguity," *Quarterly Journal of Economics* 105:4 (November 1990), pp. 829–50.

Alexander, R. J. *Arturo Alessandri: A Biography*. 2 vols. Ann Arbor: Rutgers University/University Microfilms International, 1977.

Allardt, E. and Rokkan, S., eds. *Mass Politics: Studies in Political Sociology*. New York: Free Press, 1970.

Alves, M. T. *Viva-fying the Other*. London: Kala Press, 1994.

Angel, R., ed. *Rebeldes y domesticados: Los intelectuales frente al poder*. Buenos Aires: Ediciones El Cielo por Asalto, 1992.

Angell, A. and Pollack, B. "The Chilean Elections of 1993: From Polarisation to Consensus," *Bulletin of Latin American Research* 14:2 (May, 1995), pp. 105–25.

Arditi, B. *Estado Omnívoro, sociedad estatizada, poder y orden político en el Paraguay.* Asunción: Centro de Documentación y Estudios, 1989.

Arditi, B. *Adiós a Stroessner. La reconstrucción de la política en el Paraguay.* Asunción: Centro de Documentación y Estudios, 1992.

Arditi, B. *Cálculo y contingencia en las transiciones a la democracia.* Asunción: Centro de Documentación y Estudios, 1994.

Baklanoff, E. N. "Model for Economic Stagnation: the Chilean Experience with Multiple Exchange Rates," *Inter-American Economic Affairs* 13:1 (Summer 1959), pp. 58–82.

Baloyra, E. A. and Morris, J. A. *Conflict and Change in Cuba.* Albuquerque: University of New Mexico Press, 1993.

Barbieri, T. de and Oliveira, O. de., eds. *Presencia política de las mujeres.* San José: FLACSO, 1991.

Barrett, M. and Phillips, A., eds. *Destabilizing Theory: Contemporary Feminist Debates.* Cambridge: Polity, 1992.

Barrios, A. and Brunner, J. J. *La sociología en Chile.* Santiago: FLACSO, 1988.

Bartra, R. "Luis Villoro piensa en México," *La Gaceta del Fondo de Cultura Económica* 301 (January 1996).

Becker, G. *The Economics of Discrimination.* Chicago: University of Chicago Press, 1957.

Bell, D. *The End of Ideology: On the Exhaustion of Political Ideas in the Fifties.* New York: The Free Press, 1962.

Bergquist, C. *Labor in Latin America. Comparative Essays on Chile, Argentina, Venezuela and Colombia.* Stanford: Stanford University Press, 1986.

Bernstein, H., ed. *Underdevelopment and Development.* Harmondsworth: Penguin, 1976.

Bethell, L., ed. *The Cambridge History of Latin America*, vol. 4. Cambridge: Cambridge University Press, 1986.

Bethell, L., ed. *Mexico since Independence.* Cambridge: Cambridge University Press, 1991.

Bethell, L., ed. *Argentina since Independence.* Cambridge: Cambridge University Press, 1993.

Blachman, M. J., et al., eds. *Confronting Revolution: Security through Diplomacy in Central America.* New York: Pantheon Books, 1986.

Blanchard, P. "A Populist Precursor: Guillermo Billinghurst," *Journal of Latin American Studies* 9:2 (1977).

Blanchard, P. *The Origins of the Peruvian Labor Movement, 1883–1919.* Pittsburgh: Pittsburgh University Press, 1982.

Booth, J. A. and Seligson, M. A., eds. *Elections and Democracy in Central America.* Chapel Hill: University of North Carolina Press, 1989.

Bourdieu, P. *Distinction: A Social Critique of the Judgement of Taste.* London: Routledge and Kegan Paul, 1984.

Brohman, J. "Universalism, Eurocentrism, and Ideological Bias in Development Studies: from Modernisation to Neoliberalism," *Third World Quarterly* 16:1 (March, 1995).

Buchanan, J. M. and Tollison, R. D., eds. *The Theory of Public Choice II.* Ann Arbor: University of Michigan Press, 1984.

Bucholtz, M. et al., eds. *Cultural Performances.* Berkeley: University of California Press, 1994.

Butler, J. *Gender Trouble: Feminism and the Subversion of Identity.* London: Routledge, 1990.

Butler, J. *Bodies That Matter: On the Discursive Limits of "Sex."* London: Routledge, 1993.

Caballero, E. *Dictadura, Estado Prebendario y Crisis Política.* Asunción: Mimeo, 1986.

Camp, R. *Intellectuals and the State in Twentieth Century Mexico.* Austin: University of Texas Press, 1985.

Camp, R., Hale, C. A. and Vázquez, J. Z., eds. *Los intelectuales y el poder en México.* Mexico City: El Colegio de México/UCLA Latin American Center Publications, 1991.

Carey, G. *Chile sin UF: Vivencias.* Santiago: Zig-Zag, 1989.

Castañeda, J. *Utopia Unarmed: The Latin American Left after the Cold War.* New York: Knopf, 1993.

Castillo, D. A. *Talking Back: Toward a Latin American Feminist Criticism.* Ithaca: Cornell University Press, 1992.

Castro, F. *History Will Absolve Me.* London: Jonathan Cape, 1967.

Castro, F. and Debray, R. *On Trial.* London: Lorrimer Publishing, 1968.

Chakravorty Spivak, G. *Outside in the Teaching Machine.* London: Routledge, 1993.

Chaney, E. *Supermadre.* Mexico City: Fondo de Cultura Económica, 1983.

Chant, S. "Women, Work and Household Survival Strategies in Mexico, 1982–1992: Past Trends, Current Tendencies and Future Research," *Bulletin of Latin American Research* 13:2 (May, 1994), pp. 203–33.

Chomsky, N. *The Culture of Terrorism.* London: Pluto Press, 1987.

Chomsky, N. *On Power and Ideology: The Managua Lectures.* Boston: South End Press, 1987.

Chomsky, N. *Necessary Illusions: Thought Control in Democratic Societies.* Boston: South End Press, 1989.

Cockcroft, J. D. *Intellectual Precursors of the Mexican Revolution, 1900–1913.* Austin: University of Texas Press, 1968.

Corominas de Hernández, M. "La nacionalización de la enseñanza en Cuba," *Revista Bimestre Cubana* 37:1 (1936).

Crahan, M. E. "Religious Penetration and Nationalism in Cuba: U.S. Methodist Activities, 1898–1958," *Revista/Review Interamericana* 8:2 (Summer 1978).

Crawford, V. P. and Sobel, J. "Strategic information transmission," *Econometrica* 50:6 (November 1982), pp. 1431–51.

Cubitt, T. *Latin American Society.* Harlow: Longman Scientific, 1995.

Cullis J. and Jones, P. *Public Finance and Public Choice: Analytical Perspectives.* London: McGraw-Hill, 1992.

Davies, M., ed. *Third World, Second Sex: Women's Struggles and National Liberation: Third World Women Speak Out.* London: Zed Books, 1983.

Davies, P., ed. *An American Quarter Century.* Manchester: Manchester University Press, 1995.

Davies, P. *Representing and Imagining America.* Keele: Keele University Press, 1996.

De Shazo, P. *Urban Workers and Labor Unions in Chile, 1902–1927.* Madison: Wisconsin University Press, 1983.

Desnoes, E. *Punto de Vista.* Havana: Instituto del Libro, 1967.

Dore, E. and Weeks, J. *The Red and the Black: The Sandinistas and the Nicaraguan Revolution.* London: ILAS, 1992.

Dostal, W., ed. *The Situation of the Indian in South America.* Geneva: World Council of Churches, 1972.

Draper, T. *Castro's Revolution: Myths and Realities.* New York: Frederick A. Praeger, 1962.

Draper, T. *Castroism: Theory and Practice.* New York: Frederick A. Praeger, 1965.

Dulles, J.F.W. *Anarchists and Communists in Brazil, 1900–1935*. Austin: Texas University Press, 1973.

Dunkerley, J. *Power in the Isthmus: A Political History of Modern Central America*. London: Verso, 1988.

Eagleton, T. *Ideology: An Introduction*. London: Verso, 1991.

Eatwell, R. and Wright, A., eds. *Contemporary Political Ideologies*. London: Printer Publishers, 1993.

Eccleshall, R. et al., eds. *Political Ideologies, An Introduction*. London: Hutchinson, 1984.

Eckstein, S., ed. *Power and Popular Protest: Latin American Social Movements*. Berkeley: University of California Press, 1989.

Espindola, R., ed. *Problems of Democracy in Latin America*. Stockholm: Institute for Latin American Studies, University of Stockholm, 1996.

Espinosa y Rodríguez, C. *La crisis de la segunda enseñanza en Cuba y su posible solución*. Havana: Cultural, 1942.

Fagen, R. R. *The Transformation of Political Culture in Cuba*. Stanford: Stanford University Press, 1969.

Fisher, J. *Out of the Shadows: Women, Resistance and Politics in South America*. London: Latin American Bureau, 1993.

Fisher, J. "Women and Democracy: For Home and Country," *NACLA: Report on the Americas* 27:1 (1993), pp. 30–36.

Flecha, V. J., Martini, C. and Silvero Salgueiro, J. *Autoritarismo, transición y constitución en el Paraguay*. Asunción: BASE ECTA, 1993.

Foweraker, J. *Theorizing Social Movements*. London: Pluto, 1995.

Fowler, W. "Dreams of Stability: Mexican Political Thought during the 'Forgotten Years.' An Analysis of the Beliefs of the Creole Intelligentsia (1821–1853)," *Bulletin of Latin American Research* 14:3 (September 1995), pp. 287–312.

Fowler, W. "Introduction: The Forgotten Century, 1810–1910," *Bulletin of Latin American Research* 15:1 (January 1996), pp. 1–6.

Fowler, W. "Valentín Gómez Farías: Perceptions of Radicalism in Independent Mexico, 1821–1847," *Bulletin of Latin American Research* 15:1 (January 1996), pp. 39–62.

Fowler, W. *The Mexican Press and the Collapse of Representative Government during the Presidential Elections of 1828*. Research Paper no. 21. Liverpool: Institute of Latin American Studies, 1996.

Fowler, W., ed. *Authoritarianism in Latin America since Independence*. Westport, CT: Greenwood, 1996.

Fowler, W. "The Compañía Lancasteriana and the Élite in Independent Mexico, 1822–1845" *TESSERAE Journal of Iberian and Latin American Studies* 2:2 (Summer, 1996), pp. 81–110.

Fowler, W. *Military Political Identity and Reformism in Independent Mexico. An Analysis of the Memorias de Guerra 1821–1855*. London: Institute of Latin American Studies, 1996.

Fowler, W. *The Liberal Origins of Mexican Conservatism, 1821–1832*. Glasgow: Institute of Latin American Studies, 1997.

Fowler, W. and Morales Moreno, H., eds. *El conservadurismo mexicano del siglo diecinueve*. Puebla: Universidad Autónoma de Puebla/Instituto Nacional de Antropología e Historia, in press.

Fukuyama, F. *The End of History and the Last Man*. Harmondsworth: Penguin, 1992.

Galeano, E. *We Say No: Chronicles, 1963–1991*. New York: W. W. Norton, 1992.

García Canclini, N. *Culturas híbridas: Estrategias para entrar y salir de la modernidad.* Buenos Aires: Editorial Sudamericana, 1992.

García Canclini, N. *Hybrid Cultures: Strategies for Entering and Leaving Modernity.* Minneapolis: University of Minnesota Press, 1995.

García Márquez, G. *One Hundred Years of Solitude.* London: Picador, 1978.

Geertz, C. *The Interpretation of Cultures.* London: Fontana, 1993.

Gellner, E. *Nations and Nationalism.* Oxford: Blackwell, 1983.

Gillespie, R., ed. *Cuba after Thirty Years: Rectification and Revolution.* London: Frank Cass, 1990.

Gleijeses, P. *Shattered Hope: The Guatemalan Revolution and the United States, 1944–1954.* Princeton: Princeton University Press, 1991.

Godio, J. *Historia del movimiento obrero argentino, migrantes asalariados y lucha de clases, 1880–1910.* Buenos Aires: Editorial Tiempo Contemporáneo, 1973.

Gonzales Prada, M. *Anarchy.* Tucson: IWW, 1972.

González, N. *El Paraguay Eterno.* Asunción: Cuadernos Republicanos, 1986.

Gordon, E. A. "Anarchism in Brazil: Theory and Practice, 1890–1920," Unpubl. Ph.D. Diss., Tulane University, 1978.

Gramsci, A. *Selections from the Prison Notebooks.* London: Lawrence and Wishart, 1971.

Grosz, E. *Volatile Bodies: Toward a Corporeal Feminism.* New York: Cloumbia University Press, 1994.

Guzmán, J. *Escritos personales.* Santiago: Zig-Zag, 1992.

Harasym, S. ed. *The Post-colonial Critic: Interviews, Strategies, Dialogues.* London: Routledge, 1990.

Hartz, L. *The Liberal Tradition in America: An Interpretation of American Political Thought since the Revolution.* New York: Harcourt, Brace and Company, 1955.

Hayward, J. *After the French Revolution, Six critics of Democracy and Nationalism.* London: Harvester Wheatsheaf, 1991.

Held, D., ed. *Prospects for Democracy: North, South, East, West.* Cambridge: Polity Press, 1992.

Hicks, F. "Interpersonal Relationships and Caudillismo in Paraguay," *Journal of Inter-American Studies and World Affairs* 13:1 (1971).

Hobsbawm, E. J. *Primitive Rebels.* Manchester: Manchester University Press, 1959.

Hobsbawm, E. and Ranger, T., eds. *The Invention of Tradition.* Cambridge: Cambridge University Press, 1983.

Hogan, M. J. and Paterson, T. G., eds. *Explaining the History of American Foreign Relations.* Cambridge: Cambridge University Press, 1991.

Hojman, D. E. *Chile: The Political Economy of Development and Democracy in the 1990s.* London and Pittsburgh: Macmillan and Pittsburgh University Press, 1993.

Hojman, D. E. "The Political Economy of Recent Conversions to Market Economics in Latin America," *Journal of Latin American Studies* 26:1 (February 1994), pp. 191–219.

Hojman, D. E., ed. *Neo-liberalism with a Human Face? The Politics and Economics of the Chilean Model.* Liverpool: Institute of Latin American Studies, University of Liverpool, 1995.

Hojman, D. E. "Chile under Frei (Again): The First Latin American Tiger—or Just Another Cat?" *Bulletin of Latin American Research* 14:2 (May 1995), pp. 127–42.

Hojman, D. E. "Poverty and Inequality in Chile: Are Democratic Politics and Neo-liberal Economics Good for You?" *Journal of Inter-American Studies and World Affairs* 38 (in press).

Hunt, M. H. *Ideology and U.S. Foreign Policy*. New Haven: Yale University Press, 1987.

Immerman, R. *The CIA in Guatemala: The Foreign Policy of Intervention*. Austin: University of Texas Press, 1982.

Immerman, R., ed. *John Foster Dulles and the Diplomacy of the Cold War*. Princeton: Princeton University Press, 1990.

Ipola, E. de. *Ideología y discurso populista*. Mexico City: Folios Ediciones, 1982.

Irigaray, L. *Je, tu, nous: Towards a Culture of Difference*. London: Routledge, 1993.

Jacobsen, C. G. *Soviet Attitudes towards, Aid to, and Contacts with Central American Revolutionaries*. Washington DC: U.S. Department of State, 1984.

Jacquette, J. S. *The Women's Movement in Latin America: Feminism and the Transition to Democracy*. Boston: Unwin Hyman, 1989.

Jelin, E., ed. *Women and Social Change in Latin America*. London: Zed Books, 1990.

Johnson, L. J. "Problems of Import Substitution: The Chilean Automobile Industry," *Economic Development and Cultural Change* 15 (1967), pp. 202–16.

Johnston, L. "*Por la Escuela Cubana en Cuba Libre*: Themes in the History of Primary and Secondary Education in Cuba, 1899–1958." Unpubl. Ph.D. Diss., University of London, 1996.

Kay, D. *Chileans in Exile*. Basingstoke: Macmillan, 1987.

Klaren, P. F. and Bossert, T. J., eds. *Promise of Development: Theories of Change in Latin America*. Boulder, CO: Westview Press, 1986.

Knight, A. *The Mexican Revolution*. 2 Vols. Cambridge: Cambridge University Press, 1986.

Krauze, E. *Caudillos culturales en la Revolución Mexicana*. Mexico City: Editorial Siglo XXI, 1985.

Krauze, E. *Textos heréticos*. Mexico City: Editorial Grijalbo, 1992.

Küppers, G. *Compañeras: Voices from the Latin American Women's Movement*. London: Latin American Bureau, 1994.

LaFeber, W. *America, Russia, and the Cold War, 1945–1990*. New York: McGraw-Hill, 1991.

LaFeber, W. *Inevitable Revolutions: The United States in Central America*. New York: W. W. Norton, 1993.

LaFeber, W. *The American Search for Opportunity, 1865–1913*. Cambridge: Cambridge University Press, 1993.

Laffitte, R. "El grup com a procés d'autoaprenentatge," *Papers d'innovació social* 35. Barcelona: Eco Concern, 1996, pp. 3–11.

Laíno, D. *Paraguay: Represión, Estafa y Anticomuni$mo*. Asunción: Ediciones Cerro Corá, 1979.

Latin American and Caribbean Women's Collective. *Slaves of Slaves: The Challenge of Latin American Women*. London: Zed Books, 1980.

Lavrin, A. "Women, Labor and the Left: Argentina and Chile, 1890–1925," *Journal of Women's History* 1:2 (1989).

Leffler, M. P. *A Preponderance of Power: National Security, the Truman Administration, and the Cold War*. Stanford: Stanford University Press, 1992.

Levy, D. C. *University and Government in Mexico: Autonomy in an Authoritarian System*. New York: Praeger, 1980.

Levy, D. C. *Higher Education and the State in Latin America: Private Challenges to Public Dominance*. Chicago: University of Chicago Press, 1986.

Lewis, P. *Paraguay under Stroessner*. Chapel Hill: University of North Carolina Press, 1980.

Linden, M. van der, and Thorpe, W., eds. *Revolutionary Syndicalism: An International Perspective*. Aldershot: Scolar Press, 1990.

López Cámara, F. "La UNAM en la política mexicana," *Revista Universidad de México.* September 1992.

Maier, J. and Weatherhead, R. W., eds. *The Latin American University.* Albuquerque: University of New Mexico Press, 1979.

Maram, S. L. "Anarchists, Immigrants and the Brazilian Labor Movement." Unpubl. Ph.D. Diss., University of California at Santa Barbara, 1972.

Marchand, M. H. and Parpart, J. L., eds. *Feminism/Postmodernism/Development.* London: Routledge, 1995.

Marinello, J. *Por una enseñanza democrática.* Havana: Editorial Páginas, 1945.

Marinello, J. *La reforma educacional en Inglaterra: la inspección de la enseñanza privada.* Havana: Editorial Páginas, 1945.

Martí, J. *Páginas Escogidas.* Buenos Aires: Espasa Calpe, 1954.

Martínez Estrada, E. *X-Ray of the Pampa.* Austin: University of Texas Press, 1971.

Masi, F. *Autoritarismo y transición política en el Paraguay.* Asunción: IDIAL, 1989.

Masi, F. *Stroessner: La extincción de un modelo político en Paraguay.* Asunción: Nandutí Vive/Intercontinental Editora, 1989.

Mattelart, M. *Women, Media, Crisis.* London: Comedia Publishing Group, 1986.

McCormick, T. J. *America's Half Century: United States Foreign Policy in the Cold War.* Baltimore: Johns Hopkins University Press, 1989.

Melrose, D. *Nicaragua: The Threat of a Good Example.* Oxford: Oxfam, 1985.

Meyer, D., ed. *Lives on the Line.* Berkeley: University of California Press, 1988.

Meza, R. A. *El triángulo de la opresión.* Asunción: Imprenta Salesiana, 1990.

Miller, N. *Soviet Relations with Latin America, 1959–1987.* Cambridge: Cambridge University Press, 1989.

Miranda, C. R. *Paraguay y la era de Stroessner.* Asunción: PRP Ediciones, 1990.

Mohanty, C., Russo, A. and Torres, L., eds. *Third World Women and the Politics of Feminism.* Indiannapolis: Indiana University Press, 1991.

Molyneux, M. "Mobilization without Emancipation? Women's Interests, the State and the Revolution in Nicaragua," *Feminist Studies* 11:2 (1985), pp. 227–54.

Molyneux, M. "No God, No Boss, No Husband. Anarchist Feminism in Nineteenth Century Argentina," *Latin American Perspectives* 13:1 (1986).

Momson, J. H. and Kinnaird, V., eds. *Different Places, Different Voices: Gender and Development in Africa, Asia and Latin America.* London: Routledge, 1993.

Montecinos, V. "Economic Policy Elites and Democratization," *Studies in Comparative International Development* 28:1 (Spring 1993), pp. 25–53.

Montori, A. *El problema de la educación nacional.* Havana: Cuba Pedagógica, 1920.

Montori, A. "La educación en Cuba," *Cuba Contemporánea* 38:150 (June, 1925).

Morris, J. O. *Elites, Intellectuals and Consensus. A Study of the Social Question and the Industrial Relations System in Chile.* Ithaca: Cornell University Press, 1966.

Mueller, D. C. *Public Choice II.* Cambridge: Cambridge University Press, 1989.

Munslow, B. and Finch, H., eds. *Proletarianisation in the Third World. Studies in the Creation of a Labour Force under Dependent Capitalism.* London: Croon Helm, 1984.

Nash, J. and Safa, H., eds. *Sex and Class in Latin America.* New York: Gergins, 1980.

Nash, J. and Safa, H., eds. *Women and Change in Latin America.* South Hadley, MA: Bergin and Garvey, 1986.

Nelson, L. *Rural Cuba.* New York: Octagon Books, 1970.

Nicholson, L., ed. *Feminism/Postmodernism.* London: Routledge, 1990.

Nicholson, L. and Seidman, S., eds. *Social Postmodernism: Beyond Identity Politics.* Cambridge: Cambridge University Press, 1995.

Nickson, R. A. "Brazilian Colonization of the Eastern Border Region of Paraguay," *Journal of Latin American Studies* 13:1 (1981), pp. 111–31.

Nickson, R. A. "Tyranny and Longevity: Stroessner's Paraguay," *Third World Quarterly* 10:1 (1988).

Nickson, R. A. "The Overthrow of the Stroessner Regime: Reestablishing the Status Quo," *Bulletin of Latin American Research* 8:2 (1989).

Nickson, R. A. *Historical Dictionary of Paraguay.* London: Scarecrow Press, 1993.

Novik, P. *That Noble Dream: The "Objectivity Question" and the American Historical Profession.* Cambridge: Cambridge University Press, 1988.

O'Leary, J. *Prosa Polémica.* Asunción: Napa, 1982.

Park, J. W. *Latin American Underdevelopment: A History of Perspectives in the United States, 1870–1965.* Baton Rouge: Louisiana State University Press, 1995.

Pérez, L. A., Jr. *Cuba under the Platt Amendment, 1902–1934.* Pittsburgh: Pittsburgh University Press, 1986.

Pichardo, H., ed. *Documentos para la historia de Cuba.* Vol. 4. Havana: Editorial Pueblo y Educación, 1986.

Portuondo Linares, S. *Los independientes de color: Historia del Patrido Independiente de Color.* Havana: Ministerio de Educación, Dirección de Cultura, 1950.

Potters, J. "Fixed Cost Messages," *Economics Letters* 38 (1992), pp. 43–47.

Potters, J. and van Winden, F. "Lobbying and Asymmetric Information," *Public Choice* 74 (1992), pp. 269–92.

Posse, A. *La pasión según Eva.* Barcelona: Planeta, 1995.

Psacharopoulos, G. and Tzannatos, Z., eds. *Case Studies on Women's Employment and Pay in Latin America.* Washington, DC: The World Bank, 1992.

Puryear, J. M. *Thinking Politics: Intellectuals and Democracy in Chile, 1973–1988.* Baltimore: The Johns Hopkins University Press, 1994.

Radcliffe, S. A. and Westwood, S. *Viva: Women and Popular Protest in Latin America.* London: Routledge, 1993.

Riff, M. A. *A Dictionary of Modern Ideologies.* Manchester: Manchester University Press, 1987.

Riquelme, M. A. *Stronismo, golpe militar y apertura tutelada.* Asunción: CDE/RP Ediciones, 1992.

Roberts, G. and Edwards, A. *A Dictionary of Political Analysis.* New York: Routledge, Chapman and Hall, 1991.

Robinson, W. I. *A Faustian Bargain: US Intervention in the Nicaraguan Elections and American Foreign Policy in the Post–Cold War Era.* Boulder, CO: Westview Press, 1992.

Rock, D. *Politics in Argentina, 1890–1930. The Rise and Fall of Radicalism.* Cambridge: Cambridge University Press, 1975.

Rodríguez Alcalá, G. *Ideología autoritaria.* Asunción: RP Ediciones, 1987.

Rodríguez Ledesma, X. "El poder como espejo de los intelectuales," *Revista Mexicana de Ciencias Políticas y Sociales* 39:158 (October–December 1994).

Roett, R. "Paraguay after Stroessner," *Foreign Affairs* 68:2 (1989).

Roig de Leuchsenring, E. *Males y vicios de Cuba republicana: sus causas y sus remedios.* Havana: Oficina del Historiador de la Ciudad, 1959.

Rovira, G. *¡Zapata vive! La rebelión indígena de Chiapas contada por sus protagonistas*. Barcelona: Virus Editorial, 1995.

Ryan, D. *US-Sandinista Diplomatic Relations: Voice of Intolerance*. Basingstoke: Macmillan, 1995.

Said, E. *Orientalism: Western Conceptions of the Orient*. Harmondsworth: Penguin, 1995.

Said, E. W. *Culture and Imperialism*. London: Chatto and Windus, 1993.

Sanders, T. G. "The Fall of Stroessner: Continuity and Change in Paraguay," *Field Staff Reports* 2 (1989–90).

Saporta Sternbach, N., Navarro-Aranguren, M., Chuchryk, P. and Alvarez, S. "Feminisms in Latin America: from Bogotá to San Bernardo," *Signs: Journal of Women in Culture and Society* 27:1 (1992), pp. 393–434.

Schlesinger, S. and Kinzer, S. *Bitter Fruit: The Untold Story of the American Coup in Guatemala*. New York: Doubleday, 1982.

Schoultz, L. *National Security and United States Policy toward Latin America*. Princeton: Princeton University Press, 1987.

Scott, J. W. "The Evidence of Experience," *Critical Enquiry* 17 (1991), pp. 159–77.

Scruton, R. *A Dictionary of Political Thought*. Basingstoke: Macmillan, 1982.

Seiferheld, A. *La caída de Federico Chávez: Una visión documental norteamericana*. Asunción: Ediciones Históricas, 1987.

Shipley, R. E. "On the Outside Looking In: A Social History of the Porteño Worker during the 'Golden Age' of Argentine Development, 1914–1930." Unpubl. Ph.D. Diss., Rutgers University, 1977.

Sklar, H. *Washington's War on Nicaragua*. Boston: South End Press, 1988.

Smith, W., ed. *The Russians Aren't Coming: New Soviet Policy in Latin America*. Boulder, CO: Lynne Rienner, 1992.

Sondrol, P. C. "Authoritarianism in Paraguay: An Analysis of Three Contending Paradigms," *Review of Latin American Studies* 3:1 (1990), pp. 83–105.

Sondrol, P. C. "Totalitarian and Authoritarian Dictators: A Comparison of Fidel Castro and Alfredo Stroessner," *Journal of Latin American Studies* 23:3 (1991), pp. 599–620.

Soto, L. *La Revolución del 33*. Havana: Editorial Pueblo y Educación, 1977.

Spalding, H., Jr. *Organized Labor in Latin America. Historical Case Studies of Urban Workers in Dependent Societies*. London: Harper and Row, 1977.

Suckle Ortiz, B. "Changing Consciousness of Central American Women," *Economic and Political Weekly* 20:17 (India, 1985), pp. 2–8.

Talpade Mohanty, C., Russo, A. and Torres, L., eds. *Third World Women and the Politics of Feminism*. Bloomington: Indiana University Press, 1991.

Teitelboim, V. *Neruda: An Intimate Biography*. Austin: University of Texas Press, 1991.

Thompson, E. P. *The Making of the English Working Class*. Harmondsworth Penguin, 1968.

Thompson, R. "The Limitations of Ideology in the Early Argentine Labour Movement: Anarchism in the Trade Unions, 1890–1920," *Journal of Latin American Studies* 16:1 (1984).

Townsend, W. C. *Lázaro Cárdenas: Mexican Democrat*. Ann Arbor: George Wahr Publishing Company, 1952.

Valdés, J. G. *La Escuela de Chicago: Operación Chile*. Buenos Aires: Editorial Zeta, 1989.

Vargas Llosa, M. *Contra viento y marea*. 2 Vols. Barcelona: Editorial Seix Barral, 1986.

Vasconcelos, J. *Memorias*. Mexico City: Fondo de Cultura Económica, 1982.

Walker, T. W., ed. *Reagan versus the Sandinistas: The Undeclared War on Nicaragua*. Boulder, CO: Westview Press, 1987.

Walker, T. W., ed. *Revolution and Counterrevolution in Nicaragua*. Boulder, CO: Westview Press, 1991.

Weinbaum, B. *The Curious Courtship of Women's Liberationism and Socialism*. York: South End Press, 1978.

Wiarda, H. and Kline, H., eds. *Latin American Politics and Development*. Boston: Houghton Miffin, 1979.

Wiesen Cook, B. *The Declassified Eisenhower: A Divided Legacy*. New York: Doubleday, 1981.

Williams, R. *Keywords: A Vocabulary of Culture and Society*. London: Flamingo, 1981.

Wolfe, J. "Anarchist Ideology, Worker Practice: The 1917 General Strike and the Formation of Sao Paulo's Working Class," *Hispanic American Historical Review* 71:4 (1991).

Wolfe, J. *Working Women, Working Men: São Paulo and the Rise of Brazil's Industrial Working Class, 1900–1955*. Durham: Duke University Press, 1993.

Yúdice, G., Franco, J. and Flores, J., eds. *On Edge: The Crisis of Contemporary Latin American Culture*. Minneapolis: University of Minnesota Press, 1992.

Zabaleta, M. *La organización de las mujeres para el proceso de Reforma Agraria*. Santiago: El Rebelde, 1972.

Zabaleta, M. "Research on Latin American Women: In Search of Our Political Independence," *Bulletin of Latin American Research* 5:2 (1986), pp. 97–103.

Zabaleta, M. "On the Process of the Construction of a Feminine Social Consciousness. The Peronist Case (Argentina, 1943–55)." Unpubl. D. Phil. Thesis, University of Sussex, 1989.

Zabaleta, M. "Women and Men in Argentina: From Modern Nation to Multinational Haven (1880–1996)," *New Left Review* (in press).

Zaid, G. *De los libros al poder*. Mexico City: Editorial Grijalbo, 1988.

Zellner, M. "Cielito lindo," *AmericaEconomia* 97 (July 1995).

Index

Ação Social Naconalista, 21
Adelman, Jeremy, 13
Afro-Cuban identity, 96, 101
Agrarianism, 84, 87
Agrarian Reform Law, 1952 Guatemalan, 116
Alba, Victor, 15
Albendea, Gabriel, 4
Alessandri, Arturo, 22, 23, 61, 161
Alfonsín, Raúl, 55
Algeria, 70
Allamand, Andrés, 169
Allende, Salvador, 67–70, 79, 140, 151, 153–155, 172
Allendismo, 65
Althusser, Louis, 98, 107
Altruism, 109
Álvarez, Sonia E., 142
Amnesty Law, 1978 Chilean, 165
Amsterdam, 15, 23
Anarchism, 6–8, 11–16, 20, 24, 70, 179
Anarcho-feminism, 16
Anarcho-syndicalism, 7, 11–14, 16–22, 24, 25
Anglo-American context, 139, 144, 145
Angola, 102

Anguita, Julio, 3
ANR (*Alianza Nacional Reformista*), 137
Anticlericalism, 59
Anticommunism. *See* Communism
Antinationalism. *See* Nationalism
AP (*Alianza Popular*), 3
Apoliticism, 52
APRA (*Alianza Popular Revolucionaria Americana*), 14, 22, 51, 68
Aquinas, Thomas, 57
Araucanian Indians, 71
Arbenz, Jacobo, 108, 113–117, 120
Arévalo, Juan José, 108, 113–116, 120
Argentina, 5, 8, 12–24, 26, 46, 47, 49, 50, 56, 57, 61, 66, 68, 70, 72–74, 76, 78, 140–142, 145, 175, 176, 178
Aristocracy, 47
Armed forces. *See* Militarism
Army. *See* Militarism
Asia, 71
Asociación de Escuelas Privadas, 35
Asociación de Maestras Católicas, 35
Asociación Rural del Paraguay (ARP), 128, 136
Aspíllaga, Antero, 11
Asunción, 138

Auténticos, 85, 91, 99, 101
Authoritarianism, 3, 21, 46, 49, 57, 59, 69, 72, 73, 79, 110, 125, 129–131, 138, 151, 154, 155, 158, 168
Avellaneda, Nicolás, 61
Aylwin, Patricio, 161, 165, 166, 180
Aznar, José María, 3

Bahía Blanca, 18
Bakunin, Mikhail, 12
Bakuninism, 14
Balzac, Honoré de, 57
Baptist church, 101
Barbieri, Teresita de, 66, 72
Barbosa, Rui, 26
Barrios, Alicia, 60
Bartra, Roger, 60
Basque Country, 4
Bassols, Narciso, 54
Batista, Fulgencio, 51, 54, 57, 83, 85, 86, 92, 98, 99
Batlle y Ordóñez, José, 25
Bay of Pigs. *See* Playa Girón
Beauvoir, Simone de, 69
Beijing, 145
Belaunde, Fernando de, 68
Belén (Cuba), 32
Bell, Daniel, 111
Benítez, Conrado, 102
Berlin, Isaiah, 120
Berlin wall, 9, 166
Billinghurst, Guillermo, 18, 25
Blair, Tony, 2
Blanchard, Peter, 15
Bolivia, 23, 59, 93, 101, 116, 127
Bolsheviks, 21, 22
Bonaparte, Napoleon, 139
Bonchismo, 92, 101
"Boom," Latin American, 46
Boorstin, Daniel, 111
Bosnia, 4
Bowie, Robert, 113, 114
Brazil, 5, 12, 14–16, 18, 20–22, 26, 46, 47, 72, 100, 128, 129, 142, 176, 178
Britain, 2, 3, 6, 10, 35, 73, 101, 102, 141, 143
Brunner, José Joaquín, 60
Buchi, Hernán, 160, 161

Buenos Aires, 14–16, 18, 21, 25, 46, 57
Bunster, Gimena, 80
Bush, George, 2

Caballero, Bernardino, 129
Cabaña Fortress, 101
Calles, Plutarco, 53, 56
Camp, Roderic, 54
Capitalism, 4, 9, 12, 13, 15–17, 19, 20, 22, 68, 69, 116, 117, 126, 156
Cárdenas, Lázaro, 53, 54, 57
Caribbean, 9, 65, 119, 145
Carranza, Venustiano, 52
Carter, Jimmy, 114, 131, 138
Castañeda, Jorge, 61
Castro, Fidel, 5, 8, 48, 57, 70, 85, 86, 93, 95, 98–102, 114, 117
Catalonia, 4
Catholic church/faith, 27, 28, 34–37, 39, 40, 42, 46, 77, 100, 101, 142, 151–154, 156, 158, 159
Catholic University (Santiago), 152, 153, 155, 158, 180
Caudillos, 48, 52
Cayaltí, 11
"Cecilia" colony, 14
Censorship, 36, 49
Center Christian politics, 3
Center left politics, 70, 161, 163, 166, 171–174, 176, 179–181, 183
Center politics, 65, 79
Center right politics, 161, 169, 180
Central America, 8, 65, 105, 106, 108–111, 113–116, 119, 120, 138
Central Bank (Chile), 176, 179, 181
Chaco War, 127
Chamorro, Violeta, 141
Chaney, Elsa, 67–69, 78, 79
Chant, Sylvia, 144
Chávez, Martha, 141
Chechnia, 4
Chiapas, 5
Chibás, Eddy, 99
Chibasismo, 99
Chicago, 172, 181
Chicago Boys, 8, 154, 155
Chile, 5, 6, 8, 11, 12, 14, 16, 18, 20, 22–24, 46, 47, 50, 51, 58, 60, 61, 65, 67–

71, 78–80, 140–142, 145, 146, 150–
152, 156–158, 160–164, 167–169, 171–
176, 178, 179, 181–183
Chilenidad, 157
China, 71
Chomsky, Noam, 113, 118, 119
Christian Democrats, 61, 68, 137, 152,
153, 159, 160, 180, 181
Christian faith/morals, 4, 36, 39, 69, 154
Church, 28, 29, 37, 38, 48, 101
CIA, 113, 115, 117, 118
Cienfuegos, 31
Científicos, 51
Ciudad del Este, 129
Clark, Ismael, 30–34, 41
Class (interests/divisions), 7, 28, 30, 32,
34, 35, 37, 38, 41, 57, 67, 68, 72, 74,
75, 77, 84, 134, 139, 140, 142, 143,
146, 159
Clientelism, 159, 162, 163
Clinton, Bill, 2
Coalición Democrática Socialista, 99,
Cockroft, James D., 52
CODELCO, 175
Coercion, 130
Cold war, 8, 86, 97, 105–113, 119, 120,
132, 133, 166
Colina, 162
Colombia, 1, 5, 23, 46, 58, 68
Colorado party (Paraguay), 125–131, 136
Colosio, Luis Donaldo, 6
COMECON, 94, 102
Commission of Truth and Reconciliation
(Chile), 165
Committees of the Defense of the Revolu-
tion (CDR), 87, 88, 100
Communalism, 87
Communism, 2, 3, 6, 21, 22, 34, 36, 38,
46, 53, 56, 69, 86, 94, 98, 106, 108,
112–119, 130, 131, 133–135, 137, 159,
166
Communist party: in Chile, 14, 51, 159,
162, 181; in Cuba, 35, 36, 42, 51, 85,
87, 94, 99, 101; in Paraguay, 127, 132,
137; in Venezuela, 101
Communitarianism, 155
Concepción, 71

Concertación, 161, 163, 167
*Confederación de Colegios Cubanos
Católicos*, 39
Confederación General de Trabajadores,
75
*Confederación Obrera Regional Argen-
tina*, 20
Confederación Unitaria de Trabajadores
(CUT), 174
*Consejo Nacional de Educación y Cul-
tura*, 55
Conservatism, 1–4, 32, 35, 38, 39, 54, 58,
60, 66, 68, 74, 75, 140, 142, 152, 155,
158, 159, 171
Conservative party: in Britain, 6, 10; in
Chile, 158
Constitution, 1980 Chilean, 157, 164, 165
Constitution, 1901 Cuban, 29, 32, 33, 100
Constitution, 1940 Cuban, 33–37, 39, 40,
57
Constitution, 1976 Cuban, 102
Constitution, 1824 Mexican, 62
Constitution, 1857 Mexican, 62
Constitution, 1917 Mexican, 52
Constitution, 1940 Paraguayan, 131, 137
Constitution, 1967 Paraguayan, 131, 137
Constitution, 1977 Paraguayan, 131, 132
Constitution, 1787 U.S., 62
Constitutions, 130, 132, 167, 168
Constructivism, 155
Contemporáneos, 53
Corcoran-Nantes, Yvonne, 142
Córdoba (Argentina), 26, 58
CORFO (*Corporación de Fomento*
[Chile]), 61
Corporatism, 8, 151, 152, 155–157
Corporativism, 125, 127
Corruption, 29, 30, 32, 85, 91, 92, 98, 99,
128, 133, 134, 138, 174
Cosío Villegas, Daniel, 62
Cottam, Martha, 114
Coups d'état, 6, 7, 55, 83, 92, 117, 125,
133, 151, 153
Criteros, 56
Croatia, 4
CTC (*Confederación de Trabajadores Cu-
banos*), 99

Cuba, 5, 7–9, 23, 27–42, 46, 47, 50, 51, 54, 55, 58, 64, 75, 83, 85, 87, 88, 91–103, 113, 118
Cuba Libre, 27, 28, 39, 40, 55
Cubanidad, 7, 28, 31, 32, 34, 37, 38, 41
Cubanismo, 83–88, 91–94, 96, 98
Cuban Missile Crisis, 86, 100
Culture, 32, 45, 47–53, 56–58, 60–63, 72, 84, 88, 91, 94, 96, 106, 107, 109–112, 118, 120, 129, 161, 165, 166, 179
Czechoslovakia, 115

Dante, Alighieri, 57
Delgado de Odría, María, 68
Democracia y Progreso, 161
Democracy, 2, 4, 5, 28, 34, 36–38, 40, 49, 56, 58–60, 65, 72, 73, 92, 105, 109–111, 114, 116, 117, 119, 120, 130, 131, 133–135, 138, 141, 144, 151, 155, 157, 158, 160, 161, 163–169, 172
Democratic party (U.S.), 3, 119
Democratization. *See* Democracy
Departamento de la Mujer (El Salvador), 149
DEU (*Directorio Estudiantil Universitario*), 98–100
Diario de la Marina, 32, 35, 36, 38
Díaz, Porfirio, 5, 51–53
Dictatorship, 3–5, 51, 61, 69, 73, 91, 116, 119, 125–127, 130–133, 135
Di Tella Institute, 46
Dominican Republic, 79
Dore, Elizabeth, 116
DRE (*Directorio Revolucionario Estudiantil*), 98–100
Dreyfus Affair, 47, 51
Dulles, John Foster, 114, 117, 118
Eagleton, Terry, 105, 107, 111, 115
Eastern bloc, 102, 103, 115
Eastern Europe, 46, 98, 102, 166
Eatwell, Roger, 2, 4
Economic Planification and Development System (SDPE), 94, 102
Economics/economy, 2–6, 14, 16, 17, 19, 20, 27–29, 31, 33, 37, 38, 40, 46–48, 53, 59, 72, 76, 77, 84, 85, 87, 88, 91, 93, 94, 96–100, 102, 106, 109, 111–

113, 117–119, 128, 132–134, 136, 137, 143, 154–160, 163, 165–167, 171–183
Ecuador, 5, 23
Education: general, 8, 27, 30–34, 38–41, 45, 47, 50–52, 54, 55, 57, 72, 75, 76, 88, 93, 97, 100–102, 116, 117, 136, 153, 163, 175, 177, 179–181, 183; private, 7, 27–41; public, 7, 27–29, 33, 34, 36–38, 40–42
Egalitarianism, 92, 111, 139
Egypt, 108
Eisenhower, Dwight, 114, 117, 119
El Abra, 175
El Bosque, 162
Elites, 1, 7, 11, 13, 14, 17, 18, 21–23, 28, 30, 32, 36, 49, 50, 52, 54, 63, 85, 90–92, 106, 126, 127, 152, 155, 159, 162
El Mercurio, 8, 153, 171–177, 180–183
El Mundo (Cuba), 36, 38
El Poder Femenino, 140
El Salvador, 115, 149
Engels, Friedrich, 70, 139
Enlightenment, 28, 111, 139, 147
Epifanistas, 136
Errázuriz, Francisco Javier, 161
Escalante, Aníbal, 100
Escrivá de Balaguer, José María, 159
Escuela Santa María, 18
Ethiopia, 102
Ethnicity, 29, 46, 72, 74, 79, 143
Europe, 5, 8, 12, 14, 15, 46, 47, 54, 58, 66, 69, 71, 102, 112, 139, 143–145, 172
Eyzaguirre, Jaime, 152, 156

Falangists, 38, 159
Falcón, Ramón, 25
Fascism, 3, 6, 38, 69, 74
Febreristas, 127
Federación de Mujeres Cubanas, 75
Federación Estudiantil de la Universidad Católica (FEUC), 153
Federación Obrera Regional Argentina, 17
Federalism, 26
Femenism, 145–147, 150
Feminism, 8, 16, 66, 67, 69–77, 79, 80, 139, 140, 142–150
FENAMAD, 143
Fisher, Jo, 142

Florida, 103
Fondo de Cultura Económica, 57
Foweraker, J., 144
Foxley, Alejandro, 180
Fraga Iribarne, Manuel, 3
France, 30, 47, 111, 151, 152
Franco, Francisco, 4
Francoism (from Franco, Francisco), 3
Freemasons, 1, 70
Frei, Eduardo, 68, 152, 153, 166, 181
Frei, Jr., Eduardo, 161, 177, 180
Freire, Paulo, 100
Freismo, 65
French Revolution (1789), 62
Frente Juvenil de Unidad Nacional, 154
Frente Popular, 51, 61
Frondizi, Arturo, 50
Fuentes, Carlos, 61
Fukuyama, Francis, 111
Fundación Luz Caballero, 32, 33

Galeano, Eduardo, 118
Gallegos, Rómulo, 55
García, Álvaro, 180
García Calderón, Francisco, 54
García Canclini, Néstor, 58
García Márquez, Gabriel, 1
Gauchero politics, 73
Geertz, Clifford, 107, 111, 120
Gellner, Ernest, 54
Gender, 7, 41, 65, 66–68, 70, 72–78, 140–143, 145, 146
Generación del Centenario, 92
Generationalism, 91, 94
Germany, 6, 23, 136
Gleijeses, Piero, 114, 116, 119
Gonzales Prada, Manuel, 12, 14
González, Natalicio, 127, 128
González Videla, Pedro, 51
Gorbachev, Mikhail, 120
Gordon, E. A., 16
Goulart, Joao, 67
Gramsci, Antonio, 47, 70, 98
Grau San Martín, Ramón, 58, 92, 99
Greece, 114
Green politics, 9
Gremialistas, 8, 151–157, 160, 165
Guanabacoa, 30

Guaraní Indians/Language, 127, 128, 135
Guatemala, 58, 108, 112–120
Guerra y Sánchez, Ramiro, 54
Guevara, Che, 48, 93–97, 100–102
Guionistas, 136
Guiteras, Antonio, 85, 99
Guzmán, Jaime, 8, 151–154, 156, 158–160, 164, 165, 168

Halle, Louis, 113, 114
Hartz, Louis, 110
Havana, 35, 86, 97, 101, 103, 113
The Havana Post, 36
Haya de la Torre, Víctor Raúl, 14, 22, 26, 50
Hayward, Jack, 5
Hembrismo, 79
Heraldo de Cuba, 30
Hilton, Isabel, 137
Hispanic world, 100
Hispanoamericanism, 59
Hitchens, Christopher, 116
Hitler, Adolf, 108
Hobsbawm, Eric, 15, 45
Hollander, N. C., 75, 76
Huerta, Victoriano, 52
Hugo, Victor, 62
Human rights, 55, 109, 117, 131, 132, 138, 142, 143, 159, 164
Hunt, Michael, 106, 107, 109, 110, 112, 118

Ibáñez, Carlos, 22, 61
Idealism, 2
Ideals, 2, 28, 77, 90, 110, 111, 119, 130, 154, 155, 167
Ideological discourse, ix, 1–3, 5–9, 65, 66, 68, 72, 74, 76, 77, 79, 85, 90, 106, 107, 131, 135, 155, 158
Ideologies, ix, x, 2–8, 15, 28, 35, 61, 62, 65–72, 74, 76–79, 83–98, 101, 102, 105–113, 115, 116, 118–120, 125–136, 138–148, 151, 152, 155, 156, 159, 161–163, 165, 166, 179
Ideologues, ix, 16, 67, 83, 111, 144, 154
IMF (International Monetary Fund), 143
Immerman, Richard, 108
Independencia, 162

India, 56,
Indigenous interests, 143
Individualism, 20, 111, 116, 155, 156
Industrial Workers of the World (Wob-
  blies), 14, 16, 22, 25
Instituto de Bienestar Rural, 133, 134
Instituto de la Mujer (Spain), 150
Intellectuals, 7, 8, 12–15, 28, 32, 42, 45–
  60, 84, 93, 98, 120, 126, 147, 152
Intelligentsia, 48
Inter-American Development Bank (IDB),
  133
Inter-American Relationship, 105–107,
  120
Iquique, 18
Isla de Pascua, 162
Israel, 101
Itaipú Dam, 128
Italy, 7, 14, 15, 23, 98
Izquierda Unida, 3

Jacobsen, Carl, 115
Jacquette, Jane, 69
Jelin, Elizabeth, 141
Jesuits, 31, 38, 42
Jews, 29
Joven Cuba, 99
JPAS (*Juntas de Abastecimiento y Pre-
  cios*), 71
Juárez, Benito, 51
Judeo-Christianity, 93

Kennan, George, 109
Kirkwood, Julieta, 144, 149
Knox, John, 57
Krauze, Enrique, 48, 63
Kremlin, 108, 114
Kronstadt Rising, 21
Krushchev, Nikita, 120
Kuppers, Gaby, 143

Labor code, Guatemalan 1947, 116
Labor movements, 12, 13, 18–22, 25, 76
Labor party (Britain), 2, 3, 6, 10
La Cisterna, 162
LaFeber, Walter, 116
La Granja, 162
Laíno, Domingo, 133

Laissez-faire principles, 18, 111, 126
La Pasionaria (Ibarruri, Dolores), 3
Larrain, Felipe, 180
Larroulet, Cristian, 180
Las Condes/Vitacura, 162
Latin America, ix, 2–9, 12, 23, 28, 58, 60,
  61, 65–68, 70–75, 79, 80, 99–101, 109,
  112, 118, 120, 133, 139, 140, 143, 145,
  147, 150
La Voz de la Mujer, 16, 24
L'Avvenire, 15
Law, Sáenz Peña, 18
Leeds, ix
Leffler, Melvyn, 113
Left-wing politics, 3–5, 7, 37, 56, 61, 65,
  67–71, 79, 101, 116, 117, 132, 140–
  142, 146, 159, 160, 162, 166, 171, 181
Leguía, Augusto, 22, 58
Lenin, Vladimir Ilyich, 70
Leninism, 159
Leo XIII, 152
Lesbianism, 142
Letelier, Valentín, 54
Leturia, Javier, 153
Levy, Daniel, 59
Liberal party (PL/Paraguay), 126, 127, 136
Liberalism, 1, 2, 28, 34, 37–39, 49, 51, 54,
  60, 62, 86, 98, 100, 107, 110, 116, 127,
  135, 137, 154, 156, 160, 164
Liberation theology, 117
Liga da Defensa Nacional, 21
Liga Patriótica Argentina, 21
Ligas Agrarias (Paraguay), 128, 136
Linz, J. J., 134
Lipset, Seymour Martin, 111
Literacy Campaign, 1961 Cuban, 88
Lo Espejo, 162
Lombardo Toledano, Vicente, 56
London, 143
Los Angeles (Chile), 162
Luther, Martin, 57
Luz y Caballero, José de la, 37

Machado, Gerardo, 47, 54, 64, 83, 91, 98
Machado, Vieira, 142
Machismo, 67, 70, 79
Macul, 162
Madero, Francisco I., 52, 53

Madrid, 3
Makhno, Nestor, 21
Malatesta, Errico, 14
Manifest destiny, 106, 110, 112
Mannheim, Karl, 111
Marcos, Subcomandante, 5
Marianismo, 67
Mariátegui, José Carlos, 14
Marinello, Juan, 34–39, 51
Martí, José, 38, 54, 55, 64, 83, 91–96, 99,
    101
Martianismo, 91–93
Martínez Estrada, Ezequiel, 57
Marx, Karl, 13, 14, 70, 139
Marxism, 14, 60, 66, 80, 88, 94, 110, 117,
    131, 142
Marxism-Leninism, 98, 118
Massad, Carlos, 180, 181
Mattelart, M., 68, 69, 79
McCarthyism, 118
McCormick, Thomas, 113
Mechanisms of control, 49, 55, 59, 90,
    125, 126, 128
Mediterranean countries, 6
Melipilla, 162
Mella, Julio Antonio, 50, 91, 101
MEMCH-83, 141
Menchú, Rigoberta, 79
Menem, Carlos, 73
Mentalities, 126, 134, 135, 138
Mercado, Manuel, 101
MERCOSUR, 178, 179, 182
Messianism, 111, 119, 134
Mexicanidad, 53
Mexican Revolution (1910–1920), 51–53
Mexico, ix, 5, 6, 9, 23, 46, 47, 49–58, 60–
    62, 64, 141, 144, 150, 176
Meyer, Jean, 53, 56
Miami, 100
Middle classes, 8, 18, 21, 45–47, 50, 52,
    53, 58, 59, 62, 67, 69, 73, 101, 115,
    140, 142, 143, 163
Militarism, 3, 22, 28, 29, 46, 50, 51, 55,
    57, 59, 61, 72, 80, 85, 87, 88, 100, 102,
    108, 113, 115, 125, 127, 128, 130, 136,
    137, 151, 153, 157, 158, 160, 162–169,
    172
Milton, John, 57

Miranda, Carlos, 125
Miristas, 69
MNR (*Movimiento Nacional Revolucion-
    ario*), 99
Molina, Sergio, 180, 181
Molina Enríquez, Andrés, 62
Molyneux, Maxine, 74
MOMUPO, 146, 150
Moncada Barracks, 92, 99
Monroe Doctrine, 106, 109, 118
Montenegro, Sofía, 144
Montevideo, 69
Montori, Arturo, 31, 32
MOPOCO, 137
Morínigo, Higinio, 125, 127, 135
Morris, James, 12
Morrow, Dwight, 56
Moscovisados, 22
Moscow, 94, 95, 101, 102, 113, 115
Movement, 26 July, 85, 88, 98–100
Mujerista politics, 8, 150
Mulchen, 162
Munck, R., 17
Muslim (faith), 4
Myth, political use of, 6, 8, 10, 49, 67, 83–
    85, 89, 90, 92–98, 102, 133–135, 146

Nasser, Gamal Abdel, 108
National Institute of Agrarian Reform
    (INRA), 87, 100, 101
National Security Council (NSC), 113
National Security Doctrine (NSD), 132
Nationalism, 4, 7–9, 31, 33, 34, 36, 38–41,
    47, 59, 65, 83–85, 87, 90–92, 97, 106,
    110–113, 116–120, 126–130, 134, 135,
    158, 167
NATO, 3
Navarrete, Jorge, 179
Nazism, 38
Neoliberalism, 4–6, 8, 9, 46, 113, 116,
    117, 120, 146, 147, 154–158, 160, 171,
    172, 182, 183
Neruda, Pablo, 51, 62
New Deal, 116
Nicaragua, 112–115, 117–120, 144
Northern Ireland, 4
North Korea, 71
Novik, Peter, 107, 110, 111

Obregón, Álvaro, 52, 54, 63
Ocampo, Victoria, 70
O'Leary, Juan, 126, 127
Oligarchies, 11, 21, 47, 49–51, 54, 56, 58, 60, 156
Oliveira, Orlandina de, 66, 72
Opportunism, 125, 126
Opus Dei, 159
Organization of American States (OAS), 86, 118, 133
Organization of Integrated Revolutionary Organizations (ORI), 87, 100
Ortiz, Fernando, 33, 34, 36, 37, 40
Ortiz Mena, Antonio, 133
Ortodoxos, 86, 92, 98, 99
Oxfam, 150

Paine, 162
Paine, Thomas, 57
Paraguay, 8, 23, 59, 125–138, 178
Paraguayan civil war (1947), 127, 128
Paraguayidad, 126, 127, 129
Paris, 143
Parsons, Talcott, 78
Partido del Pueblo Cubano, 99
Partido Independiente de Color, 30
Partido Obrero Socialista (Chile), 25
Partido Popular (Mexico), 56
Partido Revolucionario Cubano, 99, 101
Parties (political), 2–7, 9, 20–22, 26, 30, 50, 51, 53, 56, 60, 61, 67, 70, 72, 77, 78, 88, 95, 99, 102, 127, 130–132, 137, 140, 141, 151, 158–169, 179–181, 183
Patria, 127
Patriotism, 32, 130
Patronage, 129, 130, 134
Paz, Octavio, 54, 56
PDC (Christian Democratic Party/Chile), 161, 162, 180, 181
Peñaflor, 162
Perestroika, 120
Perón, Eva, 66–68, 72, 73, 75–77, 79
Perón, Juan, 56, 57, 73, 77, 78
Peronism, 8, 22, 65, 66, 72, 74–78
Peronist Feminine party (PPF), 75, 77
Peronistas. See Peronism
Personalist politics, 8, 125, 126, 129

Peru, 8, 11–13, 15–18, 20, 21, 22, 25, 26, 46, 47, 50, 51, 55, 58, 60, 64, 68, 79, 140–143, 145
Peurifoy, John, 114
Piglia, Ricardo, 61
Piñera, José, 160, 161
Pinochet, Augusto, 6, 70, 154, 162, 164–168, 172
Pius XI, 152
Platt Amendment, 90, 91, 100
Playa Girón, 86, 92, 96, 100
Plaza de la Revolución, 93
Plaza de Mayo, 142
Plebiscite, 1988 Chilean, 164
Pliego Nacional de Peticiones, 71
PLR (*Partido Liberal Reformista*), 137
Pluralism, 105, 118, 120, 145, 147
PNR (*Partido Revolucionario Nacional*), 53
Police, 18, 25, 72, 109, 113, 130
Popper, Karl, 110
Popular Front (Chile). *See Frente Popular*
Popular Unity. *See Unidad Popular*
Populism, 8, 14, 22, 49, 65–68, 72–74, 78, 80, 83, 85, 111, 153, 157
Por la Escuela Cubana en Cuba Libre, 37, 38
Por la Patria y por la Escuela, 35, 36, 38
Portes Gil, Emilio, 56, 58
Portugal, 152
Positivism, 54, 62
Postfeminism, 143, 147
Postmodernism, 73, 140, 147
Poststructuralism, 140
PP (*Partido Popular*/Spain), 3, 4
PPD (*Partido Por la Democracia*/Chile), 161, 162, 179–181
Pragmatism, 2–9, 14, 16, 144, 146, 147, 158, 168
PRF (*Partido Reformista Febrerista*), 137
Prío Socarrás, Carlos, 99
PRONOSOL, 144
Propaganda, 13–15, 25, 88, 91, 93, 101, 127, 133, 134
Protestant faith/morals, 28, 29, 34, 42, 93, 101
PSOE (*Partido Socialista Obrero Español*), 3, 4

PSP (*Partido Socialista Popular*), 86, 88, 94, 95, 99, 100, 102
Pudahuel, 162
Puerto Rico, 23

Querétaro, 62
Quimantú, 68, 72

Rabe, Stephen, 114
Race (issues), 28, 30, 34, 35, 37, 38, 40, 41, 67, 70–73, 106, 127, 128, 143
Racism, 79
Radcliffe, Sarah, 72, 140, 147
Radicalism, 20, 25, 28, 38, 53, 58–60, 65, 68, 85, 86–88, 92, 94, 100, 102, 112, 116, 127, 140, 143, 156, 162, 167
Radowitzky, Simón, 25
Ranger, Terence, 45
Reactionary politics, 67
Reagan, Ronald, 108, 114, 115, 117, 118, 138
Reciprocity Treaty, U.S.-Cuban 1934, 85, 92, 99
Recoleta, 162
Reformism, 16, 20–24, 26, 58, 59, 68, 70, 76
Regional politics, 7
Religion, 4, 7, 12, 16, 29, 31, 32, 33, 34, 35, 36, 37, 70, 87, 89, 90, 93, 100, 101, 158
Repression, 14, 17, 18, 20–22, 34, 46, 49, 52, 55, 59, 60, 125, 127, 128, 130, 132, 133, 136
Republicanism, 28, 110, 111
Republican party (U.S.), 3, 119
Revolution, 6, 7, 15, 28, 40, 54, 61, 78, 83, 86–88, 92, 93, 95–99, 101, 105, 106, 109–111, 113–115, 117–120
Revolutionary politics, 8, 13, 16, 19, 20, 23, 27, 66, 69, 70, 76, 84–86, 91, 94–98, 100, 110, 160
Revolutionary syndicalism, 12, 16, 24
Revolutionary Women's Front (FMR), 70, 71
Ricard, Serge, 111, 112
Right-wing politics, 3–5, 53, 65, 67–69, 72, 119, 151, 153, 154, 158, 160, 161, 163, 166–169, 171, 179, 181

Rivera, Diego, 53
RN (National Renewal), 161–163, 166–169, 180–182
Rock, David, 58
Rodríguez Alcalá, Guido, 125
Rodríguez de Francia, José Gaspar, 126, 136
Roig de Leuchsenring, Emilio, 36, 37, 38, 39
Rojas de Morena, María Eugenia, 68
Roosevelt, Franklin, 116
Roosevelt, Theodore, 109
Roosevelt Corollary, 1904–1905, 106, 109
Rosario, 18
Rossi, Giovanni, 14, 24
Rousseau, Jean-Jacques, 57, 62
Rowbotham, Sheila, 143
Russia, 15, 21, 25, 114
Russian Revolution (1917), 21, 22, 70
Ruston Academy, 35

Sábato, Ernesto, 55
St. George School, 35
Salazar, Oliveira, 152
Said, Edward, 106, 119
San Bernardo, 162
Sandinismo, 65, 108, 113–120
Sandinistas. See Sandinismo
Sandino, Augusto César, 114, 117
San Fernando, 162
San Miguel, 162
Santería, 93, 101
Santiago (Chile), 22, 25, 152, 162, 164, 171, 176, 180
Santiago de Cuba, 99
Sao Paulo, 14, 15, 22
Sardinia, 4
Sarmiento, Domingo, 54, 61
Schaulson, Jorge, 180
Schlesinger, Arthur, 110
Schools of Revolutionary Instructions (EIR), 88, 100
Scotland, 4
Secularism, 28, 31, 34, 36–39, 41, 110
Serbs, 4
SERNAM (National Women's Service/Chile), 141, 145, 148, 150

Sexism, 79, 183
Shils, Edward, 111, 120
Shultz, George, 120
Sierra, Justo, 54
Sisa, Bartolina, 143
SLAS (Society for Latin American Studies), ix, x, 78
Social democratic politics, 3, 67, 117
Socialism, 2–9, 14, 20, 23, 37, 53, 54, 67, 69–74, 93, 95, 97, 101, 116, 140, 151, 155, 167, 172, 179, 181
Socialist party: in Argentina, 19, 25; in Chile, 14, 22
Sociedad de Fomento Fabril (SFF/Chile), 182
Sociedad Económica de Amigos del País (Cuba), 29
Sociedad Nacional Minera (SNM/Chile), 182
Solano López, Francisco, 126, 136
Somoza Debayle, Anastasio, 116
Sondrol, P. C., 138
Sonora, 52
South Africa, 137
South America, 11–16, 17, 18, 19, 20, 21, 22, 176
Southern Cone, 69, 130, 131, 138
South Pacific Mail, 11
Soviet Union, 6, 86, 95–97, 100, 102, 108, 112, 115
Spain, 3, 7, 14, 15, 23, 27–30, 38, 42, 101, 150–152, 159
Spalding, Hobart, 12
Spanish America, 45–51, 53–61
Spanish Civil War, 3, 38, 101
Spanish Regional Association (Cuba), 29
Stalinism, 86
State, 5–8, 13, 14, 17, 18, 21–23, 26, 28, 31, 33–38, 40, 41, 45–56, 58–61, 68–72, 76, 84, 114, 117, 118, 125, 127, 128, 136, 152–157, 174, 175
Storni, Alfonsina, 70
Strikes, 10, 11, 13, 17, 19–21, 25, 26, 29, 30, 55, 71, 153, 174
Stroessner, Alfredo, 8, 125–131, 133–138
Stronato, 125, 128, 132, 134, 135
Stronismo, 126, 131

Structuralism, 98
Suckle Ortiz, Bobbye, 79
Sweezy, Paul, 79
Syndicalism, 13, 14, 16, 17, 20, 21

Taiwan, 137
Technocracy, 2–6, 8, 61, 95, 111, 155, 156, 158, 173
Televisión Nacional (Chile), 179
Thatcher, Margaret, 3
Thompson, E. P., 12
Thorpe, Wayne, 13, 17
Tlatelolco Massacre, 1968, 56
Toriello, Guillermo, 117, 118
Totalitarianism, 36, 110, 116, 138, 157, 168
Trade-Unionism, 7, 14
Trade Unions, 3, 10, 13, 16–18, 20, 22, 23, 24, 47, 51, 71, 75, 88, 99, 101, 132, 140, 141, 144, 145, 152, 153, 157, 181
Trotsky, Leon, 70
Trotskyists, 69
Truman Doctrine, 108, 114

UCC (Center Center Union), 161
UDI (Independent Democratic Union), 158–169
UGT (*Unión General de Trabajadores*), 3
Unidad Popular, 67, 69, 70, 78, 79, 153, 155
Unified Revolutionary Socialist Party (PURS), 87
Unión Cívica Radical, 19
Unión de Juventud Comunista, 97
Unión Progreso de Chile, 161
United Fruit Company (UFCO), 116, 119
United Nations, 133
United States, 3, 6, 8, 27–29, 31, 32, 35, 46, 56, 59, 60, 62, 66, 71, 85, 86, 91, 92, 99–103, 105–120, 125, 128, 131–133, 138, 140, 141, 143, 147, 149, 172, 179
Universidad Popular (Mexico), 64
Universidad Popular (Peru), 64
Universidad Popular José Martí (Cuba), 64
University of Chicago, 181, 183
University Reform Movement (Argentina), 58, 59

Upper Classes, 39, 67, 162
Uruguay, 23, 25, 46, 58, 69, 178
Utopia, 7, 13, 14, 16, 120

Valparaíso, 22, 25, 162, 171
Values, political, 9, 13, 14, 84, 89, 96, 97, 102, 107, 109, 112, 116, 126, 128, 129, 134, 157, 165, 179
Van der Linden, Marcel, 13, 17
Vargas, Getúlio, 72
Vargas, Virginia, 145, 149
Vargas Llosa, Mario, 5, 55
Varguismo, 65
Vasconcelos, José, 51, 52, 54, 56, 58
Vatican, 42
Venezuela, 5, 59, 101
Videla, Jorge Rafael, 73
Vietnam, 71, 118
Vietnam War, 108, 114
Villa, Francisco, 52
Villavicencio, Maritza, 140
Vitacura, 162
Vitalismo, 116

Wales, 4
Walker, Alice, 150
War of Independence, 1868–1878 Cuban, 83, 101

War of Independence, 1895–1898 Cuban, 83, 91, 101
Washington, 86, 99, 106, 109, 110, 112, 113, 115–119
Weeks, John, 116
Welfare State, 5, 144, 174
Western world, 2, 4–6, 8, 46, 97, 115, 116, 120
Westwood, S., 72, 140
Whitehead, Laurence, 47
Wolfe, J., 14
Womanist politics, 8, 146, 150
Women, 8, 15, 16, 22, 24, 41, 42, 65–78, 80, 96, 139–146, 148
Woolf, Virginia, 70
Working classes, 11, 12, 14–16, 19, 21, 22, 40, 50, 69, 70, 75, 142, 144, 159, 162
World Bank, 6, 39, 133
World War I, 11, 17, 18, 20, 23
World War II, 48, 52, 59, 101, 110
Wright, Anthony, 2, 4
Writers' Union (UNEAC), 51

Yrigoyen, Hipólito, 14, 19, 20, 22, 58
Yugoslavia, 4

Zola, Emile, 62

Editor and Contributors

WILL FOWLER is Lecturer in Spanish at the University of St. Andrews. He is the editor of *Authoritarianism in Latin America since Independence* (Greenwood, 1996) and the *Bulletin of Latin American Research*'s special issue, "Mexican Politics in the Nineteenth Century" (January, 1996). He has published several articles on Mexican political history in the early national period and is currently working on a book on ideologues and ideologies in independent Mexico, 1821–1853. He was Head of the Hispanic Section at De Montfort University before moving to St. Andrews, and has been Secretary of the Society for Latin American Studies since 1995.

PAUL HENDERSON is Lecturer in History at the University of Wolverhampton. His early publications were concerned with the impact of World War I on economic and social conditions in Peru and Chile. He recently developed interests in the economic history of Ecuador and the history of anarcho-syndicalism in Latin America, and is currently writing a book on the subject. He is a committee member of the Society for Latin American Studies.

DAVID E. HOJMAN is Senior Lecturer in Economics and Latin American Studies at the University of Liverpool. He has published articles and books on agriculture, mineral exports, the Dutch Disease, open-economy macroeconomics, economic integration, labor markets, education, poverty, inequality, infant mortality, public choice and rent-seeking, and the political economy of recent conversions to free-market open-economy policies. He is the author of *Chile: The Political Economy of Development and Democracy in the 1990s,* and the editor of *Neo-liberalism with a Human Face? The Politics and Economics of the Chilean Model.*

LAURIE JOHNSTON teaches Latin American and Caribbean History at University College, London. She is currently researching communist activity in Cuba during the 1930s.

ANNY BROOKSBANK JONES is Reader in Hispanic Studies and Head of Spanish at Nottingham Trent University. She has published widely on Spanish and Latin American women and feminist theory, and is coeditor of *Feminist Readings in Latin American Women's Writing.* She is currently completing a study of women and social change in contemporary Spain.

ANTONI KAPCIA is Principal Lecturer in Spanish and Latin American Studies at the University of Wolverhampton. He has been actively carrying out research on Cuba since 1971, especially in the areas of pre-1959 history, intellectual and cultural history, the evolution of ideology, and the politics of the revolution. He has published extensively in these areas.

PETER LAMBERT is a Lecturer in Spanish and Latin American Studies at the University of the West of England, Bristol. He is currently in the process of writing a comparative study of democracy and democratization in Latin America from 1987 to 1991. Previously he lived in Asunción, Paraguay, where he worked as a political researcher and analyst at the Centro de Documentación y Estudios (CDE).

NICOLA MILLER is Lecturer in Latin American History at University College, London. Her research interests include the intellectual history of Latin America and the international relations of Latin America. She is the author of *Soviet Relations with Latin America, 1959–1987,* and is currently writing a comparative history of the relationship between intellectuals and national identity in Spanish America during the twentieth century.

MARCELO POLLACK is a rsearcher for the Institute for European-Latin American Relations (IRELA) in Madrid. He was Latin American Editor for Oxford Analytica until last year and has published work on democratic transition processes. He is currently preparing an article on the new Chilean right for publication. He is also engaged in research on right-wing think tanks in post-authoritarian Chile for a book on the role of technocracy in that country.

DAVID RYAN is Senior Lecturer at De Montfort University, Leicester, specializing in U.S. Foreign Relations and International History. He is the author of *US-Sandinista Diplomatic Relations: Voice of Intolerance,* and is in the process of writing two other books on the Cold War and U.S. Foreign relations in world history. He is primarily concerned with questions of democracy, freedom, and justice in world history. His research encompasses a range of theoretical considerations coupled with U.S. policy.

MARTA ZABALETA is Senior Lecturer in Spanish and Latin American Studies at Middlesex University, and has been adviser of CHANGE International Reports (U.K.) since 1980. She has been actively carrying out research on women's issues in the context of Latin American underdevelopment since 1964, especially in the areas of economic history, popular education, agrarian reform, reformism and revolution, and representation. Her work has greatly benefited from her belonging to several women's networks around the world. She has published extensively on Latin American women and her most recent publication is entitled *An Analysis of the Speeches of Eva Perón*.

ISBN 0-313-30063-1

90000>

EAN

9 780313 300639

HARDCOVER BAR CODE